An Introduction to
Social Geography

An Introduction to Social Geography

EMRYS JONES
and
JOHN EYLES

OXFORD UNIVERSITY PRESS

Oxford University Press, Walton Street, Oxford OX2 6DP

OXFORD LONDON GLASGOW
NEW YORK TORONTO MELBOURNE WELLINGTON
KUALA LUMPUR SINGAPORE JAKARTA HONG KONG TOKYO
DELHI BOMBAY CALCUTTA MADRAS KARACHI
NAIROBI DAR ES SALAAM CAPE TOWN

First published 1977
Reprinted 1979

British Library Cataloguing in Publication Data
Jones, Emrys, b.1920
   An introduction to social geography.
   Bibl. — Index.
   ISBN 0-19-874062-X
   ISBN 0-19-874063-8 Pbk
   1. Title   2. Eyles, John
   301   GF41
   Anthropo-geography

*Set by Hope Services, Wantage, and
Printed in Great Britain by
Billing & Sons Ltd., Guildford and Worcester*

To my mother
and the memory
of my father
EJ

To my mother
and the memory
of my father
JE

Preface

The relative lack of agreement about the structure and content of social geography has led us to explain in brief our own perspective. This task is carried out in the Foreword which we consider to be an integral part of the text. Our purposes in writing a short preface are more modest and specific. We would like to acknowledge the assistance given us by David Smith of Queen Mary College, London, and David Herbert of University College, Swansea. At short notice and with great diligence, they pointed, in a most constructive fashion, to some of the gaps and shortcomings of an earlier draft. They were kind enough to regard our framework of concepts, patterns, processes, and planning as given. We both feel that this is the best framework for social geography at the present time. In fact, this book is the result of detailed collaboration between us at all points. Although each of us had particular responsibilities, with Emrys Jones writing most of Chapters 3, 4, 5, 7, and 8 and John Eyles most of 1, 2, 6, 9, and 10, the emphasis must firmly be placed on 'most of'. We feel that the book has benefited greatly from being the product of two minds, with discussions on many points leading to substantial rewriting and contributions from both in nearly every chapter. We would like to take this opportunity to thank Valerie Armes, Mrs. D. Emery, Mrs. G. Cornwell, Mrs. P. Farnworth, and Dorothy Eyles for their efficient and patient typing, and Don Shewan of Queen Mary College and Mrs. E. Wilson and staff of the cartographic unit of the London School of Economics for drawing the original figures that appear in this book. Finally, our thanks go to our respective families for their support and encouragement.

London
March 1976

Emrys Jones
John Eyles

Acknowledgements

The author and publishers gratefully acknowledge permission to reproduce copyright material.

Figure 2.1, Theodorson: 'Studies in Human Ecology', in Park *and* Burgess *The City*, p.41. Reprinted by permission of the University of Chicago Press.

Figure 2.2, 4.5, from David E. Sopher: *Geography of Religions*. Reprinted by permission of David E. Sopher and Prentice-Hall, Inc.

Figures 2.3, 2.4a, 2.4b, from Yi-Fu Tuan, *Topophilia: A Study of Environmental Perception, Attitudes, and Values*, © 1974, pp. 36, 38, 165. Reprinted by permission of Prentice-Hall, Inc., Englewood Cliffs, New Jersey

Figure 2.6, from *Irish Geography* 1969 edited by Stephens and Glassock. Reprinted by permission of Queen's University of Belfast.

Figure 2.7, from Gerald D. Suttles: *Social Order of the Slum* p.17. Reprinted by permission of the University of Chicago Press.

Figure 2.8, from Goodey: *Perception of the Environment*. Reprinted by permission of the University of Birmingham.

Figure 2.9, from *Image of the City* by Kevin Lynch. Reprinted by permission of M.I.T. Press, Cambridge, Massachusetts.

Figure 2.12, from Peter Gould and Rodney White: *Mental Maps* Copyright © Peter Gould and Rodney White, 1974. Reprinted by permission of Penguin Books Limited.

Figure 2.12b, c, e, from Gould and White: *Mental Maps*. Reprinted by permission of Regional Studies, University of Reading.

Figures 3.1, 9.1, 9.2, from Coates & Rawstron: *Regional Variations in Britain*. Reprinted by permission of Batsford Limited.

Figures 3.2, 3.3, 4.11, 4.12, 4.13, 4.19, 4.20, 7.2a, 7.2b, from Shepherd, Westaway & Lee: *A Social Atlas of London*. Reprinted by permission of Oxford University Press.

Figures 3.4, 3.5, 6.4, from the *Scottish Geographical Magazine* Vol. 74. Reprinted by permission of The Scottish Geographical Society.

Figure 3.7, from Wreford Watson and Sissons: *The British Isles: A Systematic Geography*. Reprinted by permission of Thomas Nelson & Sons Limited, London.

Figure 3.8, from John Gay: *Geography of Religion in England*. Reprinted by permission of Gerald Duckworth & Co. Limited.

Figure 3.11, from Jones: *Social Geography of Belfast*. Reprinted by permission of Oxford University Press.

Figure 4.1, from Sir Lawrence Stamp: *Some Aspects of Medical Geography*. Reprinted by permission of the Athlone Press.

Figure 4.2, from G.M. Howe in *Transactions of Institute of British Geographers*, 1960. Reprinted by permission of the Institute of British Geographers.

Figures 4.3, 4.4, based upon material taken from the *Complete Atlas of the British Isles*. Reprinted by permission of The Reader's Digest Association Limited.

Figures 4.6, 4.7, from Carter & Thomas: *Regional Studies* 1968. Reprinted by permission of Pergamon Press Limited.

Figure 4.8, from Emrys Jones: 'The changing distribution of the Celtic Languages in the British Isles' in *Transactions of the Honourable Society of Cymmrodorion* 1967. Reprinted by permission of Transactions of the Honorable Society of Cymmrodorion.

Figures 4.9, 4.25, 8.10, 8.11, from David Herbert: *Urban Geography*. Reprinted by permission of David Herbert.

Figure 4.10, from Harries; *Geography of Crime and Justice*. Reprinted by permission of McGraw-Hill Book Company.

Figure 4.14, from Peach: *Urban Segregation*. Reprinted by permission of Longman Group Limited.

Figures 4.15, 4.16, from *The Atlas of Jerusalem*. Reprinted by permission of Walter de Gruyter, Inc., New York.

Figure 4.17, from *The City in Modern Africa* (Library of African Affairs, 1967).Ed. Miner. Reprinted by permission of Pall Mall Press Limited.

Figure 4.18, from Emrys Jones: *Human Geography*. Reprinted by permission of Chatto & Windus Limited.

Figures 4.21, 4.22, 4.24, from Philip H. Rees's Master's Thesis 1968: The Factorial Ecology of Metropolitan Chicago. Reprinted by permission of the University of Chicago (Joseph Regenstein Library).

Figure 4.26, from Frederic J. Osborn and Arnold Whittick: *The New Towns*. Reprinted by permission of Leonard Hill and Publishers.

Figure 4.27, from the Plan of Heighington, Co. Durham, from Thomas Sharpe: *The Anatomy of the Village*. Copyright © Thomas Sharpe, 1946. Reprinted by permission of Penguin Books Limited.

Figures 4.28, 4.29, from Jenkins, Jones, Hughes and Owen: *Welsh Rural Communities* A.D. Rees: *Life in the Welsh Countryside*. Reprinted by permission of the University of Wales Press.

Figure 5.2, from *Compact City: A Plan for a Liveable Urban Environment.* by George B. Dantzig and Thomas L. Saaty. Reprinted by permission of W.H. Freeman & Company Copyright © 1973

Figure 6.2, from Dickinson: *Statistical Mapping and the Presentation of Statistics* Crown copyright reproduced with the permission of the Controller of Her Majesty's Stationery Office.

Figure 6.3, from *Studies in Human Geography* By Chisholm & Rodgers. Reprinted by permission of Heinemann Educational Books Limited.

Figure 7.1, from *Social Forces* 45 (March 1967): '412-23 Ethnic Concentration and Assimilation: An Australian Case Study' by F. Lancaster Jones. Copyright © The University of North Carolina Press.

Figure 7.3, from the *Sociological Review 1V*, No.2 (1956) by Jones. Reprinted by permission of the Sociological Review, University of Keele.

Figure 7.4, from R.J. Johnston: *Urban Residential Patterns*. Reprinted by permission of G. Bell & Sons Limited.

Figure 8.1, from *Geographic Perspectives on Urban Systems: With Integrated Readings*, by Berry & Horton. Reprinted by permission of Prentice-Hall, Inc., Englewood Cliffs, New Jersey.

Figures 8.2, 8.3, from R. Mansell Prothero: *Migrants and Malaria in Africa*. Reprinted by permission of the University of Pittsburgh Press. © 1968 by the University of Pittsburgh Press.

Figure 8.4, from *Social Geography of Zambia* by George Kay. Reprinted by permission of Hodder & Stoughton Educational.

Figure 8.5, from Broeck & Webb: *Geography of Mankind*. Reprinted by permission of McGraw-Hill Book Company.

Figure 8.6, from Jones: *Towns and Cities*. Reprinted by permission of Oxford University Press.

Figure 8.7, from *Greater London* by J.T. Coppock and Hugh C. Prince. Reprinted by permission of Faber and Faber Limited.

Figures 8.8a, 8.8b, 8.9, from *Ekistics*, Vol.18, No.109, December 1964. Published by The Athens Center of Ekistics, Athens, Greece.

Figure 9.3, from Smith: *Geography of Social Well-being*. Reprinted by permission of McGraw-Hill Book Company.

Figure 10.1, from Coates and Silburn: *County Deprived Area Study 1975. Poverty, Deprivation and Morale in a Nottingham Community*. Reprinted by permission of the University of Nottingham.

Figure 10.2, from Paul L. Knox: *Social Well-being: a spatial perspective*. Reprinted by permission of Oxford University Press and Greater London Council.

Contents

7.   SEGREGATION   165
     Degree Assimilation   165
     Ghettos   169
     The Black Belt   170
     Measuring and Mapping Segregation   171
     Processes and Models   175

8.   MACRO-PROCESSES   184
     Migration   184
     Typology of Migration   185
     Models of Migration   194
     Urbanization   196
     The Growth of Cities   197
     Urbanization as a Social Process   199
     The Rural–Urban Continuum   201
     Effects of Urbanization in the Non-Western City   205
     Increasing Social Scale: Its Spatial Implications 211

                    IV. Planning

9.   A FAIR SOCIETY – CONCEPTS AND MEASUREMENT   221
     Social Justice and a Fair Society   221
     Measurement and Social Monitoring   233

10. PUBLIC POLICY AND SOCIAL PLANNING   242
     Social Planning as Social Engineering   242
     Social Remedial Planning   244
     Participation and Pressure Groups   250
     Social Development Planning   257
     The Efficacy of Social Planning   258
     Social Geography and Public Policy   262

     SELECTED BIBLIOGRAPHY   265

     INDEXES   267

Foreword

'Social geography is what social geographers do' is both a fair description and a fair criticism of the state of inquiry in this particular field. It is possibly a stage through which most new disciplines pass before there is general agreement about the substantive issues, about methodology and about the conceptual framework which justifies the recognition of a distinctive area of study. For some years both research and teaching have shown the total inadequacy of equating social geography with human geography and the need to relate studies more firmly to processes in society itself. The empirical work has been uneven and theoretical work slow to evolve, but at the same time courses in social geography have multiplied rapidly. In universities and in polytechnics these courses — albeit very varied in their approach — have attracted large numbers of students, possibly indicating an increasing awareness of the immediacy of social problems and the possible role of geographers in analysing such problems, particularly in our cities. In this respect, at least, the 'relevance' of geography is a live issue, and a deeper under-standing of the spatial implications of social processes is eagerly sought. In the same way the widening of the concept of planning in more recent years to include a new emphasis on social planning has involved geographers to a greater extent in the spatial allocation of social resources.

In spite of this awakening interest there are very few books available which introduce social geography at a simple level, and students are left with a bewildering number of articles and detailed studies, none of which aims at a broad and general field. This small volume is meant to fill that gap and to suggest to both students and teachers a broad framework into which the detailed studies can be fitted. Within the limits of size and the constraint of lack of consensus on concepts, the authors' attempts are deliberately modest. The approach is not a theoretical one, but leans heavily on sociological theory. At so pre-liminary a stage, it is difficult to see what satisfactory theory may emerge which is not subsumed under current sociological thoery. Rather, we have emphasized an empirical approach, drawing on as wide a range as possible of studies which fall within our framework. The emphasis on patterns is an indication of the descriptive and explana-tory nature of much of the work being done in social geography, but the patterns also imply much that is discussed under processes. The

whole is tied together by an approach which assumes certain characteristics of space — dealt with in the second chapter — and of the structure
of society. Finally, we indicate the relevance of these studies for
planning. Throughout, we are aware of the cursory nature of the
treatment: studies of each aspect in depth would have enlarged the
book several times. We have tried to offset this to some extent by
giving as many references as were thought necessary to complement the
text. The student, by referring to these, can follow through the full
implications of any particular aspect. The brief bibliographic list shows,
in more general terms, the kind of literature which will help the student
to broaden his approach.

This book is largely about urban society. The virtual exclusion of the
rural world was the result of a deliberate decision, mainly dictated by
space, but also reflecting the weight and distribution of studies in social
geography. This does not unduly distort the real situation because we
live in a predominantly urban society, and most of our problems lie in
the city. But it emphasizes a final point: that our concern is also overwhelmingly with Western society. References to other societies and to
the pre-industrial city do not redress a balance, but merely set the main
arguments of the book in a yet wider setting.

Largely within the confines of our own society, then, and with an
emphasis on British and American cities, we hope that this tentative
outline will introduce students to a new and exciting field of study.

I · CONCEPTS

1 Social Geography – a group approach

DEFINITIONS

Geography often seems to be involved in a process of questioning its own existence and subject-matter. Its boundaries are ill-defined and the discipline shares common concerns with other subjects — geology, history, economics, anthropology, sociology, planning, botany, politics, demography, and so on. Thus geography cannot be easily located in the camp of either the earth sciences or the social sciences or, for that matter, the geometric sciences. The same is true when we examine the specialisms within geography. There is not, for example, an exact correspondence between geography and economics which produces economic geography. Economic geography also involves consideration of past trends, government intervention, and workforce characteristics and so has links with history, politics and planning, and demography The difficulties of defining the area of study are even more acute in social geography, a fairly young specialism, whose links with other disciplines are still being forged. The obvious academic connection is between geography and sociology and we shall argue that most social geographical theory is likely to be sociological in its derivation (see pp. 12-23). But there are other necessary ties with, for example, planning (see p. 243), history (see p. 143), demography (see p. 197), and economics (see p. 224). Such eclecticism means that there is no subject-matter that all social geographers would accept. Some might say, therefore, that social geography is what social geographers do.

There have, however, been attempts to provide definitions of social geography, although it can be argued that these are coloured by the particular concerns of their authors. Watson, for example, has defined the subject as 'the identification of different regions of the earth's surface according to associations of social phenomena related to the total environment'.[1] His stress is placed on the idea of areal differentiation, this simply being made social. Pahl's conception of the specialism is as 'the study of the patterns and processes in understanding socially defined populations in a spatial setting'.[2] He emphasizes a sociological orientation, in which 'spatial setting' is merely the framework for social analysis. Buttimer has said that social geography is 'the study of the areal (spatial) patterns and functional relations of social groups in the context of their social environment; the internal structure and external relations of the nodes of social activity, and the articulation of various channels of social communication.'[3] This definition directs attention to the meaning of the environment to groups and their activities in it. It is, however, two other definitions which are, not surprisingly, closest to our aims in this book. Eyles sees social geography as 'the analysis of the social patterns and processes arising from the distribution of, and access to, scarce resources',[4] while Jones has taken it to mean 'the understanding of the patterns which arise from the use social groups make of space as they see it, and of the processes involved in making and changing such patterns'.[5] Jones's approach places emphasis on the social group (see pp. 12–23), while the addition of the view of Eyles makes social geography explicitly problem-oriented: in other words, it must tackle the socio-spatial outcomes of the scarcity and inequitable distribution of desirable resources (goods, services, facilities) in Western society.

We can point to four dominant themes in this book. First, social geography, like its parent discipline, is primarily concerned with space. In our case, we need to know the meanings that different groups attach to space as well as the activities that groups carry out in their environments. There are other important constraints besides perception that affect activity as our discussion of where people live in the city shows (see Chapter 6).

Second, a function of social scientists is to search for order in their subject-matter, i.e. to establish patterns. A primary stage in most scientific inquiries is to sort and sift the available information to see if a coherent pattern emerges. If, for example, we are interested in the distribution of black immigrants in the city, we must firstly decide on the meanings of the terms 'black' and 'immigrant' and secondly on the scale of analysis, e.g. borough, ward, enumeration district (see p. 75). It is then necessary to describe the distribution of black immigrants, often by mapping their numbers in each sub-division. This distribution forms our pattern (p. 70).

Third, perhaps a greater function of the social scientist is to try to explain the patterns so established, i.e. to examine those processes that appear to produce a particular pattern. Thus, for example, from our pattern of black migrants, we need to know if they form significant proportions in the subdivisions in which they live. Once this has been established, we must seek the reasons for their presence, absence, or concentration in particular areas. Black immigrants may well be segregated in particular districts, because of their earning power, white attitudes, political decisions, personal preference, and so on (see pp. 169).

Fourth, given the desire for a problem-oriented approach, social problems and their areal concentration must be identified. This perspective demands that the attempts to ameliorate encountered problems be assessed, i.e. we must consider social planning, for in complex societies collective welfare and the welfare of the weakest members can be maintained and improved only by specified societal action. For example, it may be found that there are particular districts in a city that suffer from many disadvantages (unemployment, slum housing, overcrowding, high incidence of crime) to a greater extent than other areas. It may be thought that the deprivation of these areas can best be tackled by improving educational facilities. Educational reform is thus seen as a way of breaking into the vicious circle of deprivation. In the UK, this argument has led to the setting up of educational priority areas which are discussed at length elsewhere (see pp. 247–9).

THE NATURE OF SOCIAL GEOGRAPHY

Our view of the nature of social geography is based partly on its historical antecedents. It has close connections with the human geography taught by the French school early in this century. We shall refer later to the radically new trend set by Paul Vidal de la Blache when he emphasized the importance of man–environment relationships and the significance of social and cultural elements in the way certain regions had distinctive ways of life (see p. 27). He and his followers demonstrated how the 'personality' of the region is the outcome of the way in which society exploited resources, how society reacted to its habitat, and how it organized itself — an outcome, in fact, of its culture. The French school had great influence on British geography, as did the ideas of the French sociologist, Frédéric le Play. These ideas particularly impressed H.J. Fleure and Patrick Geddes, both of whom adopted a holistic approach. Fleure contended that geography, history, and anthropology formed an inseparable trilogy and his approach, like that of Geddes, was essentially through man in society. This is nowhere better exemplified than in a study of simple societies by C. Daryll Forde, Fleure's successor at the School of Geography and Anthropology in Wales. The theme of man in society was further given expression in modern societies by a series of studies of rural life in England and Wales.[6]

The tendency of the French school to balance the man–environment equation in favour of man encouraged much work in historical and cultural geography. In Britain, the work of Estyn Evans can be cited. He has made a notable contribution to our understanding of the part played by society from prehistoric times to the present day in the shaping of the regions of Ireland.[7] With its emphasis on man's material equipment and the effects of man's work on the landscape, Evans' work might properly be identified as 'cultural geography', a term more familiar to American geographers. In Carl Sauer's view, cultural geography deals with those elements of material culture that give character to an area through being inscribed into the earth's surface. It is concerned with man's adjustment to and of the environment or, in Sauer's often-quoted phrase, 'the transformation of the natural landscape into the cultural landscape'.[8] It is the application of the idea of culture to geographical problems, and it is fair to say that cultural geography concentrates on the works of man rather than man himself. This is perhaps the main distinguishing feature between cultural and social geography, the latter tending to emphasize man.

When the city and its peoples became the focus of attention, the old problem of man and the environment appeared again but in a rather more subtle form as the urban environment is itself man-made. It seemed impossible, however, to think of specific groups of city dwellers apart from the environs in which they lived. The very poor and the socially deprived lived in slums; immigrants began urban life in the so-called zones of transition near city centres; black people lived in ghettos; the middle classes lived in suburbs. In urban sociology, human ecology dominated thought for two of the most fruitful decades in the study of the city. But the application of ecological principles to human society by the Chicago school of sociologists implied a deterministic approach which has led to major criticism (see pp. 28–32). The model which Burgess drew of Chicago is primarily descriptive, but it implies a mechanistic process of change firmly linked with the habitat which is the city itself. The concentric zones, the bases of the model, are derived largely from the growth of the city and the age of its constituent parts, which become progressively more recent as one moves away from the centre. The exception is the centre itself, usually rebuilt as a commercial core, so that the oldest and most obsolete zone is that immediately around the core. The physical nature of the zones and their distance from the centre are of primary importance in the disposition of social groups and in controlling their movement. The zones themselves and the activities they contain are the outcome of economic forces related to the accessibility of the centre (see p. 30).

There were reactions to such views, firstly and notably by Walter Firey, who claimed that the character of some parts of the city is not the inevitable outcome of economic forces, but reflects the social values which people attach to certain areas (see pp. 33). Approaching city structure through social values enables us to stress cultural definitions of space. Such views have been considerably strengthened more recently by perception studies: the world is not necessarily the neatly measured and categorized universe of the geographer; many varied and 'distorted' visions reflect how different groups see the world and how they are taught to deal with it (see p. 34ff).

Still more recently it has been realized that man's actions and reactions even to and within his perceived universe are often not the ones he would wish to follow. His actions, particularly his ability to choose certain courses of action, are often hedged with constraints. Income and colour are two such constraints that limit an individual's or group's freedom of action. They affect where a person may live and the activities he may pursue (see p. 148). Certain groups can be seen to have greater degrees of choice than others who suffer many such constraints and deprivations. The coincidence of these deprivations has led some researchers to ask whether the problems produced by the operation of these constraints are inherent in the very nature of society itself (see pp. 258ff). These problems must, however, be given due cognizance because the social geographer must look upon squatting and slums, deprivation and poverty, as spatial components of social life.

This has been the briefest résumé of what interests a social geographer because each aspect will be dealt with in greater detail in subsequent chapters. They have been mentioned here to show how they arose from the initial premises of human geography and to demonstrate the additive nature of social geography. Gradually attention has become focused on the activities of people in groups and on the search for the processes that give rise to patterns of activities. Each component of social experience which has spatial implications — ethnicity, class, interest-group activity, language, religion etc. — can be examined in terms of the patterns that arise from group differentiation and activities (see pp. 19–21). This in turn leads to a search for processes.

SPACE, PATTERN, AND PROCESS

It is perhaps foolhardy to attempt to separate space, pattern, and process, especially pattern and process. Any attempt to discuss process usually begins with the elaboration of a particular state of affairs, a pattern, while few studies of pattern ignore explanation totally. Thus interest in explaining how choice is limited in the housing market will need to be prefaced by a discussion of the access of different groups to this market, i.e. of a social classification of tenure-types, residential districts, and so on. Conversely, regional variations in the provision of dental care are likely to raise questions, such as why the good care is concentrated in south-east England and the county towns and the poor in industrial areas like Lancashire, West Yorkshire, and South Wales. Such questions may lead to tentative explanations in terms of the operation of particular processes. We have, therefore, isolated pattern and process simply for the purposes of analysis and clarity. This is also true for the concepts of space. Clarity is very important in this context, as the role of space in a social setting has been given several interpretations.

Without going into detail on the philosophical arguments about what space is, we can, on a simple level, think of two main approaches. The first is that space is a container of things, and a commonsense approach has found this a useful conception. In fact, geographers have traditionally accepted this view. As Preston James has said: 'The kind of space that geographers are concerned with is earth space. Earth space can be infinitely subdivided into segments of various sizes. Such a segment is known as an area, and those not arbitarily separated, but identified by specific criteria, are called regions.'[9] Space, with respect to this approach, can be divided into a number of pigeon-holes according to whim or intent, and in them we place all things environmental and all spatial behaviour. This view seems convenient for descriptive and classificatory purposes, although the problem of regional division is one of the oldest in geography. Interest in total regions, i.e. a division of the area of study into mutually exclusive regions on the basis of criteria that catalogue all physical and human geographical facts, has declined. This means of course that the division of space will vary according to the purpose of our study.[10]

For social geographical purposes, it can be argued that the idea of space as a container of things begs other questions. It leaves unanswered many of the questions geographers are now asking concerning man's behaviour. We are, therefore, turning increasingly to the second concept of space — that it is an attribute of things. The spaces which have meanings for us are those we create by our activites. Our movements to work, shop, play help to bring order to our environment. Our activities — work, holidays, family life, walks — can add to our knowledge of space as well as endowing it with meaning. The significance of space, as opposed to a more objective point of reference system, is an outcome of the way people think about and use space. This 'social space', therefore, has become central to themes in social geography and is dealt with more fully in the next chapter.

Similar problems also arise in the attempt to separate micro-processes, i.e. emphasis on the individual and group, from macro-processes, i.e. emphasis on society in general. Like all areas of separation, there are fields where the division between micro and macro may seem arbitrary. Taken at the extremes the division is simple enough. At one end, processes involve the behaviour of the individual himself, e.g. his move to a new home (see p. 156), while at the other, we are generalizing about large sections of the population e.g. the migration stream from Europe to the USA (see p. 191). If we are interested in explaining the process, then at the micro-level there is a danger of being drawn into explanations about individual motivation, which not only reduces the problem to one of unique situations, but may force us into purely psychological explanations. To take a crude example, the desire for property ownership may be attributed to the needs of security of and identity with the family and, therefore, to the psychological traits of fear and love. This ignores social and economic considerations such as the relative cost of different housing types, social pressures from one's peers, and status needs.[11] Thus even at the micro-level, it is essential to be able to generalize and to relate explanations to phenomena that are socially derived.

It is possible to think of macro-processes as being made up of behaviour at the micro-level, although some would argue that there is an added element: for example, mass hysteria or crowd reaction is more than the sum of individual behaviour. Yet the link between micro and macro in conceptual terms is extremely difficult to find. There may be a parallel here between social studies and physics. In the world in which we live and move, the classical laws of physics, based on vast generalizations and regularities, are enough of an explanation of process. Yet in quantum physics the movements of particles seem to be arbitrary and do not conform to the classical laws.[12] The randomness of these processes disappear at the macro-scale. It may well be that if particles are represented by individuals, then unique behaviour — decisions, motivations, etc. — is absorbed in a more generalized pattern at the macro-scale. To give a very simple example, the individual reason why a family moves from a city centre to a suburb may be anyone of a hundred, many of which are unique to certain families and to specific circumstances. Dealing with census or similar data the geographer is bound to be concerned with a limited number of generalizations which subsume such detail. He emerges with hypotheses governing, perhaps, suburban movement as a whole, and suggests that changes in socio-economic status or in family size are common and fundamental underlying causes. Such generalizations ignore of necessity both reasons lying outside this framework of explanation, and the individual who behaves completely contrary to it. Individual variation is lost in a statistical approach.

Curry, in agreeing that 'the transition from individual man making decisions to groups of men which are the main concern of human geography is not an easy one', reminds us that the economists' 'optimizing man' is an old favourite to bridge the gap.[13] Here is a completely 'rational' being who obtains his goal of optimal results through complete knowledge of all the elements involved and through a series of logical decisions. Uncertainty and irrationality are ruled out, meaning that we are ruling out the human being himself. As an alternative, Curry suggests 'summation man', a 'convolution of the situation of many individuals' whose 'choices at this more general level have a considerable random component'. The implied uncertainty in this approach points more to a probabilistic way of dealing with decision-making, although it may be that we are dealing with the decisions of aggregates and not of groups (see p. 17).

Our methods of analysis at the micro-level are still crude, particularly compared with the sophisticated techniques of handling data at an aggregate level. In spite of this, the former needs more exploring. The behaviour of groups must be understood as derived from individual behaviour, irrationalities and all. Studies along these lines may lead to new models of man: at least they will lead to an appreciation of the fundamental complexity of explanation at any scale.

The problems of separating micro from macro and of deciding the relationships between the processes operating at these levels raises the general geographical problem of scale. Scale 'obtrudes into geographical research in three main ways: in the problem of covering the earth's surface; in the problem of linking results obtained at one scale to those obtained at another; and in standardising information that is available only on a mixed series of scales.'[14] Our main concern so far in the discussion of micro- and macro- processes has been with the second of these — the scale linkage problem. We must be wary of assuming, then, that associations existing at one scale will produce association at another scale or that the magnitude of association or problem will be the same at different scales. Thus unemployment figures at the regional level will mask pockets of greater or less unemployment at a more disaggregated level. The scale linkage and the coverage problems are discussed in more detail later in an example of the distribution of West Indians (p. 68).

SOCIAL GEOGRAPHY — A GROUP FRAMEWORK

We have so far said that our structure of the subject matter of social geography for this book is that of space, pattern, and process. But it is central to ask: patterns of what and what kind of processes? We are not raising empirical questions at this point — these are of course discussed at length in the following chapters — but conceptual and methodological ones. Social geography is concerned with the patterns of the attributes and action of *people*. But is it enough simply to say that we are dealing with people? This introduces another scale problem — a social scale problem, for people range in quantity from one individual to the entire world. It is true to say that however interesting the study of individuals' attributes and activities may be, such an approach will provide us with a chaotic assemblage of behavioural and social data which would be extremely difficult to analyse and structure. We would be in a position then of having too much detail and not enough structure. If we take as our social reference framework the total population of the world, we would encounter the opposite problem. To handle so much information it would be necessary to arrange the attributes and activities into very broad categories. This means of course that we would obtain little detail about these phenomena. It is therefore necessary to strike a happy medium, to produce a social framework that is a meaningful categorization of the population and at the same time provides sufficient detail to form the basis of useful analysis. It is necessary to do this before we begin our studies of spatial behaviour, and it is our belief that this framework should be the group structure of a society. Thus social groups must provide the social reference points for social geography.

Social groups, however, also vary in size, but for the purposes of social geographical study a broad two-type categorization seems appropriate. The basis of the distinction is the general type of social relationships and interaction within each group. On one level, there is the primary group or group-in-the-mind, on the other, the secondary group or group by association. The primary group is dominated by informal, personal face-to-face contact between members and is a vital component of society. Thus, the family is a primary group. In the family there is obvious face-to-face contact. It is the primary group that provides most people with their initial socialization and affective care. These bonds of care and love bind the members of the family together, although other motives may be important. The family, at least in its nuclear form — husband, wife, offspring — is found in virtually every society[15] and like most other social institutions is continuously changing, i.e. adapting and adjusting to wider social changes[16] (see p. 211).

Of greater interest to the social geographer, however, is the neighbourhood group (or community). We do not wish to become deeply involved in the debate on the meaning of community (see p. 120). There have been many attempts to produce a definition. Many of these are of limited use because they are project-specific. Hillery reviewed ninety-four definitions of community and came up with the conclusion that 'all of the definitions deal with people. Beyond this common basis, there is no agreement.' He did find, however, three major elements present in most definitions — area, common ties, and social inter-action.[17] A community is, therefore, small-scale, involving a close pattern of social relationships. This has led some, notably Gans and Pahl, to consider that community *per se* cannot exist in modern society.[18] Many of the community studies which form the basis of our views were made in the 1930s and before. It is equally true to say, as Gans does, that 'ways of life do not coincide with settlement patterns'. But as Pahl has suggested, a group, a small social system, can either be nationally or locally oriented in its outlook and it is the locally oriented group, i.e. with roots and ties in a locality rather than in national values, that remains the basis of present-day community. As Stacey has pointed out, it is doubtful if this local social system will ever be totally eclipsed, although outside processes will influence the local population.[19] The term 'community' can probably be reserved for small-scale, socially intensive groups, and we can define community as a spatially delimited set of interacting primary groups.

This view of community is close to that of Tönnies's idea of *Gemeinschaft*, in which human relationships are long-lasting, inclusive, and intimate.[20] Families and informal primary groups make up the important social units within *Gemeinschaft*. Social relationships, though, are based on a clear understanding of where each person stands in society. Roles are specific and consonant with one another. They are inclusive and not segmental, i.e. involve many aspects of behaviour rather than a limited segment of an individual's total activities. This means that people interact with one another in a wide variety of contexts. It is also worth pointing out that the culture of *Gemeinschaft* is relatively homogeneous and its members relatively immobile, both physically and socially. In such a community, with its enduring loyalties to people and place, behaviour is regulated largely by custom, with the family, church, and primary group being strong moral custodians. Tradition — cumulative experience of *Gemeinschaft* — is therefore central and reinforces the moral code. Intimacy, face-to-face association, and co-operation dominate and really mean therefore that a community is small-scale. Such entities are perhaps more typical of parts of the underdeveloped world rather than the developed. Even in those countries — e.g. Mexico — there is a fierce debate as to the type of community in existence, in other words as to the complexity of social ties in small-scale societies.[21] It would be wrong to extend the term 'community' to larger-scale societies which by definition involve more people with a concomitant decline in face-to-face association. The breakdown is caused by the increasing complexity and interdependence of modern society. Redfield's folk society was ideally self-sufficient. This is no longer possible in the industrial world. People leave their home areas to work, shop, and so on; i.e. their links with the outside world increase, and with the increasing spread of the mass forms of communication, national and international ideas reach even remote and peripheral areas.

Increasing societal complexity does not mean that primary groups disappear; but their functions do change. They operate at a different level of social activity than they did in folk society. The nuclear family becomes the most important primary group as it is the one least affected, in structure at least, by the social and economic changes of the modern world. But individuals do come together to form other groups by their own efforts or those of others. They come together for quite different reasons than did the members of primary groups. Self-interest now dominates. Groupings are important if they help protect or advance the interests of individuals who are similarly placed on the cultural, economic, or political ladders. Thus, for example, blacks are forced into a group because they are stigmatized by white society. Although such groups may eventually become interest-based, their group membership is 'ascribed', i.e. it is determined, by factors over which they have little or no control. Thus we are mainly dealing with biological characteristics that take on or are given social meaning. Racial and ethnic groups are, therefore, the main examples. It can be argued, though, that group membership that is determined by beliefs is, in some ways, 'ascribed'. Believers are considered to be the in-group while those with different values are thought to be different, apart, or the out-group. Throughout history the Jews, for example, have been thought of as a group on the basis of their beliefs. Other factors are important of course — life-style, desire for separation — but these are closely related to the particular pattern of beliefs. Thus religious and, in more general terms, cultural groups belong in the same category as racial groups. It is strange to think of culture as being 'ascribed' because it is essentially learnt. But we argue that an individual has little choice over which culture, set of beliefs, and so on he learns. He is born and socialized into a particular culture. It is the task of social geography to examine the distribution of all these particular groups and then consider the processes that led to their areal concentration, dispersal, or regrouping. If we discover that the Jewish group in London has dispersed from its old concentration in Aldgate and Stepney we must ask why (see p. 179). Similarly, if we find that Italian migrants to American cities seek out concentrations of previous Italian immigrants, we must again ask why (see p. 181). We must attempt to link consideration of spatial pattern and process in a group framework.

Other people group together to achieve certain ends, i.e. they have common interests. This category can be subdivided into those who group for expressive ends, in which there is intrinsic satisfaction in the group activity itself, and those who group for material ends in which group activities are not themselves ends but are means of achieving common goals. Some clarification is in order. Voluntary associations are examples of expressive groups. These consist of individuals who come together because of a shared interest which they consider is best pursued in a group context. All types of clubs and societies fall into this category. Research has shown how voluntary associations tend to be run by and for the particular social groups, especially the middle class.[21] They are, therefore, particularly prevalent in certain localities because of the close correspondence between social segregation and residential segregation (see p. 152).

More common, however, are those who group together for material ends, for example, trade unions, business associations, pressure groups, gangs, political parties, and to some extent classes.[23] Thus, for example, a pressure group is formed to achieve aims which are shared but which the members as individuals could not hope to obtain (see p. 255). It is necessary for social geography to examine the distribution of such activities to discover the situations and environments in which they arise, i.e. the social and spatial contexts of such activities. This is likely to involve both problem and planning perspectives (see Chapters 9 and 10). Gangs are also groups made up of individuals who pursue shared goals and aims. We may discover that gangs are found mainly in run-down housing areas near the city centre. Having discovered such a pattern, we must again ask why. Do these neighbourhoods lack legitimate opportunities for success? Is the cultural context from which such groups emerge significantly different from the values of the wider society? These are complex issues[24] and our concern is simply to show the social geographical context of the study of such groups.

We can call all these groups — 'ascribed', expressive, materialist — groups by association (or secondary groups). This brief classification suggests a more clear-cut division than exists in reality. Individuals associate for a mix of all these reasons and groups are formed by the self-same mix. Groups by association exist particularly, however, in societies dominated by large-scale, transitory, impersonal and contractual relationships (Tönnies's *Gesellschaft*). Thus individuals are categorized as belonging to different sections of society and are required to occupy different statuses and play many different, frequently unrelated roles. Individuals, therefore, group together when they see a particular need — to share a hobby or interest, pursue a wage claim, strengthen their beliefs, or when they are categorized as a group by the rest of society. It is the spatial components of group attributes, activities, and interactions that should be central to social geography.

We do not pretend that these ideas are new. The group has a long history of study in both social psychology and sociology. In the latter subject, in fact, Durkheim introduced the topic of social morphology, the analysis of the distribution of social forms (or *substrat social*). He viewed the *substrat social* as the group framework for his study of social interaction and differentiation. This group framework is, however, independent of any consideration of the physical environment, a point later rectified by Sorre in his conception of social space[25] (see p. 34). Rather than physical environment we consider that it is spatial setting — the use and meaning of space (see p. 62) — that must be tied to the group framework to produce a group-oriented social geography.

The second aspect to methodological and conceptual problems that we raised concerned processes, i.e. how patterns are explained. Social geography is beginning to put forward explanations, as will be seen in our chapters on processes, but as yet has tended, like the parent discipline, to adopt a pragmatic approach to the problems it tackles. This may mean that explanation is piecemeal, suggesting one set of processes for one set of circumstances and another set for changing circumstances. In some ways, this book reflects, indeed must reflect, this approach because it is a statement of where the discipline is as well as, hopefully, an encouragement to future exploration. Social geography then lacks a strong theoretical basis because of its past pragmatism and also because of its straddling of both micro and macro concerns. But if we take the group to be the social framework of social geography some theoretical suggestions can be made. Many of these are implicit in the following chapters, but we take this opportunity to make them explicit.

Group Structure. Our first conceptual concern must be what binds individuals together in groups? It must be remembered that we are not dealing with individuals *per se* but with individuals as members of groups. Studies that have examined spatial behaviour beyond the level of the individual have, in the main, produced conclusions about aggregates and not about groups. Put another way, behavioural geography has tried to explain aggregate behaviour and not group behaviour. Part of the reason can be found in the data used. Thus, for example, census data tell us about age aggregations and not age groups. Another reason is that the object of many studies has not been to differentiate group behaviour in space but to distinguish between spatial objects on the basis of their attractiveness or otherwise to collectivities of individuals. In the case of consumer behaviour, for example, the spatial object — town, service centre hierarchy — has been the primary focus of attention, although there has been some change in interest toward treating shopping as a search procedure on the part of people.[26] Even here it is perhaps important to stress that emphasis should be placed on the search procedures of groups and not aggregates, i.e. the definition of shopping groups must become a research task for the social geographer.

It appears, however, that the major determinants of internal group cohesion are both economic and cultural. First, it seems that individuals of similar socio-economic position are more likely to group themselves together than those of divergent status. Second, those who come together to form a group will probably possess similar ideas about the world and how to behave in the world. The spatial aspects of these shared beliefs are discussed in the next chapter. This normative structure of the group is an important cohesive element. What are its guidelines for action (norms)?; what is its view of the world (values)? A theory of group action that stresses the importance of group norms is Parsons's normative theory of social action.[27] In this, interaction occurs when one person needs or wishes to take account of the action of another. Then if both these people have some regular need to consider each other's actions, certain mutual expectations — norms — emerge, which define the conditions of interaction. This emergence and acceptance of norms is not a piecemeal development but each person gains other benefits from his participation. It is of great help if the relationship becomes predictable, i.e. it becomes easier to manage, and the members are also said to gain gratification from the interaction process. These elements, along with socialization and social control, are the ways in which the pattern of norms — the social equilibrium — is maintained. Parsons used this interaction process between two people as a microcosm of a social system. The elements in this process — beliefs, values, and norms — make up the system. The social system is seen, therefore, as a set of rules. No social life is possible without a normative system.

This view has had many criticisms levelled against it, especially from the point of view of inter-group relationships. The crux of this criticism is that the emphasis on consensual, normative elements means that the interests that produce social conflict and instability are ignored.[28] While such criticisms have great validity, we can still conclude that for the mechanics of a group's internal structure the normative theory has relevance. Even if groups in society are in conflict, the members of each group must be bound together or the groups would not exist. The binding principles, integrative mechanisms, are both objective and subjective, concern both socio-economic position and norms and values. The latter place emphasis on the psychological and cultural aspects of group action; because a normative structure is produced by the internalizing in individual minds, of guidelines, rules, and perspectives, these being produced and strengthened by the interaction of group members, i.e. by their culture. Thus, the conceptual framework for a study of groups in space must include cultural and psychological dimensions in order to discover shared views and perspectives and the integrative mechanisms operating in different environments. To date the most important geographical research in this context is perhaps that concentrating on image and perception (see Chapter 2).

Group Categorization and Differences. As we said, however, there is an objective dimension to the definition of group structure. This is best seen when we move to the next level of analysis and consider inter-group relationships, i.e. the interaction *between* groups. The view that stresses that different social groups are more often than not in harmonious accord (i.e. have a strong normative relationship) has been severely challenged. It must be pointed out that a discussion of group differences involves two elements. First, we need to know how different groups are categorized by the rest of society. This was examined earlier in our exposition of the importance of groups in social geography. Conceptually, then, the categorization of groups involves us in a consideration of *Gemeinschaft, Gesellschaft*, group-in-the-mind, groups by association. It was in fact pointed out that groups by assocation — interest groups or secondary groups — tend to dominate modern society, whereas groups-in-the-mind are more prevalent in folk society. Second, we must also examine the effects of group differences on the spatial structure. The best starting-point for examining such effects seems to be the nature of the relationships between groups. The consensual normative view has been challenged. Parsons has, for example, been criticized for ignoring the substratum of social action, especially in the way in which this may condition interests likely to produce social conflict and instability. This substratum has been defined as 'the factual disposition of means in the situation of action, that produces interests of a non-normative kind'.[29] Thus too great an emphasis on norms means that the relationships of power and conflict inherent in the scarcity of means (and of course ends) in society are underemphasized.

In all societies resources are limited. In some societies this may not matter. In hunting and gathering societies, there was often a balance between resources and population. Other societies may be organized on egalitarian principles, perhaps on principles of social justice (see p. 221), so that all members receive a 'fair' share of the resources available. It is in competitive societies like those of the industrialized West that the limitation of available goods and services has special significance. In these societies, there is no principle of social justice and there is conflict over who gets what. This conflict need not manifest itself if there is a consensus on the allocation criteria that decide who gets what. It can be argued that there is no such consensus in the modern industrial capitalist societies, that there is an unprincipled scramble for goods and services with the groups with the most power obtaining a greater share of these resources. Some have argued that this conflict can have important, positive uses for the society in which it occurs.[30] It can lead to innovation and point the way to necessary change. Thus, for example, the conflict over desirable housing space may lead to attempts to develop cheaper, more accessible forms of private housing, or the competition for world grain supplies may lead to attempts to increase yields and acreage. In this view, conflict is seen as a way in which the normative structure adjusts to meet new conditions. It should be pointed out, however, that although conflict does increase the innovative potential of a society, the direction of change is not always easy to predict. In our housing example, it is just as likely that conflict over desirable housing would lead to its greater concentration among particular social groups simply because those who begin as winners usually remain winners and losers remain losers[31].

We have argued that the relative positions of different social groups in this conflict over scarce and desirable resources of both spatial and non-spatial kinds is determined to a large extent by the amount of power each of them possesses. The power of groups depends greatly on their position in the market, i.e. their ability to obtain scarce resources depends on their relative standing in the competitive process. This has led many to conclude that class is the most important form of group as it is placement in the economic structure that is the prime determinant of competitive ability. So the amount of money obtained from work conditions the type of housing obtained or educational resources enjoyed, and so power is thus seen as being dependent on class membership, on position in the labour market. But modern society is more complex. Other factors, including cultural phenomena, affect an individual's group membership and social position (see pp. 145-7). Thus class and status largely determine social position. The position of an individual or a group in the social structure greatly influences the ability of the individual or group to obtain the scarce and desirable resources of society. Position in the social structure, therefore, determines access to scarce resources, such as power and wealth, which in turn influence position in the spatial structure and access to spatial resources.[32] If those with power distribute resources to their own advantage, as might be expected, the spatial structure would then reflect the distribution of power in society. But the welfare and planning agencies attempt to reduce great differences in the share of scarce resources enjoyed by different groups. For example, public housing is built, social security benefits paid, and health, educational, and other facilities are provided. While the efficacy of such measures for eradicating inequality can be questioned (see Chapter 10), they have certainly altered the relationships between groups in their competition for resources. It now appears that there are many different markets in which groups compete for the resources and facilities of that market — labour market, housing market, welfare services market, and so on. The conflict between groups is often tempered by social and political considerations which modify the effects of economic forces. It is of course still true to say that the labour market is the dominant market because social and political interference in other markets is often a reaction to the situation produced by labour market relationships. On the whole though, the Weberian notion of market situation (see p. 145) seems more appropriate for our discussion of group conflicts and differences that does economically determined class. In summary, then, a consideration of inter-group relationships consists of two parts: the first involves such concepts as *Gemeinschaft, Gesellschaft*, and the categorization of groups, and the second includes such concepts as conflict (the basic competition for scarce resources in a market-dominated society), power (the relative standing of groups in this competition), inequality (the resulting distribution of resources produced by unequal power positions), and market situation (the relative position of groups in different resource markets).

Groups in society. The third and final aspect of our group-oriented approach to social geography is to consider the wider issue of groups in relation to society itself and particularly to social, economic, political, and cultural changes that affect society. Of course, these changes will affect different groups in different ways and it seems likely that the type and magnitude of effect will depend on the group's structure and its position in relation to other groups. The major changes that have affected most industrial (and to a lesser extent industrializing) societies are industrialization and urbanization. Industrialization has the impact of reducing a society's reliance on the land and creating situations that demand new social relationships. In an agricultural society, primary groups with close links with the land predominate. There is also a hierarchical arrangement of groups with each knowing quite clearly its position and role with respect to the others. Thus in feudal society, there were three major groupings — nobility, clergy, and commoners — each with a defined function and a regulated pattern of rights and obligations as far as the others were concerned. The family was often the unit of production and the local community had a strong hold over its members. With industrialization, individuals enter rather different relationships. The cultural and political links between superordinate and subordinate groups start to break down as monetary, contractual relations begin to dominate. The family changes in both structure and function, as does the community (see p. 120). A usual concomitant of industrialization is the growth of towns, bringing people from different regions and cultures into contact with one another. In Chicago's Near North Side slum, there were twenty-eight different nationalities in the 1920s (see p. 29). This mixing may be increased by long-distance permanent migration (Chapter 8), which has led to the social heterogeneity of American cities and the development of primate cities in the Latin America and Africa of today.

As the industrialization of a society continues, there is likely to be an increasing specialization of labour to increase efficiency and improve production. There is then an increasing division of labour. As this happens, there is a growing interdependence among different sections of society. No one section produces all its needs. In fact it produces more and more of less and less. This interdependent association is, however, based normally on the vested interests of each section or group. Primary groups, excluding the nuclear family, weaken, and groups by association become more important, and the relative power of these groups will determine the impact that these processes of industrialization, urbanization, and specialization have. As society becomes more complex, as it increases in scale (see Chapter 8), there is an increasing need for organization, i.e. for the orderly arrangement of affairs. This organization is necessary both in the economic sphere and in the political sphere, the latter becoming increasingly important to regulate group relationships as societal complexity increases. This is the introduction of bureaucratic management and of planning — to arrange affairs, decide priorities, control any abuses. It is from the political bureaucracy that groups which lack power in economic sphere expect recompense (see Chapter 10). In summary, there are three major processes acting on groups in a changing society — industrialization, urbanization, and bureaucratization. It is these that must form the basis of our analysis of change.

Table 1.1. *Summary of the Three Identified levels of Social Activity*

Level of Social Activity	Concepts/Processes
Group Structure	Normative Structure
	Shared Values
	Cultural Definition
Group Categorization and Differences	Primary and Secondary Groups
	Class and Market Situation
	Conflict and Power
Groups in Society	Processes of Change
	Industrialization
	Urbanization
	Bureaucratization

It is obvious from our discussion of the conceptual basis of social geography that the three levels — group structure, group categorization and differences, and groups in society — are interrelated; the elements at one level condition, and are modified by, elements at the other (see Table 1.1). Any analysis involves an ordering — a classification — of information and ideas into manageable sections. We feel that this is less arbitrary than most because it deals with meaningful levels of social activities. The following chapters reflect this conceptual ordering. Group structure, especially the shared, cultural meaning of space, is discussed in Chapter 2. Group categorization and differences are examined in Chapters 3, 4, 5, 6, and 7, especially from the viewpoint of the patterns of group attributes and differences and important processes such as residential selection and segregation. Groups in society, particularly in urban and political affairs, are discussed in Chapters 8, 9, and 10. It may be that not all the studies we utilize fit into our scheme of things: it would be strange if they did. The fact that five chapters are in one topic area shows the present concentration of interest. We also introduce material to point to other methodological and empirical problems. These help to portray particular approaches to and dimensions of social geography. It is of course hoped that much future research will fit into a group- and problem-oriented framework.

NOTES AND REFERENCES

[1] J.W. Watson (1957), 'The Sociological Aspects of Geography' in G. Taylor (ed.), *Geography in the Twentieth Century*, 3rd ed., London, pp. 463–99.

[2] R.E. Pahl (1965), 'Trends in Social Geography' in R.J. Chorley and P. Haggett (eds.), *Frontiers in Geographical Teaching*, London, pp. 81–100.

[3] A Buttimer (1968), 'Social Geography' in D.L. Sills (ed.), *International Encyclopaedia of the Social Sciences*, New York, Vol. 6, pp. 134–45.

[4] J. Eyles (1974), 'Social Theory and Social Geography', *Progress in Geography* 6, pp. 22–87.

[5] E. Jones (1975), Introduction in E. Jones (ed.), *Readings in Social Geography*, London, pp. 1–12.

[6] See, P. Vidal de la Blache (1926), *Principles of Human Geography*, London; H. Peake and H.J. Fleure (1927–36), *The Corridors of Time*, Oxford; C.D. Forde (1934), *Habitat, Economy and Society*, London; A. Rees (1950), *Life in a Welsh Countryside*, Cardiff. For a discussion of this geographical work see also P. James (1972), *All Possible Worlds* Indianapolis; T.W. Freeman (1961), *A hundred Years of Geography* London.

[7] E.E. Evans (1951), *Mourne Country*, Dundalk.

[8] C. Sauer (1962), 'Cultural Landscape' in P.L. Wagner and M.W. Mikesell (eds.), *Readings in Cultural Geography*, Chicago, pp. 30–3.

[9] P. James, op. cit., p. 459.

[10] The problem of regional delimitation is one that has caused much debate in geography. See P. Haggett (1965), *Locational Analysis in Human Geography*, London; M. Chisholm (1975), *Human Geography*, Harmondsworth.

[11] Eyles (1974), op. cit.

[12] E. Jones (1956), 'Cause and Effect in Human Geography', *Ann. Ass. Am. Geog.* 46.

[13] L. Curry (1967), 'Chance and Landscape' in *Northern Geographical Essays*.

[14] P. Haggett (1965), 'Scale Components in Geographical Problems' in Chorley and Haggett, op. cit., pp. 164–182.

[15] The universal presence of the nuclear family is discussed by G.P. Murdock (1949), *Social Structure*, New York.

[16] The changes in the nature and functions of the family are examined by M. Young and P. Willmott (1973), *The Symmetrical Family*, London.

[17] G.A. Hillery (1955), 'Definitions of Community: Areas of Agreement', *Rural Sociology* 20.

[18] R.E. Pahl (1970), *Patterns of Urban Life*, London: and H.J. Gans (1968) *People and Plans*, New York.

[19] M. Stacey (1969), 'The Myth of Community Studies', *British Journal of Sociology* 20, pp. 134–47.

[20] F. Tönnies (1957), *Community and Association*, New York.

[21] See the contrasting views of R. Redfield (1941), *The Folk Culture of Yucatan*, Chicago; and D. Lewis (1951), *Life in a Mexican Village: Tepoztlan Revisited*, Urbana.

[22] See Pahl (1970), op. cit.

[23] Class is perhaps a special case. Classes are not formal organizations but they involve at times the conscious actions of many individuals towards certain ends. It is more than a social aggregate. We have called it a group, others however regard it as a social category. Class also involves some 'ascription' or at least categorization by others. Thus it consists of shared beliefs and stereotyping by others. Because of these problems and its importance, it may deserve a category to itself. See our discussion on class in Chapter 6.

[24] The relative importance of these arguments has been extensively debated by sociologists and criminologists. Those interested are recommended to read J.B. Mays (1970), *Crime and its Treatment*, London.

[25] E. Durkheim (1964) *The Division of Labour in Society*, New York; M. Sorre (1957) *Recontres de la géographie et de la sociologie*, Paris. These views are brought together by A. Buttimer (1969), 'Social Space in Interdisciplinary Perspective', *Geogl. Rev.* 59, pp. 417–26.

[26] See the review of these studies of consumer behaviour by R. Davies (1973), 'The Location of Service Activities' in M. Chisholm and B. Rodgers (eds.), *Studies in Human Geography*, London, pp. 125–71.

[27] T. Parsons (1937), *The Structure of Social Action*, New York; id. (1951), *The Social System*, London.

[28] See Eyles (1974), op. cit.

[29] D. Lockwood (1956), 'Some Remarks on "the Social System" ', *British Journal of Sociology* 7, pp. 134–46.

[30] This is essentially a functionalist conception and is discussed fully in Eyles (1974), op. cit.

[31] See also K. Coates and R. Silburn (1970), *Poverty: The Forgotten Englishman*, Harmondsworth.

[32] See, J. Eyles (1971), 'Pouring New Sentiments into Old Theories: How Else Can We Look At Behavioural Patterns', *Area* 3, pp. 242–50.

2   Concepts of space

The core of concern in social geography is people in groups but to talk about people without reference to their milieux is to forsake geography altogether. Earlier in the history of the subject, i.e. in the nineteenth and early twentieth centuries this complicated debate on how man's behaviour could be related to his habitat was simplified by separating the identity of man from the environment. When this was done it seemed to most geographers that the explanation of man's behaviour lay in a causal relationship between the two. Behaviour was seen as a reaction to forces in the environment in which man lived. At its most crude this meant that man lived his life at the dictate of the environment. Through the spatial variation of resources and through climatic control, the environment determined man's economy, the materials from which he built his shelter, his thinking, and even his religious beliefs. The geographer's task, even when focused on human activities, was to study these geographical, i.e. environmental, factors.

Two of the greatest English-speaking proponents of this approach were Huntingdon and Semple. One of Huntingdon's basic theses was that great historic cycles of drought periodically drove nomadic peoples out of the heart of Asia to invade Eastern Europe. He was also convinced that civilizations could thrive only in areas of stimulating climate, and that as tropical areas could never provide this, they were doomed to remain poor. Semple, a pupil of the German geographer Ratzel, fully accepted her teacher's premiss that man had to obey a kind of environmental 'law' which dictated his actions. She summarized by saying, 'Man is a product of the earth's surface . . . the earth has mothered him, fed him, set him tasks, directed his thoughts.'[1] Thus the explanation for man's works and even his behaviour lay in the environment.

The reaction to the more extreme environmentalists was best formulated by certain French geographers, particularly Vidal de la Blache, who insisted that the relationship between man and environment was two-way, that to a large extent man decided how he wanted to live, albeit within limits set by nature. The environment, rather than compelling man to do this or that, presented him with a number of possibilities, from which he chose. This choice was largely the outcome of man's culture. In British geography, these relationships were expressed well by Fleure, who divided the world's surface into seven major regions indicating man's well-being. These were regions of hunger, debilitation, increment, effort, difficulty, wandering, and industrialization.[2] In fact, each of these is a reflection of the environment as well as man's response to it. The link with the environment as a factor remains in this two-way relationship.

The French school did not resolve the problem of environmental determinism, but, rather, focused attention on man's role in the interrelationship. The arguments for and against environmentalism were periodically echoed until the middle of this century, the subtleties of argument and the weight of evidence proving inadequate substitutes for basic belief, until the arguments themselves became sterile. To a large extent the dilemma was put aside in the 1950s when a sequence of papers by British scholars gave a new turn to the discussion of man–milieu relationship doctrine.[3] New fundamental problems were posed, new directions sought, which gave geography another perspective and added dimensions.

But in the meantime, the more flexible approach of geographers like Fleure and in particular Vidal de la Blache had led to the development of fruitful concepts about social geography. Vidal saw social relations as consisting of an intricate network of ties and ideas. These provide a stable way of perceiving and conducting daily life in a particular geographical setting. This geographical setting is of great importance. In fact Vidal saw terrestial unity — the interrelationship of all physical and environmental phenomena — as a basic factor in the study of man and environment. 'Every area with a given relief, location and climate is a composite environment where groups of elements — indigenous, ephemeral, migratory and surviving from former ages — are concentrated, diverse but united by a common adaptation to the environment.'[4] This adaptation to and contact with the environment is given concrete expression in particular patterns of living (*genres de vie*). These are sets of techniques, derived from past experience, by which man obtains the material necessities of life within a functional social order. The significance of *genres de vie* is that culture becomes the main basis of regional differentiation. Vidal de la Blache described France as a series of *pays*, traditional units of social homogeneity which had come to terms with the habitat in their own particular way. Much later Bowen applied the term *pays* to the heartland of Wales, the cultural as well as the physical core of the country where the pattern of Welsh life is least disturbed.[5] Thus repeated experiences within a particular geographical milieu can lead to the development of a community consciousness which makes a *genre de vie* an ecological system.[6]

The approach of Vidal is holistic, viewing space as a total phenomenon (*à ne pas morceler ce que la nature rassemble*), which is echoed in Britain in the work of Roxby who viewed social geography as the regional distribution and interrelation of different forms of social organization arising out of particular modes of life.[7] Vidal's approach is also concerned with the adaptation of man to his environment, not his determination by the environment. It is the possibilist way of viewing the man–land relationship — the land suggests various potentials and man has the choice of which one he realizes. But it can be argued that possibilism is only a variant of determinism because the limiting conditions are still environmentally set. It at least gave geographers the chance to stress that within such limits man was capable of exercising free will and of fashioning his way of life. *Genres de vie* are essentially projections of society.

The space in which human activities take place cannot be ignored. We have already referred to a recent definition of the subject-matter of social geography as 'the study of the patterns and processes involved in understanding socially defined populations in their spatial setting.'[8] Although this 'spatial setting' may sound uncomfortably like the old environmental stage on which history was 'acted', its environmental elements have been nullified to a neutral setting. In other words, space is looked upon as something where events take place. We suggested earlier that it may be more fruitful to look upon space as the outcome of human behaviour, much depending on man's perception of it and the values with which he invests it. But before dealing with this aspect, let us examine the contribution made by the human ecologists, who take us back to a consideration of the *role* of the habitat in determining patterns of land use and even of behaviour, because there is much in this approach that links it with environmentalism.

Briefly, human ecology is 'an attempt to investigate the processes by which the biotic balance and the social equilibrium are maintained once they are achieved and the processes by which, when the biotic balance and the social equilibrium are disturbed, the transition is made from one relatively stable order to another.'[9] The biological parallel implies, as in nature, a mechanistic sorting process in which causal relationships are strongly environmental. The human ecologists, then, applied biological analogy to the study of human society. The impersonal, rational forces affecting organisms were seen as having their parallel in forces affecting man, although he was subject to other wants besides those needed for existence. Two levels of human activity were therefore identified — the biotic (community) and the cultural (society). It is difficult to improve on Robson's excellent discussion of these terms.

The biotic gave rise to the community and was based on the sub-social forces of competition. At this level, people were regarded as 'individuals' lacking distinctively social attributes and therefore subject to the same impulses and forces as were plants or animals in their struggle for existence and for the acquisition of the most favourable circumstances in which to live. The cultural level, on the other hand, gave rise to society and was based on the strictly social processes of communication and consensus in which people become 'persons' with social attributes . . . Society . . . was seen therefore as a superstructure lying above the more basic competitive level of community.[10]

The ecologists in fact concentrated on the biotic level, the most important concept being competition for the limited space of the habitat and for access to the most desirable locations for residence and business. Because 'individuals' with similar social attributes are similarly placed in their ability to cope with these forces of competition, there results a pattern of segregation of like types of people and like types of activity. This segregation creates therefore the basic unit of ecological space — the natural area, an unplanned product of the city's growth.

In the competition for position the population is segregated over the natural areas of the city. Land values, characterising the various natural areas, tend to sift and sort the population. At the same time segregation re-emphasises trends in values. Cultural factors also play a part in this segregation, creating repulsions and attractions . . . Natural areas and natural cultural areas tend to coincide. A natural area is a geographical area characterised both by a physical individuality and by the cultural characteristics of the people who live in it.[11]

A natural area then is an area of specified population identity, in which local social organization is related to the physical structure of the city. Thus ecological forces are predominant in allocating groups to particular urban locations. The segregation of groups in natural areas is mainly caused by their differential ability to cope with competition. So the broad ecological structure, e.g. the zones of Chicago,[12] is based on economic criteria. Other aspects of segregation such as culture, race, and language operate only within the sphere of appropriate economic levels, i.e. they further segregate elements of the population but only within the economically determined pattern — e.g. Little Sicily, the Ghetto, Chinatown in Chicago's zone of transition (Fig. 2.1).

The natural area was the focus for many studies of the human ecologists. Zorbaugh, for example, examined Chicago's Near North Side, an area of transition in which the character of the people and the area's problems were both reflections and consequences of conditions imposed by the period of transition. The district was characterized by 'the isolation of the populations crowded together within these few hundred blocks, the superficiality and externality of their contacts, the

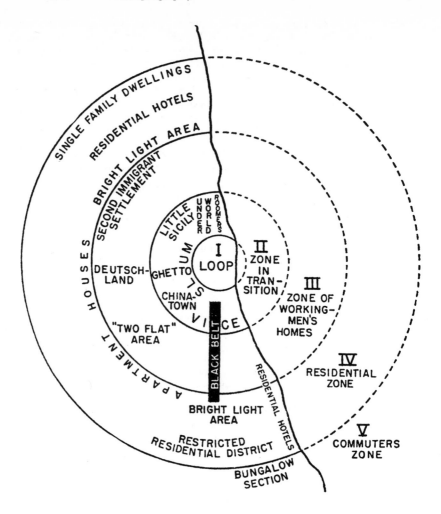

Fig. 2.1 The urban areas of Chicago (G.A. Theodorson (1961), *Studies in Human Ecology*, New York)

social distances that separate them, their absorption in the affairs of their own little worlds . . .'[13] Zorbaugh found four major natural areas. First, the Gold Coast, the area along the lakeshore. It had the highest residential land values in Chicago and many of its inhabitants were in professional jobs. The main attribute of the population was their wealth. Second, the rooming-house district, the area a few blocks inland from the lakeshore. The main residential characteristics were the lack of children and high population turnover. It was an area of transience where stays were temporary as people moved in and out as their life-cycle needs changed. Thus the area suited, amongst others, young childless couples who might move to the suburbs on the birth of a child. Third, Towertown, the bohemian bright-lights district with its restaurants, brothels, dance-halls, and so on. It was the service district with few actual residents. Fourth, the slum, inland from Towertown. This was the district in which immigrant groups congregate. Group after group claimed the slum for their own — the Irish, Germans, Swedes, Sicilians. Moving to such an area provided a known milieu for people entering a strange new world (see Chapter 7).

It should be added that, just as in plant and animal communities, some individual or species will obtain positions of maximum advantage and will become dominant. Over time, dominance leads to invasion and succession. Invasion, the encroachment of an incompatible population or land-use, represents a sudden challenge to the equilibrium of a natural area. Equilibrium will return only when succession is completed. These processes are best illustrated by the familiar example of Burgess's model of city growth. Dominance is exemplified by the fact that business competition to locate in the area of greatest accessibility will result in this central area having the highest land values. Invasion is exemplified by the changing character of the zone of transition with central city land uses invading this zone. In areas where the invasion is complete, succession is said to have occurred and the equilibrium restored.

There have of course been many criticisms of the ecological approach. It is our concern to mention briefly those that affect the ecological concept of space — the natural area. Hatt in his study of the city structure of Seattle has shown how data have been forced into a natural area pattern to conform with ecological theory.[14] Hatt used data on central Seattle to try to discern the presence of natural areas. A block-by-block examination of the district pointed to a complex pattern with only two very small areas of homogeneity — a south-western part of low status and a north-eastern one of high status. The remainder, the bulk of the district, was one of mixed characteristics. Thus to deduce a pattern of natural areas in central Seattle would create a reality where none exists. Hatt considered that the differences between his work and that of the classical ecologists were due to the fact that the latter did not distinguish between natural areas as logical statistical constructs and as a series of spatial and social factors that act as coercive influences on everyone who inhabits the geographically and culturally defined areas.

In conclusion, we can say that the human ecologists thought of the solidarity and shared interests of community members as functions of their common residence. Social solidarity including the social use of space is seen as determined by the particular pattern taken by the physical structure of the city. Common location is an important factor, but overemphasizing it means that the ability of individuals and groups to choose is largely ignored. 'Ecological explanations of social life are most applicable if the subjects under study lack the ability to make choices ... Choices ... are functions of the roles people play in the social system'[15] (see Chapter 6). Thus the ecologists saw that the forces of competition and segregation compel all individuals and groups to act in a particular way. Their work is, however, of lasting importance. If we recognize that many people have a degree of choice over, say, residential location, then we can say that the ecological approach can give some idea of the spatial constraints within which choices are made. Ecological space is, therefore, spatial space, i.e. space with little or no social meaning.

SENTIMENTS, SYMBOLISM, AND SOCIAL SPACE

Partly in reaction to the narrow determinism of the human ecologists, attempts have been made to analyse the environment in terms of the social values of the groups living in or using that environment. The pioneering work on this concept of space was carried out by Firey in Boston.[16] In Firey's view, the human ecologists saw individuals as being passive adapters to place. He thought that physical space, considered apart from its culturally defined meanings, might be quite irrelevant to social interaction. Thus space may acquire important properties through cultural definition; a social group may possess certain sentiments about its living space, giving it a symbolic, culturally defined meaning. Thus we need to know a great deal about the culture and group-milieux in which people operate before we can make useful comments about their meaning and use of space. For example, the meaning and use of agricultural land among the Dogon in Mali cannot be understood without reference to their culture and religion (their values and beliefs).

The country of the Dogon has been organised as far as possible in accordance with the principle that the world developed in the form of a spiral. In theory, the central point of development is formed by three ritual fields, assigned to three of the mythical ancestors and to the three fundamental cults. When laid out, they mark out a world in miniature on which the gradual establishment of man takes place. Starting from these three fields the fields belonging to the various kin groups, and finally various individual fields, are sited along the axis of a spiral starting from this central area [see Fig. 2.2] [17]

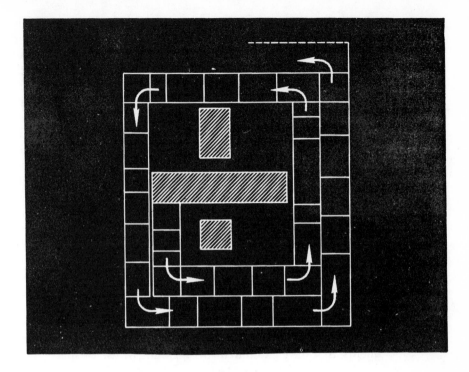

Fig. 2.2 The Dogon cosmic field pattern: counterclockwise spiral extension of cultivated land around three original fields (Sopher, 1967)

Firey suggested, that values (or volitional adaptation) comprise one of the criteria by which certain social groups choose locations. Locational patterns emerge that are meaningfully consistent with spatially referred values. He demonstrated this by his study of Beacon Hill, an area that should have been invaded by commercial land-uses according to ecological theory but which remained an upper-class residential district because of shared values about its reputation, use, and development. These values found symbolic expression in a place and therefore helped to maintain a particular kind of land-use. Social values are both a cause and consequence of specific uses and activities. Firey also suggested that although interests (or rational adaptation) dominate the spatial adaptation of certain activities, these interests themselves derive indirectly from a larger cultural system which has an important role to play in ecological change. Back Bay, an area near Boston's CBD (central business district), had been invaded and its land-use pattern was changing. The district was being taken over by middle-class apartment blocks, professional services such as doctors and dentists, and high-class shops dealing in expensive high-order goods. Firey explained the *type* of invasion with reference to the previous occupiers of Back Bay. It had been a high-class residential district, and Firey argued that the new land-uses were attracted by the area's high-class reputation. There was a rough congruence between the old and new residential uses, while the professional services and retail establishments required symbolic representation of their statuses. Back Bay provided this. Thus cultural similarity as well as interests plays a part in determining the pattern of ecological change. A British example of both Beacon Hill and Back Bay is Mayfair in London. Much of this area is still in residential use, despite its proximity to the West End. It has a reputation of being a high-class area, which may have helped to restrain the ecological invasion from nearby commercial and entertainment uses. Those parts of Mayfair that have changed their pattern of land-use are similar to Back Bay. In Mayfair, high-class hotels, diplomatic premises, and professional services predominate. Firey's work and this British example demonstrate the importance of values, i.e. cultural phenomena, in the determination of land-uses. Physical space becomes socially defined.

The social definition of space has been examined by several different researchers. We want now to look at four related geographical developments that have examined this meaning of use of space. These are social landscape; social space; territorial space; and the image and perception studies.

Social Landscape. The idea of social landscape was developed by Bobek.[18] This is a region or place in which one or several groups live and have a common set of ideas about their environment. Bobek, in fact, emphasizes social and not cultural landscape, i.e. people not things. As Preston James pointed out, Bobek is interpreting cultural landscape with the clear recognition that the human group — its attitudes, objectives, and technical skills — is the major force for change.[19] The objective is then the delimitation of regions on this basis. This has been followed up in Germany by Hartke and his followers, who consider that the occupational structure expresses social values which are in turn the primary agents of landscape differentiation on a social geographical basis.[20]

Social Space. Buttimer sees social space as the central concept of social geography and her discussion utilizes the work of French scholars, particularly Sorre and Chombart de Lauwe. Social space is seen as involving a synthesis of the perceived and objective dimensions of space. 'Sorre envisaged social space as a mosaic of areas, each homogeneous in terms of the space perceptions of its inhabitants. Within each of the areas a network of points and lines radiating from certain "points privileges" (theatres, schools, churches, and other focuses of social movement) could be identified. Each group tended to have its own specific social space which reflected its particular values, preferences, and aspirations. The density of social space reflected the complementarity, and consequently the degree of interaction between groups'.[21] Buttimer also introduces the ideas of Chombart de Lauwe on social space. His starting-point in his study of Paris was the distinction between objective social space — the social framework in which groups live; groups whose social structure and organization have been conditioned by ecological and cultural factors — and subjective social space — space as perceived by members of particular human groups. Spatial patterns were then studied on these two levels and in many instances objective and subjective spaces failed to coincide — subjective space reflecting values, aspirations, and cultural traditions that consciously or unconsciously distorted the objective dimensions of the environment. Chombart also evolved a hierarchy of spaces — familial space, neighbourhood space, economic space, and urban sector social space — within which groups live, move, and interact. It appears that Chombart has incorporated the notions of the use *and* perception of social space into a hierarchically arranged activity system. This idea of activity space has several interesting parallels with, for example, action-space (see p. 159) and territoriality. Territoriality has links with ecology, but whereas ecologists stressed biotic and economic factors, territorial space attempts to include the interactional and phenomenological aspects of human activity.

Phenomenology, the idea that knowledge does not exist independently of man, deserves to be discussed in its own right, as it is important in the study of behaviour and social space. It postulates that the world can only be understood in its reference to man and only through his attitudes and intentions. Thus man's own definition of all spatial situations is seen as vital to understanding human activity. Phenomenology provides, therefore, the philosophical underpinnings of the idea of social space. Perhaps the philosophical and practical aspects of the phenomenological world have reached their greatest expression in the work of Tuan.[22] He has looked at the world-views of different groups, presenting for example the ideas of the Yurok Indians of northern California. They conceptualize their world as a two-dimensional circular disc, despite the rugged nature of their territory (see Fig. 2.3). The river Klamath is their main source of food and means of transportation. Lacking the idea of cardinal directions, the Yurok orient themselves by this principal geographical feature, speaking of direction as upstream or downstream. The Yurok world is small (about 150 miles across) and beyond it the inhabitants are not greatly aware of social or environmental features.

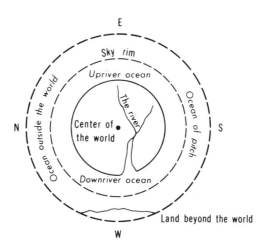

Fig. 2.3 Cosmography of the Yurok Indians, Northern California (Tuan, 1974)

The Yurok know the Klamath ends in the sea but they also believe that by going upstream for ten days or so the ocean is again reached. Water thus surrounds the circular earth, the centre of this world being on the banks of the Klamath. At this point, the sky, a solid dome, was made. The Yurok world can only be understood with reference to themselves. It is an ethnocentric world-view that places the group at the centre of a relatively isolated symmetrical world.

One further example will serve to clarify the point that we cannot understand a group's use of space outside its own definitions. 'The traditional form and layout of the Chinese city is an image of the Chinese cosmos, an ordered and consecrated world set apart by a massive earthen girdle from the contingent world beyond.'[23] The Chinese saw themselves as being at the centre of the earth, which was seen as a series of zones of decreasing 'civilization' away from the imperial capital (see Fig. 2.4a). Inside China, a royal city then required the following layout — orientation to the cardinal points; a square shape girded by walls; twelve gates to represent the twelve months; an inner precinct for the royal residences and audience halls; a public market to the north of the inner enclosure; a principal street from the

(a)

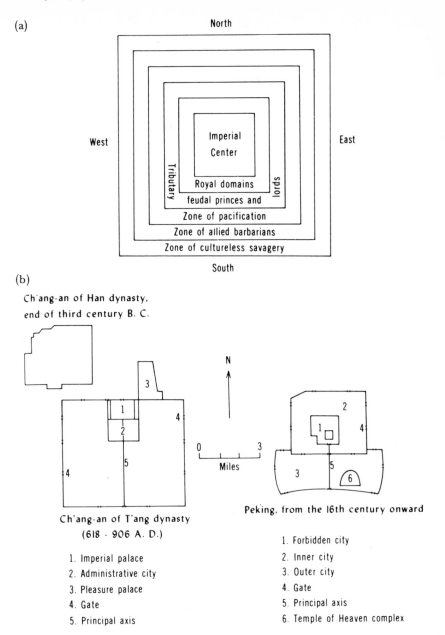

Fig. 2.4 (a) Traditional ethnocentric Chinese world view, dating back to fifth century B.C. (b) Ch'ang-an of Han dynasty, and Peking (Tuan, 1974)

south gate of the palace enclosure to the central south gate of the city wall; and two sacred places (the royal ancestral temple and the altar of the earth) on either side of the main street. The royal palace thus dominated the city and symbolically the world. The market, the centre of profane activity, was separated from the centre of religious activity and placed behind it. No city incorporated all elements of this ideal plan, as the examples of Ch'ang-an and Peking show (see Fig. 2.4b).

Territorial Space. We can begin our discussion of territoriality or territorial space by referring to the work of the ethologists, recently popularized by Robert Ardrey.[24] Ardrey sees territory as an area which an animal or group of animals defines as its exclusive preserve. This definition is expanded by reference to the work of Fraser Darling. He considered that one of the most important functions of territory is the provision of a periphery for security and stimulation. Animals at any rate are said to require a secure yet stimulating environment for a satisfactory existence (see p. 156). Ardrey has added the need for identity which animals and people feel and which territory provides. Thus territorial space can be defined in terms of the functions it serves, namely the satisfaction of the needs of identity, security, and stimulation. If we add the fact that for the most part people interact with each other in areas known to them, territory can be defined as 'the space which may be continuous or discontinuous, used by an individual or group for most interactions and which, because of this, goes a long way towards satisfying the needs of identity, stimulation and security.'[25]

But just as with social space there is a scale problem, as the type and intensity of interaction and activity will vary according to the size of the territory. Lyman and Scott have introduced a useful fourfold classification of territory types.[26] We have attempted to illustrate their four categories of body territory, interactional territory, home territory, and public territory (see Fig. 2.5). This can be seen as a territorial hierarchy. It is here that the parallels between Chombart's work and territoriality can best be seen, as this hierarchy can be considered as a graded activity system. The parts of the hierarchy provide the spatial reference points within and to which people move and at which activity occurs. At the lowest level then, there is body territory, the space immediately surrounding a person. This is an individual's most inviolate space. Hall in fact divides it into two — intimate, tactile space and personal space. Tactile space is that touching a person's skin.[27] Personal space is rather like a bubble that an individual maintains between himself and others. Much research has been carried out on personal space which is limited by invisible barriers surrounding a person's body.

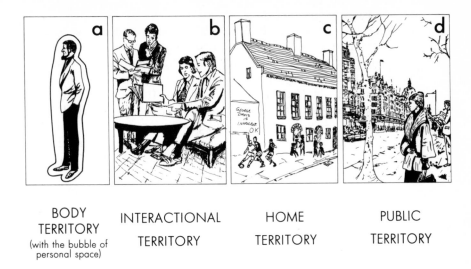

Fig. 2.5   Illustrations of four types of territory

Personal space is portable space: the individual carries it with him wherever he goes, although it can disappear under certain conditions, such as crowding. In such situations, other people in the environment are turned into non-persons; we switch off our senses as much as we can so the others become inanimate objects. In fact, there are social norms that govern behaviour in crowds, so that the lack of physical privacy is maintained by informal social regulations. In other situations, it has been found that invasion of personal space is often resented. Experiments have shown that when researchers sit too closely to subjects in libraries or on park benches, i.e. encroach on their personal space, the subjects react by shifting body position or by making defensive gestures. If the invader did not leave after these gestures were made, the subject often left instead. There is obviously a low tolerance to personal space invasion.[28] Most of these experiments have been carried out in the United States, and there may be variations in reactions as the cultural setting changes.

At a more general level, there is interactional territory (activity system) which refers to any area where a social gathering may occur. Interactional space can give territory its discontinuous property as interactions take place between different people at different times and places. Again much research has been carried out on interpersonal relations at this level, often using sociometric techniques, to try and discover interaction patterns as well as the social hierarchy of the group concerned. Such methods were used in a study on the development of friendship patterns among housewives on housing estates. The research is small-scale enough to be regarded as interactional territory, as no 'estate' involved more than thirty-five households and the majority had around ten to fifteen. It was found that five factors were especially significant in determining the level of individual interaction. These were an individual's age, her geographical mobility expectation, whether she went out to work, whether she had a relation living on the estate, and whether she had given help to a new neighbour during the early days of estate life. It was also found that on demographically heterogeneous estates, the level of activity depended on residential proximity and demographic similarity, i.e. interaction was more likely between close neighbours and those of similar age.[29]

The next level is called home territory which can perhaps be equated with our earlier definition of territorial space. It is a person's everyday behavioural frame of reference including social ties outside home and work. This is the area where the regular participants have relative freedom of action and a sense of intimacy and control over the area. It is close to Chombart's neighbourhood space and of course to the notion of community (see Chapters 1 and 4). Home territory is in fact a subset of the largest activity system — public territory in which the individual has freedom of access though not necessarily of action. Public territory is therefore relatively 'open' and can be converted by a social group into home territory. It is of course home territory that is of greatest interest to social geographers and it is at this scale that some interesting work has been carried out on the use of home territorial space and of the activities that constitute part of it.

In a study of Belfast, for example, Boal has tried to define territories in terms of site and activity characteristics of an area which lies between the Springfield and Shankill Roads.[30] Site characteristics include such phenomena as religion, newspapers read, and name given to area. Activity characteristics include movement to bus stops and grocery shops, visitor connections, and the pre-marriage addresses of interviewee and spouse. Briefly, looking at the site characteristics, there were two quite distinct religious areas, Clonard (98 per cent Roman Catholic) and Shankill I (99 per cent Protestant). The two areas met in a very narrow band restricted to one street, Cupar Street. It was found that the *Irish News* — an anti-Unionist paper with substantial coverage of Gaelic games and Catholic church news — was read by 83 per cent of the sample in Clonard and by only 3 per cent in Shankill I. The alternative local paper, the *Belfast Newsletter*, was not widely taken in either area as it had more middle-class appeal. It was also interesting to discover that on local area names, 94 per cent of those in Clonard called the area Clonard, Springfield, or Falls, while none used the term Shankill, while in Shankill I no one used Clonard, Springfield, or Falls and 77 per cent Shankill. In transitional Cupar Street, 37 per cent called the area Clonard, Springfield, or Falls, 26 per cent Shankill, and 23 per cent said the area had no name (see Fig. 2.6a). Thus on site

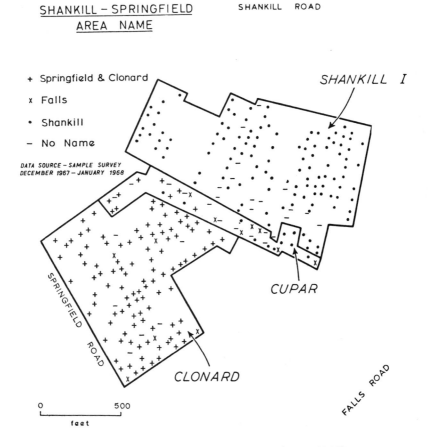

Fig. 2.6(a) Territoriality in Belfast. District Names (Boal, 1969)

characteristics two distinct territories emerge. But as Boal points out, territoriality is usually best expressed by the constraints it places on movement, on activity. Turning to activity characteristics, it was found that people were inclined to catch a bus to go to the city centre on their 'own' spine road. Thus 89 per cent in Shankill I go to Shankill while 93 per cent in Clonard go to Falls or Springfield, and not all of these are minimizing trip distance. With trips to grocery shops as well, there is a very strong focusing of each area on its own spine road. On visit connections and previous addresses (see Figs. 2.6b and c) there are two almost mutually exclusive networks. So on both site and activity characteristics, two strongly defined territorial spaces emerge, and this pattern is reinforced by the perception of residents who, when asked to define their area, stressed the divide of Cupar Street.

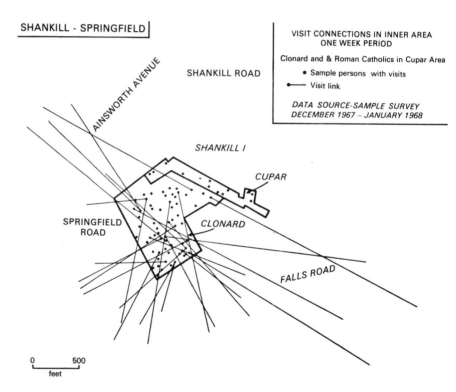

Fig. 2.6(b) Territoriality in Belfast Visitor Connections of Catholics (Boal, 1969)

Territorial space, with its relative freedom of action and sense of intimacy for its members, can also be exemplified by the urban village, in which a group, differentiated from the majority of the city population

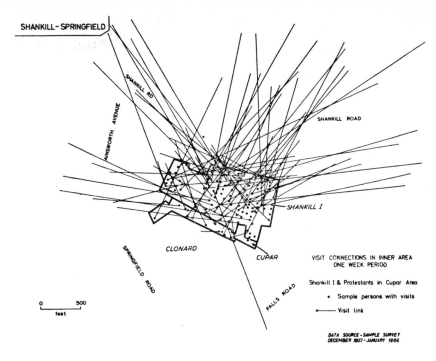

Fig. 2.6(c) Territoriality in Belfast Visitor Connections of Protestants (Boal, 1969)

by racial, ethnic, or religious characteristics, feels secure and at home. There is a sense of belonging which has cultural underpinnings such as food shops, religious and community buildings, and life-style. The Addams area of Chicago presents an example, with different ethnic groups occupying distinctive districts with their own values and social orders but retaining links with the rest of the city through work, recreation etc.[31] (See Fig. 2.7.) Italian communities in many American cities and Asian communities in some British cities can also be cited as examples.

Territorial space can also concern groups smaller than these ethnic and religious communities. Gang turf is a further example of territorial space. This illustrates well the symbolic aspects of territoriality. (In fact in the modern world, territory may, for most people, only have symbolic portrayal and significance). The turf represents the cohesion of the gang, for it is one of the reasons for the gang's existence. It becomes a cause and consequence of the gang's existence and there are parallels in this respect with Beacon Hill and Mayfair. The turf is delineated by group symbols, often graffiti. It has been shown that the

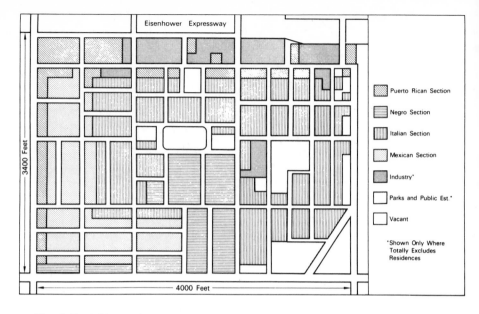

Fig. 2.7   Addams, Chicago: ethnic sections as defined by local residents (Suttles, 1968)

discovery of the graffiti of several different gangs in the same area indicates a zone of tension between groups.[32] This observation, however, leads to a point of wider significance. It appears that territorial space is especially important in situations of strain and tension, of social division, where clear distinctions between in-group and out-group, Us and Them, are required. Thus some middle-class home territories in American cities are differentiated from the surrounding area by fences, alarms, and closed-circuit television.[33] To alleviate strain and stress, therefore, the security and internal identity of one's group are emphasized. If the stress becomes too intense, then this group and territorial identification may be insufficient. The stress can result in migration away from the district. The relationship between stress and migration is more complex than suggested here (see p. 158), and in fact movement can itself cause grief.[34]

The emphasis here on division, stress, and defence must not lead us to the conclusion that territorial space is irrelevant to the bulk of the population. For most people, home territory is precisely what it says — the home, the family's dwelling unit. In a world in which social life is mainly home-centred, it is not surprising that people feel secure in and identify with this small unit and its extensions, especially the car. The amount of time spent at this element of territorial space is large and the spatial and temporal significance of this and other 'stations' of known territory has been examined by Hägerstrand (see p.134). Territorial space thus becomes a series of foci to which people move and at which activities occur (as with Chombart's scheme), although in addition there is the satisfaction of certain needs.

A rather different way of looking at the territorial hierarchy, however, is implicitly provided by Goodey.[35] His study gives us a useful link to our next section. Goodey sees the individual at the centre of his micro-area or personal space (Fig. 2.8). This is the area a person knows best.

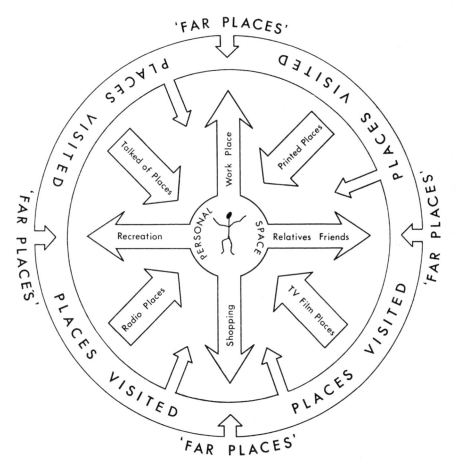

Fig. 2.8   Man's Perceptual Map (Goodey, 1971)

It will include his home, room, furniture, his close friends and relatives. From this area there may be other portions of the environment to which he moves with some regularity — journeys to work, shop, friends' homes etc. As well as these avenues from personal space, there are incursions into an individual's known space by holiday visits, media messages etc. In this scheme, emphasis is placed on how parts of the environment become known to an individual, on the build-up of environmental images.

The Image and Perception Studies. The concept of the image is central to the behavioural revolution in geography, i.e. to the attempt to explain behaviour in terms of meaningful social and psychological variables. The use of the term 'image' in such a context derives from the work of Boulding who said that behaviour depends on the image, on the picture of the world we carry round in our heads.[36] The image is reality perceived through a filter of socialization and experience. Thus space is given meaning by the image and is only meaningful when considered as an amalgam of both the phenomenal environment, the natural and man-made world, and the behavioural environment, the phenomenal as seen by man.[37] So 'the surface of the earth is shaped for each person by refraction through cultural and personal lenses of custom and fancy.'[38] There are of course more objective constraints that shape the surface of earth (e.g. economic and political factors), but we can conclude that the image is, in the main, culturally produced.

'Environmental images are the result of a two-way process between the observer and his environment. The environment suggests distinctions and relations, and the observer . . . selects, organises and endows with meaning what he sees.'[39] In this process experience is important, with nothing being experienced by itself but always in relation to its surroundings, the sequence of events leading up to it and the memory of past experiences. Thus every individual creates his own image, but of course, because of broadly similar patterns of socialization and experience, there will be a broad measure of image agreement within a social group. These group images are vital if an individual is to operate successfully in his environment and co-operate with others. In summary, images are purposive simplifications, enabling people to move easily about their environment. They are the bases of cultural definitions of physical space. We are dealing, therefore, with perceived or perceptual space. Again there are links with activity and territorial space. We cannot in any successful way perceive space without using it, despite the messages of far-away places received from the mass media, nor can we use space successfully without knowing it, i.e. perceiving it and endowing it with meaning

One view is that there are basically three approaches to the study of geographic space perception: the structural, evaluative and preference approaches.[40]

(i) The Structural Approach. This approach is concerned with the identity and structure of geographic space perceptions. The basic theme in this work on the mental or cognitive organization of space is that man must orient himself successfully in order to implement decisions as behaviour. The most famous study of orientation is that of Lynch. He carried out field studies and interviews in three cities, Boston, Jersey City, and Los Angeles. From these studies, he arrived at five types of element which form the structural bases of the mental images. These structural elements are: (a) paths — channels along which the observer moves; (b) edges — linear elements not used or considered as paths and which can be barriers or links between two phases; (c) districts — medium-sized or large sections of a city which are identifiable from the inside; (d) nodes — strategic spots (intensive foci) in the city; (e) landmarks — point references, usually simply defined physical objects. Figure 2.9 shows the results of Lynch's work in Boston; 2.9a is an outline plan of Boston; 2.9b is the visual form of Boston as recorded by Lynch and his colleagues; 2.9c is the image of respondents derived from verbal interviews; 2.9d is the image produced by analysing respondents' sketch maps; and finally 2.9e shows the parts of Boston known to most respondents, i.e. it is the shared image. Examination of these maps shows that none of the elements exist in isolation. They are simply the raw material of the city image and must be patterned together to provide a satisfactory form and a sharp purposive image.

These maps also demonstrate the importance of perception in the use of and orientation in a particular physical setting. Perceptual space is highly selective and this has been demonstrated in many other studies that attempt to define one particular element, such as a district, from the viewpoint of residents in that district. Eyles, for example, attempted to discover the inhabitants' image of Highgate village, a district of North London.[41] He found that there was a core area strongly perceived by 95 per cent of the respondents. There was also a 'peripheral area', which two-thirds of the respondents perceived as being part of the village (see Fig. 2.10). The areal extent of the perceived village was influenced by such factors as the location of the interviewee with there being a tendency to 'pull' the district — a desirable one — towards one's own residence, length of residence, and class. When asked their reasons for the size and shape of the presented

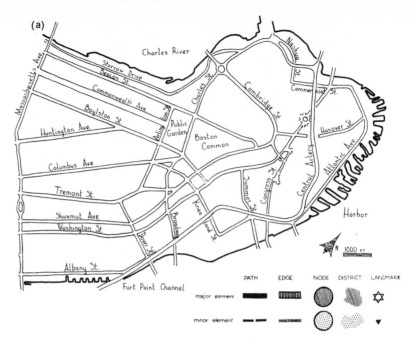

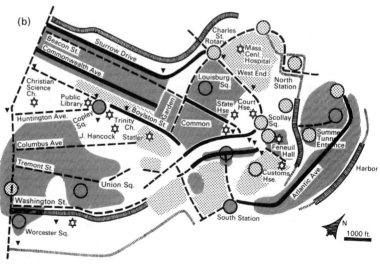

Fig. 2.9 Images of Boston (Lynch, 1960) (a) Outline map of the Boston peninsula (b) The visual form of Boston as seen in the field (c) The Boston image as derived from verbal interviews (d) The Boston image as derived from sketch maps (e) The Boston that everyone knows

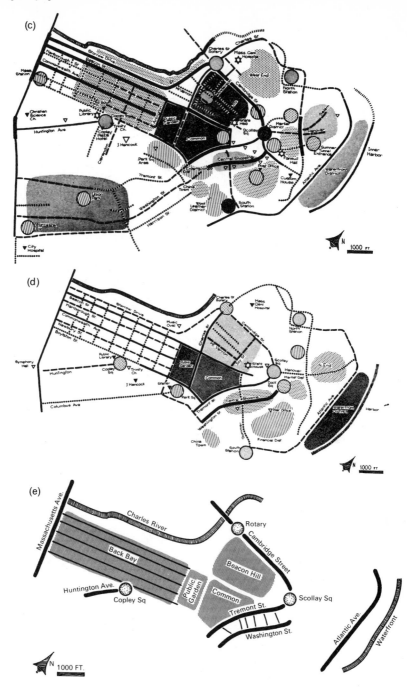

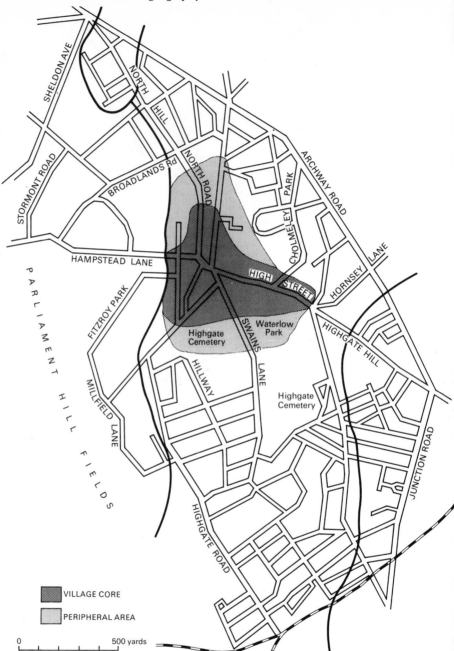

Fig. 2.10 The generalized form of the village core and peripheral area as seen by the percipients (Eyles, 1968)

image, 29 per cent were unsure (it was simply the Village). This category was called 'unknown' subjective criteria. Twenty-six per cent said that their delimitation was of the quiet area of the village centre with its quality shopping, 21 per cent gave shopping alone as their criterion, and 11 percent used a topographical reference, thinking of the district as the area on the hill.

Other researchers have attempted to discover how different social groups structure (perceive) particular spatial settings. Orleans, for example, found that different groups have very different images of the structure of Los Angeles.[42] He discovered that the perception of upper-class white residents of Westwood was rich and detailed (Fig. 2.11a), while black people from Avalon had a much more restricted view, with only the main streets being prominent (Fig. 2.11c). They had little knowledge of other districts. The smallest image, though, belonged to the Chicanos of Boyle Heights. Their shared image included only their immediate area, City Hall, and the bus depot (Fig. 2.11b). The perceptual spaces of the blacks and Chicanos are limited to their own neighbourhoods and environments; only the residents of upper-class Westwood have a detailed citywide image.

(ii) **The Evaluative Approach.** This approach is concerned with the evaluation of the environment using spatial images. Evaluation is related to decision-making and behaviour. 'Many of the decisions that men make seem to be related, at least in part, to the way in which they perceive the space around them and to the differential evaluation they place on various portions of it.'[43] Much of the work in this field has been carried out on hazard perception (floods or droughts). It has been found, for example, that decisions based on people's perceptions of hazards often led them to make behavioural adjustments that were neither optimal nor disastrous.[44] It has also been discovered that perceptions are often distorted so as to avoid the need for adjustment as in the case of affluent residents of coastal sites on the periphery of the American megalopolis. This perceptual distortion occurred so that residents did not have to choose between amenity and safety.[45]

The implicit recognition in this work is that man's knowledge of the environment, of the real world, is imperfect, and that he must rely on his own hypotheses (images) about how it works. We construct a simplified model of reality based on our learning (socialization and experience), perception, and, of course, aims. Our perception of the real world may be wrong, based on limited or incorrect knowledge. It is also certain to mean that our behaviour will be sub-optimal. For example, as Wolpert has shown, the places to which people can migrate

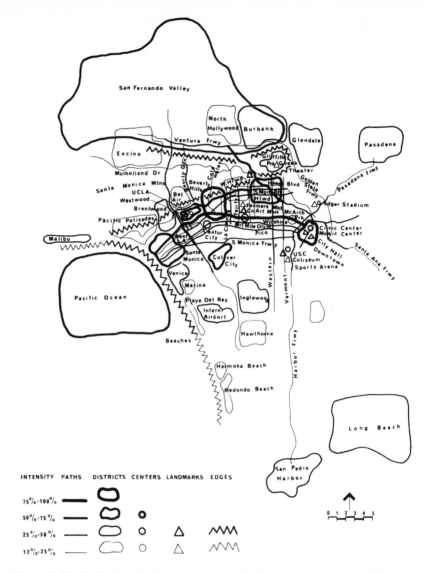

Fig. 2.11(a) Variations in the perception of the urban structure of Los Angeles Westwood (Downs and Stea, 1973)

are limited by their perception and knowledge of locational alterna-tives[46] (see also p. 134). Hence, groups are likely to migrate to areas that they perceive and know as friendly or with ample work opportunities. Their decision therefore is based on their evaluation of

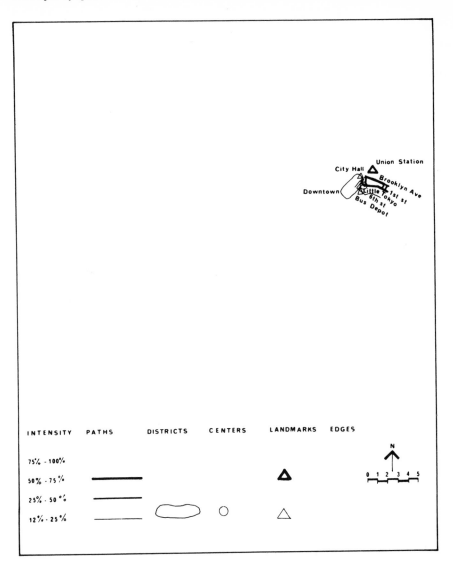

Fig. 2.11(b) Variations in the perception of the urban structure of Los Angeles Boyle Heights (Downs and Stea, 1973)

alternatives, their perception of which is an important ingredient of their total 'knowledge' of places. Thus, for example, West Indian immigrants to Britain go to places they perceive as hospitable, i.e. where their fellow islanders are, with Jamaicans migrating to Brixton (80 per

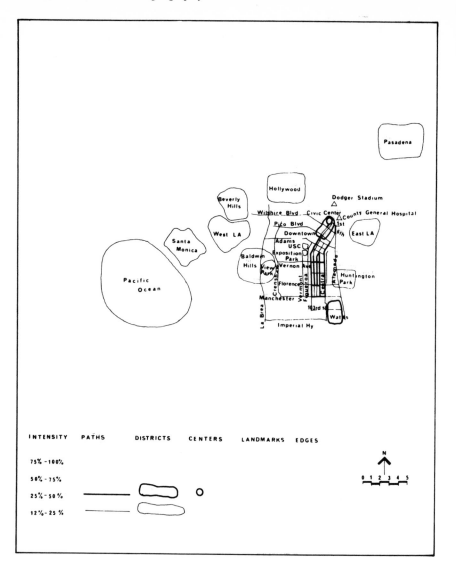

Fig. 2.11(c) Variations in the perception of the urban structure of Los Angeles Avalon (Downs and Stea, 1973)

cent of all the West Indians in the area), St. Vincentians to High Wycombe (85 per cent), St. Kittians to Leeds, and Anguillans to Slough.[47]

(iii) **The Preference Approach.** If individuals and groups have some particular objective in mind, it is likely that part of the evaluation process will involve them in assessing the relative attractiveness of spatial phenomena, i.e. they will rank these phenomena on a scale of preference. Many studies of preference space have involved asking respondents, often students, to rank states or counties in terms of perceived residential desirability. Gould and White, for example, questioned several hundred school-leavers at twenty-three schools all over Britain.[48] The respondents were given county maps of Britain and were asked to record directly on the map their personal preferences for residence. We shall look at two examples — those of the Bristol and Inverness school-leavers. In Bristol there was a strong preference for the area immediately around Bristol and Somerset, although the highest point of desirability was in Devon and Cornwall. In fact, there is a high ridge on the mental map all the way along the south coast. The trend of the preference surface is downwards as one goes north, although the gradual decline is not regular. There are areas of higher desirability — Cambridge, Hereford, the Lake District (Fig. 2.12a). In Inverness, preference for the local area is prominent. There is great differentiation of the Scottish counties and ridges can be seen in Edinburgh (Midlothian) and Ayrshire. All of North and Midland England and Wales scores low, and areas of high preference are the south coast and East Anglia (Fig. 2.12b). Gould and White also constructed a national mental map by combining all the individual school viewpoints. This is, in essence, a weighted cartographic average of all the viewpoints (Fig. 2.12c). They found a southern area of high desirability with prongs into East Anglia and the Welsh Borderland, with the Midlands being, in their terms, a mental cirque. In the south-east London is described as a sinkhole. From the Midlands northwards the surface falls quite smoothly and regularly except for the Lake District. To discover the importance of the local effect, they charted the differences between this national preference surface and the local viewpoints. Obviously the further north you go, the greater will be the difference, given the shape of the national surface. This is borne out by the Bristol and Inverness examples (Figs. 2.12d and e).

The preference approach can be seen as an indirect method of discovering people's evaluations of different parts of their environment. A rather different approach to discovering preferences must, however, be examined. Rushton was concerned with how individuals evaluate different spatial alternatives.[49] In his example, these alternatives are towns used for various shopping purposes.

He attempted to construct a preference function which would

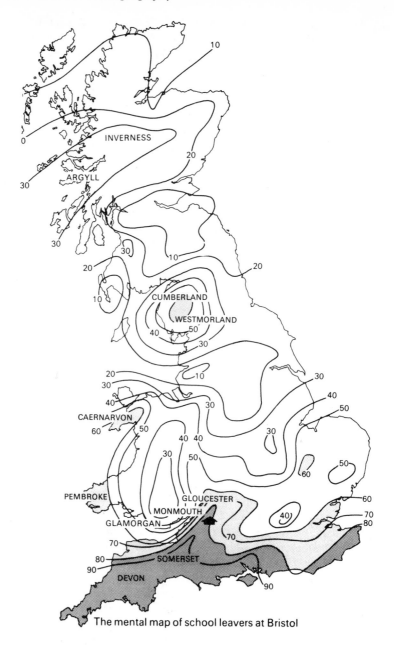

The mental map of school leavers at Bristol

Fig. 2.12(a)   Residential preferences of British school-leavers. The mental map of school leavers at Bristol (Gould and White, 1974)

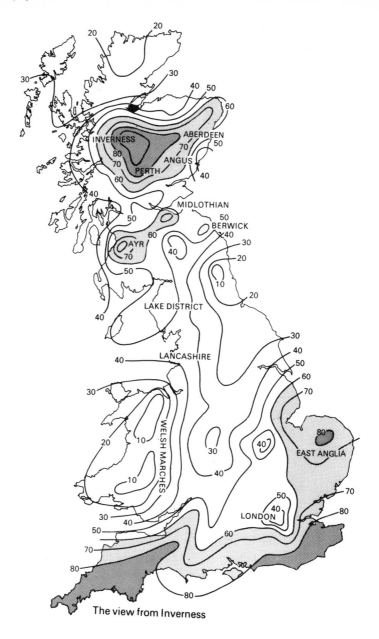

The view from Inverness

Fig. 2.12(b) Residential preferences of British school-leavers. The view from Inverness (Gould and White, 1974)

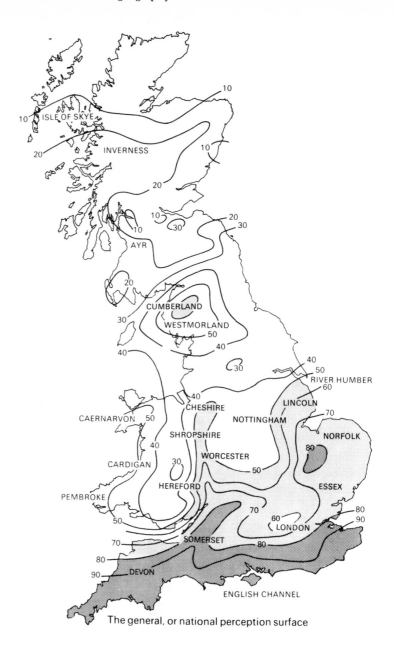

The general, or national perception surface

Fig. 2.12(c) Residential preferences of British school-leavers. The general or national perception surface (Gould and White, 1974)

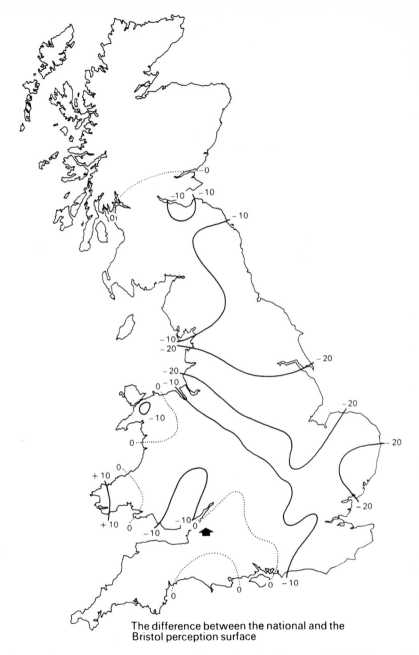

The difference between the national and the
Bristol perception surface

Fig. 2.12(d) Residential preferences of British school-leavers. The difference between the national and the Bristol perception surface (Gould and White, 1974)

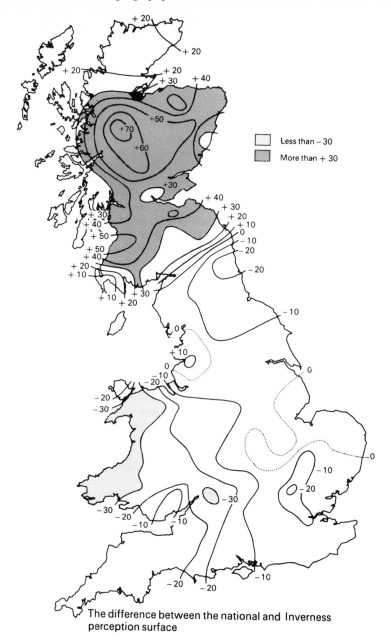

The difference between the national and Inverness
perception surface

Fig. 2.12(e) Residential preferences of British school-leavers. The difference between the national and Inverness perception surface (Gould and White, 1974)

indicate the alternative that gave the greatest satisfaction. His indifference surface approximated the shopping behaviour of rural Iowans but the model employed, based on revealed space preference, assumed the independence of spatial situations. This is a difficult condition to fulfil for, as Rushton himself admitted, the presence of one spatial alternative increases or decreases the probability that some other spatial situations will also be present. It has been further pointed out that the concept of revealed space preference does not go far enough because it does not incorporate the idea of repressed preferences or impossible opportunities.[50] This is because if an individual does not have an opportunity to behave in a certain way, his preference for this cannot be revealed. Repressed preferences, then, are those courses of action or opportunities seen as impossible to activate given the individual's present social and economic circumstances and level of knowledge. Eyles has, in fact, suggested a typology of revealed preferences, based on a survey of shopping data of residents of Isle of Dogs, London.

There are two major subdivisions of revealed preferences, absolute and relative. Absolute preferences are those in which people perceive that they have no choice or no need of choice. This was represented by 3 per cent of the Isle of Dogs sample, all elderly, who did not go off the Island to shop, despite its poor facilities that dissatisfied two-thirds of the total sample. Absolute preferences, however, will reveal the bottom and top sections of society, for in another case an individual could have such easy access to facilities that he preferred to go only to the 'best' centre.

Relative preferences occur in spatial situations where people perceive that they have or need a choice. There are two types. Firstly manifest preferences represent those courses of action that are usually pursued. The opportunity structure is such that one course of action is often seen as the easiest, perhaps the cheapest in terms of time and money. In the case of the Isle of Dogs shoppers this is represented by the street market, over 73 per cent of the sample making a majority of their purchases at one or more of these. Secondly, latent preferences represent those courses of action perceived as a choice, but which remain dormant until some specific need arises or level of knowledge changes. For the Isle of Dogs shoppers this is exemplified by the centres of East Ham and the West End visited for the infrequent purchase of a higher-order good.

An often referred to phenomenon throughout this discussion on repressed and revealed preference has been opportunity. Any attempt to investigate an individual's evaluation of spatial alternatives, i.e. his preference space, must take into account his perception of the alternatives and the opportunity he has for enjoying those alternatives. Spatial opportunity — the *possibility* of behaving in a particular way in a particular place — must be married to image for a meaningful study of the evaluation of environmental choices by individuals and groups. The idea of opportunity is a central one in social geography, and it is given implicit as well as explicit treatment in the following chapters of this book.

Our discussion of concepts of space has been wide-ranging. It has attempted to describe and exemplify some of the concepts that have been and are influential in social geography. The discussion has ranged from human ecology, important as it points to the *spatial* constraints on choice, social, territorial, and preference spaces, all stressing different aspects of how individuals and groups perceive, structure, and use space, to opportunity, with its emphasis on the *socio-spatial* constraints on freedom of action. It is necessary to try to relate these different concepts of space. 'Social space' can be thought of as an umbrella term meaning the social definition of space, i.e. how individuals and groups pattern space by their perceptions and activities. Thus there are two elements in social space — activity space and perceptual space. Their joint operation in turn gives rise to preference space, i.e. the evaluation of different parts of one's space on the basis of use and perception, and territorial space, i.e. the evaluation of part of one's environment as fulfilling the needs of security, identity and stimulation or, put simply as home. So far we have examined space on the basis of complete freedom of choice. The complexity of social space, however, is affected by certain constraints that limit and modify perceptions and activities. The major constraint is thought to be socio-economic (limitations

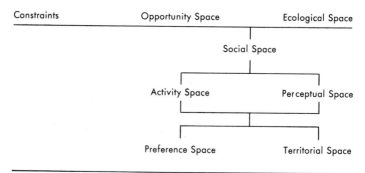

Fig. 2.13 Concepts of Space

placed upon us by income and status). These constraints give rise to opportunity space. Where we live is also important. The fact that we live in one area, say Mayfair, will give us added benefits while living in, say, Stepney will give us added costs.[51] Thus position in the spatial structure reinforces other constraints. This is, in essence, the role of ecological space (see Fig. 2.13).

As with our summary table in Chapter 1 (p. 23), different elements in this summary figure will be stressed in different places in the following chapters. Together these first two chapters provide our view of the conceptual boundaries of social geography. They provide the scheme which we shall use in our attempt to order social geographical subject-matter. Existing material does not always fit into our ordering. We do believe, though, that every discipline requires a conceptual framework in which to examine its patterns and distributions and the processes causing, and the responses to, these patterns.

NOTES AND REFERENCES

[1] E. Semple (1911), *Influences of Geographic Environment*, New York, p. 1. See E. Huntington (1915), *Civilisation and Climate*, New York.

[2] H.J. Fleure (1919), 'Human Regions', *Scott. Geogl. Mag.* 35, pp. 94–105.

[3] See H. Sprout and M. Sprout (1965), *The Ecological Perspective on Human Affairs*, Princeton, p. 142.

[4] P. Vidal de la Blache (1926), *Principles of Human Geography*, London, p. 10.

[5] E.G. Bowen (1959), 'Le Pays de Galle', *Trans. Inst. of Brit. Geogs.*, 26, pp.

[6] Some of the French material is reviewed by A. Buttimer (1968), 'Social Geography' in D. Sills (ed.), *International Encyclopaedia of the Social Sciences*, New York, Vol. 6, pp. 134–45.

[7] P.M. Roxby (1930), 'The Scope and Aims of Human Geography', *Scott. Geogl. Mag.* 46, pp. 276–90.

[8] R.E. Pahl (1965), 'Trends in Social Geography' in R.J. Chorley & P. Haggett (eds.), *Frontiers in Geographical Teaching*, London, p. 81.

[9] R.E. Park (1952), *Human Communities*, New York, p. 158.

[10] B.T. Robson (1969), *Urban Analysis*, Cambridge, p. 10.

[11] H. Zorbaugh (1961), 'The Natural Areas of the City,' in G.A. Theodorson (ed.), *Studies in Human Ecology*, Evanston, pp. 45–9.

[12] E.W. Burgess (1961), 'The Growth of the City: An Introduction to a Research Project' in Theodorson, op. cit., pp. 37–44.

[13] H. Zorbaugh (1929) *The Gold Coast and the Slum*, Chicago.

[14] P. Hatt (1946), 'The Concept of Natural Area', *Am. Soc. Rev.* 11, pp. 423–7. Reprinted in Theodorson, op. cit. The critics of the classical ecologists are discussed by Robson (1969), op.. cit.

[15] H.J. Gans (1968), *People and Plans*, New York, p. 44.

[16] W. Firey (1947), *Land Use in Central Boston*, Cambridge, Mass.

[17] D.E. Sopher (1967), *Geography of Religions*, Englewood Cliffs, p. 31.

[18] H. Bobek (1948), 'Stellung und Bedeutung der Sozialgeographie', *Erdkunde* 2, pp. 118–25. The work of the German social geographers is reviewed by J.G. Hajdu (1968), 'Towards a Definition of Post-War German Social Geography', *Ann. Ass. Am. Geogs.*, 58.

[19] P. James (1972), *All Possible Worlds*, Indianapolis p. 241

[20] W. Hartke (1959), 'Die sozialgeographische Differenzierung von Räumen gleichen sozialgeographischen Verhalten', *Erdkunde* 13, pp. 426–36.

[21] A. Buttimer (1969), 'Social Space in Interdisciplinary Perspective', *Geog. Rev.* 59, p. 419.

[22] Y.F. Tuan (1974), *Topophilia*, Englewood Cliffs.

[23] Ibid, p. 164.

[24] R. Ardrey (1967), *The Territorial Imperative*, London.

[25] J. Eyles (1970), Space, Territory and Conflict, *University of Reading, Geographical Paper* 1, p. 2.

[26] S.M. Lyman and M.B. Scott (1967), 'Territoriality: A Neglected Sociological Dimension', *Social Problems* 15, pp. 236–49.

[27] E.T. Hall (1966), *The Hidden Dimension*, New York.

[28] See particularly R. Sommer (1969), *Personal Space: The Behavioural Basis of Design*, Englewood Cliffs.

[29] This study was carried out by L. Carey and R. Mapes (1972), *The Sociology of Planning*, London.

[30] F.W. Boal (1969), 'Territoriality on the Shankill–Falls Divide', *Irish Geog.* 6, pp. 30–50.

[31] See G.D. Suttles (1968), *The Social Order of the Slum*, Chicago.

[32] See D. Ley and R. Cybriwsky (1974), 'Urban Graffiti as Territorial Markers', *Ann. Assoc. Am. Geogs.* 64, pp. 491–505.

[33] The 'sealing off' of middle class districts is reported by R. Gold (1973), 'Urban Violence and Contemporary Defensive Cities' in M. Albaum (ed.), *Geography and Contemporary Issues*, New York, pp. 309–26.

[34] Involuntary movement, occasioned by urban renewal projects, can cause stress and reactions of grief. See, for example, M. Fried (1963), 'Grieving for a Lost Home' in L.J. Duhl (ed.), *The Urban Condition*, New York, pp. 151–71.

[35] B. Goodey (1971), Perception of the Environment, *University of Birmingham, Centre for Urban and Research Studies, Occasional Paper* 17.

[36] K. Boulding (1956), *The Image*, Ann Arbor.

[37] The notions of phenomenal environment and behavioural environment are taken from W. Kirk (1963), 'Problems in Geography', *Geog.* 48, pp. 357–71.

[38] D. Lowenthal (1961), 'Geography, Experience and Imagination', *Ann. Assoc. Am. Geogs.* 51, pp. 241–60.

[39] K. Lynch (1960), *The Image of the City*, Cambridge, Mass, p. 6.

[40] See R.M. Downs (1970), 'Geographic Space Perception — Past Approaches and Future Prospects', *Progress in Geography* 2, pp. 65–108.

[41] J. Eyles (1968), The Inhabitants Perception of Highgate Village (London), *London School of Economics, Department of Geography, Discussion Paper* 15.

[42] P. Orleans (1973), 'Differential Cognition or Urban Residents: Effects of Social Scale on Mapping' in R.M. Downs and D. Stea (eds.), *Image and Environment*, London, pp. 115–30.

[43] P. Gould (1966), On Mental Maps, *Michigan Inter-University Community of Mathematical Geographers, Discussion Paper* 9, p. 30. Reprinted in Downs and Stea, op.cit.

[44] R.W. Kates (1962), Hazard and Choice Perception in Flood Plain Managements, *University of Chicago, Department of Geography, Research Paper* 78.

[45] R.W.. Kates (1967), 'The Perception of Storm Hazard on the Shores of Megalopolis' in D. Lowenthal (ed.), Environmental Perception and Behaviour, *University of Chicago, Department of Geography, Research Paper* 109, pp. 60–74.

[46] J. Wolpert (1965), Behavioural Aspects of the Decision to Migrate. *Papers of the Regional Science Association* 15, pp. 159–172.

[47] These figures can be found in D. Hiro (1971), *Black British, White British*, London.

[48] P. Gould and R. White (1968), 'The Mental Maps of British School-Leavers', *Regional Studies* 2, pp. 161–82. A large part of this study is to be found in P. Gould and R. White (1974), *Mental Maps*, Harmondsworth. This book also contains résumés of several similar preference studies.

[49] G. Rushton (1969), 'Analysis of Spatial Behaviour by Revealed Space Preference', *Ann. Assoc. Am. Geogs.* 59, pp. 391–400.

[50] J. Eyles (1971), 'Pouring New Sentiments into Old Theories: How Else Can We Look At Behavioural Patterns?', *Area* 3, pp. 242–50.

[51] The idea of where we live providing us with extra benefits or costs is examined in detail by K. Cox (1973), *Conflict, Power and Politics in the City*, New York.

II · PATTERNS

3   Patterns in social geography

Of the five definitions of social geography given in the first chapter, four began with the idea of pattern, i.e. the pattern of human activity in space. Analysing the spatial element in the activities of human beings in social groups is no easy task. The activities are infinitely varied and incredibly complex, and the space in which they operate and the surface of the earth on which they take place are no less intricate. But the activities are not random and space relationships not meaningless. We begin on the assumption that there are identifiable spatial patterns of behaviour, of group interaction, of response to stimuli: and that such generalized concepts simplify an otherwise unintelligible mass of phenomena to the point where we feel we can begin to explain them rationally. However unique an individual may feel his own behaviour to be, in most circumstances he will find himself conforming to a recognized scheme of things: the physiological link between the rhythm of waking and sleeping hours and day and night is not immutable, but it is an acceptable generalization applying to the majority of people. The movement from home to school or from home to work or from home to the theatre all follow a design familiar to many groups of peoples. The fact that people living in close contact have the same language or that the people living in the same neighbourhood have a similar standard of living enables us to identify certain areas with specific social characteristics. We begin simply by recognizing that patterns exist in space: that is, that social activities are related in space in an easily identifiable way. The social geographer's starting-point is the spatial patterning of human activities.

Such patterns are mainly the outcome of processes in society, although these may be subject to constraints in the environment. As we saw in the last chapter, geography has come a long way from the old idea that such constraints may be a sufficient explanation, that the environment determines the spatial component of man's behaviour. Nor must we go too far in the other direction and assume that social interactions are divorced from the realities of our natural and built environment. The abstract models we build of nicely geometrical relationships must be brought to earth before they can help us to interpret fully man's activity. But having freed ourselves from the notion that the constraints are merely environmental, we must then explore the processes which give rise to patterns of activites. It is virtually impossible to separate patterns and process, except as an academic exercise. It is for this reason only that processes will be dealt with in a later section, but clearly they cannot be entirely ignored when discussing the patterns to which they give rise. On the other hand, we know much more about patterns than about processes. It is almost an instinct in the geographer to arrange his data spatially, to construct a map. This has its own dangers and shortcomings. In the first place geographers have sometimes been content to go no further, making the map an end in itself, a description of a particular kind, but no more. Other disciplines have sometimes taken this image at its own evaluation, and looked on the geographer as a sort of super technician providing the basic material for them to work on. The other danger is that he becomes non-selective. After all, everything is mappable! But it would be sterile to keep on mapping, pretty though the patterns may be, and leave it at that. The map is a tool. It follows that mapping must reflect a conceptual framework which suggests what things need to be mapped. In our own study we wish to deal with the attributes and actions of people, categorized into social groups.

PROBLEMS OF SCALE

Mapping such spatial patterns has its own very considerable problems, and the most difficult may well be concerned with the scale. If we are dealing with the characteristics of individual human beings, then it may seem desirable to map individuals. This is usually virtually impossible because of sheer numbers. You may reduce the numbers statistically. If you are dealing with one characteristic only, then a random sample will give you the same kind of pattern as if you map the universe of data. For example, a sample of the addresses of people who appear in *Who's Who* will serve to represent all the entries in *Who's Who*, and will result in a distribution which is interesting because of the concentration of these entries in London and the Home Counties: here is a pattern which calls for an explanation (Fig. 3.1).[1]

But the geographer usually generalizes in terms of area. The distribution of West Indians in London, for example, can be done very easily by wards. Their percentage in the total population in each ward can be indicated by classes, and the wards shaded to show the appropriate class (Fig. 3.2)[2] Again, a distinctive pattern emerges which is an outcome of certain social processes. In this latter map we have generalized from the individual to the ward: we are suggesting the characteristic, or part of the characteristic, of an area. Such areal units are very convenient and

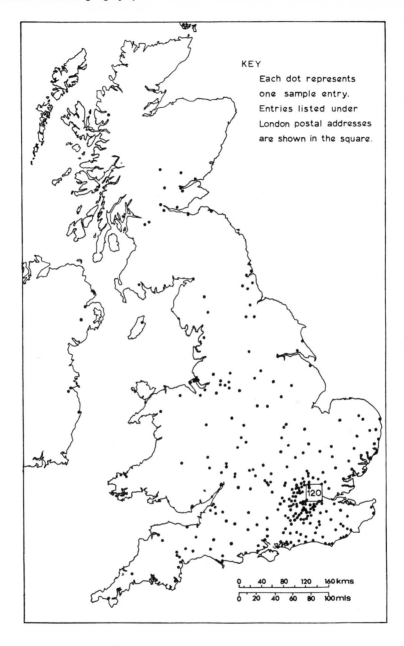

Fig. 3.1. A Residential Who's Who based on a sample analysis of entries in *Who's Who, 1964* (Coates and Rawstron, 1971)

People born in the
West Indies as a
percentage of the
total population

8·0 or more

6·0–7·9

4·0–5·9

2·0–3·9

Less than 2·0

0   1   2   3 miles

CITY

Fig. 3.2   London: Residential distributions of West Indian migrants by wards, 1971 (Shepherd *et al.*, 1974)

are often used. In the first case, the data have been collected by these units and are published in this way: secondly, the units are comparatively stable, so that you can compare distributions over time: and, lastly, they give a reasonable breakdown of London or, in order words, there are enough units to produce differences which make a pattern.

One may well be suspicious of the words 'producing' and 'making'. The fact remains that the subdivisions have an effect on the pattern. Obviously we are trying to reproduce something which does exist. It is our common experience that in London there are a very large number of West Indian migrants in a belt around the centre of the city and that they are only rarely seen in the suburbs. We are looking for a comprehensive picture of where the major concentrations are in the city as a whole. Ward figures supply this general view of the total situation. At this level of inquiry it would be inappropriate to map in greater detail even if the data allowed it.

Nevertheless, when the data are related to area, then the size of the sub-areas has a very marked effect on the pattern it has produced. Generalizing for an entire area — in the example above, giving the total number of West Indians in London — does not give us much information. At the other extreme, mapping individuals, even if we had the data, would be impossible. Generally speaking, the more fine the grain the more information the map supplies. Social geographers are always asking for more data, but their real problem is to gear the scale of the data to the kind of inquiry they are making. There certainly are advantages in producing more detail than those at ward level. Data for British cities are published for wards, but since 1961 they have also been made available for enumeration districts, that is, the areas covered by one census enumerator. A ward can vary greatly in size from a few thousand to tens of thousands, but enumeration districts usually encompass about 250 households, so we can assume a round population figure of about 1000 which rarely varies excessively (see Fig. 3.3). Obviously distribution by enumeration districts will give us a much more detailed pattern — and often a very different one — from that of wards, and this is extremely valuable to anyone studying the social geography of the city. In the example shown (Fig. 3.4) — the population density in Belfast — the first map is based on fifteen wards, and is therefore coarse-grained.[3] The information at such a generalized level is very meagre: it shows an intense concentration west of the city centre, another dense sector running south-west to the boundary and a similar area north of the centre. Belfast east of the River Lagan has only three wards, and the lesser density of the most northern of these is due to the fact that much dockland acreage is included in the

(c) Population density of enumeration districts in St. Johns Ward, Camden, 1971

(d) A census enumeration district in St. Johns Ward, Camden, 1971

(b) Population density of wards in Camden, 1971

Number of persons per hectare
110·0 or more
90·0 – 109·9
70·0 – 89·9
50·0 – 69·9
30·0 – 49·9
Less than 30·0

(a) Borough population density, 1971

Fig. 3.3 London: Census data are presented at increasing detail from borough, to ward, to enumeration district (a) Borough population density, 1971 (b) Population density of wards in Camden, 1971 (c) Population density of enumeration districts in St. Johns Ward, Camden, 1971 (d) A census enumeration district in St. Johns Ward, Camden, 1971 (Shepherd *et al.*, 1974)

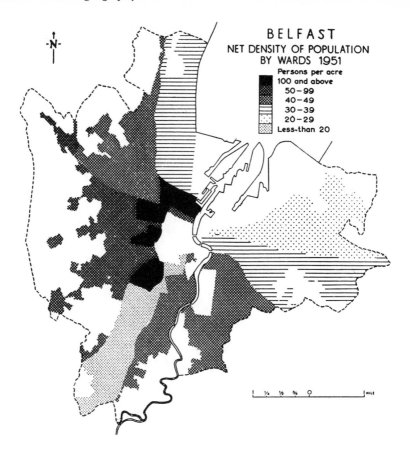

Fig. 3.4 Belfast: density of population by wards, 1951. The pattern is generalized and tends to emphasize sectors (Jones, 1961)

calculation of gross density. A map by enumeration districts, of which there are 231, reveals a very different pattern and gives much more information (see Fig. 3.5). We are able to map a greater range of densities — the lower quartile is 0·5 to 38·8 per acre, the upper quartile is 141·5 to 280·5 per acre — but more interesting is the extension of the densely peopled area in the west and the appearance of another such area south of the city centre. And even more critical is the emergence of a concentric pattern in the east with yet another core of very dense population. What it shows is simply that the sectoral shape of the three wards in the east is completely counter to the density pattern: the high figure for the hub is reduced and spread throughout the entire sector,

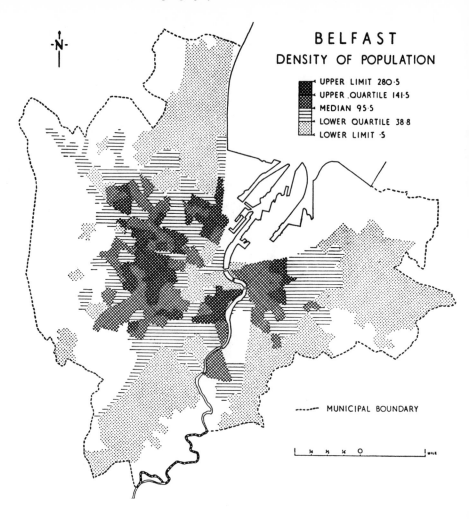

Fig. 3.5 The much finer grain of enumeration districts reveals a pattern very different from that of the wards (Jones, 1961)

giving a totally false impression.

Enumeration districts have another advantage over wards; the latter are politically decided and are sometimes used deliberately to produce certain distributions. For example, the three wards in the city of Londonderry for much of its history (they were abolished in 1971) were so drawn that one ward contained the Roman Catholic population, the other two being almost entirely Protestant. This meant that although the majority of the population of the city was Roman Catholic, it was governed by a council which always had a dominant ward-elected Protestant council.

Enumeration districts are now commonly used by British geographers for mapping[4] and for statistical analysis.[5] They are useful because they have approximately the same population base, and consequently can be expected to contain roughly the same proportion of any randomly distributed element.

In American cities social data have for more than half a century been published by census tracts, and these have been grouped into larger community areas by sociologists as a basis of their extensive social analyses of metropolitan cities. Defining such areas before analyses does rather pre-judge the issue. Enumeration districts or census tracts should be looked upon as building blocks whose groupings will themselves suggest social areas.

American studies have also sometimes made use of an even smaller unit — the city block.[6] Where a city is gridded, the regularity of this unit is temptingly convenient, and is now being paralleled in this country by the use of a grid for analysing data. Some work has already been done on this basis in England, and it makes for the fast production of computerized maps (Fig. 3.6).[7] It has the drawback that equal areas mean great variations in population, making statistical analysis difficult, though the way around this again is to build up the greater homogeneous blocks from the smaller.

Both city block and grid produce a very fine grain. But the disadvantage is simply this: that the finer the grain — that is the smaller the unit — the more probability there is of producing homogeneity within the unit. One critical area of study which is susceptible to this is segregation, or clustering, in a city (a topic which will be dealt with in greater detail in Chapter 7). If, for example, the number of West Indians in London as a whole is related to the total population, it is insignificant (less than 3 per cent in 1971), and so it would be if the West Indians were randomly distributed. Borough distributions show this is not so, but that they are found mainly in the inner boroughs, Brent with as many as 12 per cent. Ward distributions show further clustering within this inner area, mostly north-west and south of the centre, exceptionally reaching 21·13 per cent in a Brent ward. Enumeration districts produce a still finer grain which shows that some areas within the wards have even greater concentrations (some as much as 50 per cent) as one eliminates those sub-areas with very few West Indians. The last logical step in this process is to map households, and it is highly likely that these will be either wholly black or white (i.e. 100

PERCENTAGE OF TOTAL HOUSEHOLDS

23 36 49 62

KILOMETRES

MILES

Fig. 3.6 Part of a gridmap in the LINMAP system showing the proportion of households in England and Wales owning their own housing accommodation in 1966. The statistical bases of the map are the spot-values which occur within any 10-kilometre grid square. If no value occurs in any square such a square is left 'blank', in this case filled with full stop symbols (e.g. Scottish Border area). The general impression obtained from the map is much improved if it is viewed from a distance of about 4 ft. (G.C. Dickinson (1973), *Statistical Mapping and the Presentation of Statistics*, London)

per cent). In other words, what began at city level as total mix now becomes total segregation. The division between black and white has, in a way, been induced by the method of mapping. A similar example is given on pp. 173—4.

The answer to this rather complex issue is simply that the scale must meet the requirement of the problem in such a way that it does not distort, but rather reflects, the known experience: and if one is searching for something more ill-defined, then it may well be advisable to map on several scales. This example of seeming mix becoming total segregation leads us to consider some of the disadvantages of relying on published data. The areal unit — borough, ward, tract, or enumeration district — is pre-determined, and there is lack of homegeneity in size or composition. There may well be incompatability between the areal units and the socio-economic detail within them. The social significance of such units may be overemphasized because we are forced to use information on such terms irrespective of the real nature of social and economic relationships. Moreover, administrative boundaries do change, sometimes making comparative work over time extremely difficult.[8]

The discussion so far has been confined to data which are normally published and which pertain to universes of population. We have not referred to data specially collected for behavioural studies, where information is aggregated. Normally, behavioural studies are focused on small areas, sometimes unique, and they are dealt with rather differently: and one introduces different levels of explanation. One of the fascinating areas of exploration in social geography is where and how these approaches meet. More will be said later on this topic (p.133), but here it is enough to say that so far macro- and micro-studies have been asking rather different questions and consequently have been satisfied with different kinds of explanation.

THE NATURE OF THE DATA

Implicit in what has been said already is the fact that the amount of data available and the forms they take are very important factors in trying to reproduce patterns of social behaviour and characteristics of behaviour on maps. But we must also be wary of the actual meaning of official and other published statistics. A good example of the problems of data interpretation is that of crime statistics. We cannot say with certainty how much crime there is in Britain — or in any other country. Many crimes go unrecorded, or are not regarded officially as offences: statistics of offences 'known to the police' exclude those covered by discretionary attitudes. And more crimes 'known to the police' may simply mean a bigger police force, greater efficiency, more public co-operation. However accurate the recorded number of indictable and non-indictable offences, this tells us nothing of the numbers who are guilty, or how many people are never brought to court. To be useful, these statistics must be considered in terms of their own definitions, as well as in the light of the purpose of the research.[9]

Social scientists are notorious for demanding more data, and since computers now enable us to deal with so many data in such a short time, there is a danger that we may be engulfed by data to the detriment of the information we are really looking for. Yet, as in the study of crime, some characteristics are extremely difficult to quantify. Other examples are language and religion.

In the United Kingdom the census identifies those who live in Wales who are able to speak Welsh and those in Scotland able to speak Gaelic.[10] Ireland identifies Irish speakers.[11] (See Fig. 3.7.) The result is not necessarily information about, for example, the speaking of Welsh, because there are very large numbers of Welsh speakers in England. Even within Wales the issue of who speaks Welsh is not an easy one. In the first place the census is a record of those of three years of age and over who are able to speak Welsh. Secondly there are now few exceptions to the rule that all those also speak English: monoglot Welsh are merely those over three who have not yet acquired the second language. In a bilingual community it is often the case that a person will speak Welsh at home, English at work or at school, and Welsh again during attendance at Sunday service: so ability to speak a language is all that can be readily measured. The issue is even more complex in Ireland, where the number of people enumerated as being able to speak Irish need have no more than an ability acquired at school, which is in no way equivalent to that of native Irish speakers who speak it as a first language. This inflates the number of Irish speakers from a possible 20,000 or 30,000 native speakers to well over half a million; but one must question how realistic the latter figure is. Yet language can be a sensitive indicator of group differences which the social scientist is interested in. It may be a gauge of social change in rural communities[12] or a major factor in the social geography of a bilingual city such as Brussels or Quebec.

Religion is another aspect of culture which can be all-pervasive, although in many Western societies it is becoming less of an index of differentiation. Where differences are sharp and beliefs very deep-rooted, the social geographer's task is simpler even if data are difficult to obtain. Where secularization has taken place, the difficulties are immense, though justifiably one could claim that in such cases the fact

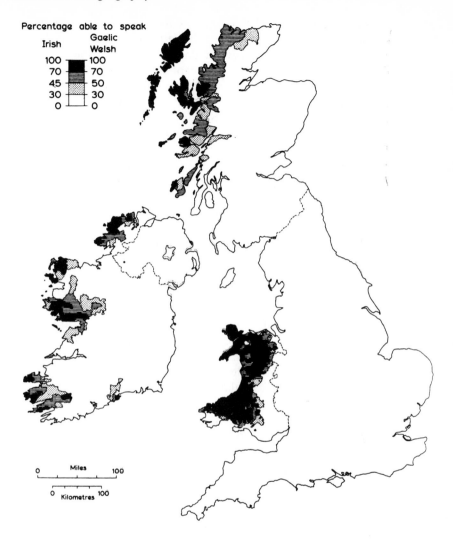

Fig. 3.7 Percentage of British population able to speak Irish, Gaelic, or Welsh, 1961. (J.W. Watson and J.B. Sissons (1964), *British Isles: Systematic Geography*, London)

ceases to be a very relevant one in social differentiation. Like the geography of language, the geography of religion is still only at a rudimentary stage. On the macro-scale the picture is very clear, but scholars like Sopher have done much to clarify distributions of religions in the United States, as well as systematizing ideas concerning, for example, the impact which religion has had on the cultural landscape, or the degrees to which different religions impinge on behaviour.[13]

In the United Kingdom data on religious beliefs are not collected by the Registrar General except in Northern Ireland,[14] a reflection of religion's relative importance in the two societies. In England and Wales the only count of religious observance was done in 1851, and was based on attendance on Sunday, 30 March in that year (see Fig. 3.8). This proved discouraging to the Establishment because of the strength of non-conformity which was revealed (and possibly explains why there was no subsequent religious census), but the census also threw into relief all the difficulties of enumeration, and there were heated debates whether a declaration of belief was preferable to the registering of attendance at religious services because apparently only one 'believer' in five attended services on Sundays! Even so, the census showed a decline of observance in the metropolitan area, and in the new industrial areas and in the north of England.[15]

Further work in this field is fraught with difficulties because denominational figures are based on varying criteria. They may give the number of communicants, of adult membership, or of total membership including children. Nor are the number and distribution of places of worship of great significance apart from the newer sects such as the Church of Latter-day Saints or Christian Scientists, where they represent considerable congregations. One attempt to avoid these difficulties is to calculate, from the monthly returns of the Registrar General, the proportions of marriages taking place by each denomination by counties. This excludes civil marriages, and in addition the fact that the two partners may well belong to different denominations makes it a crude measure. Nevertheless, if these statistical discrepancies are evenly spread, it gives us some indication of the relative strengths of religious denominations in England and Wales.[16] On a micro-scale it is easier to plot the distribution of individual congregations (see Fig. 3.9). It is well to remember that in this way we may be confining ourselves to very specific groups: the example is of a congregation of *orthodox* Jews and not of the entire population of Jews in the city.[17]

In Northern Ireland the situation is much more clear-cut. The sharpness of the traditional barrier between Roman Catholics and Protestants, emphasized by periodic conflict, leads to a clear identification of sects and an almost universal declaration of belief. Census information is satisfyingly complete. Very few people are uncommitted: about 2 per cent is normal, though in the 1971 census this became 10 per cent due to political pressure on Roman Catholics not to

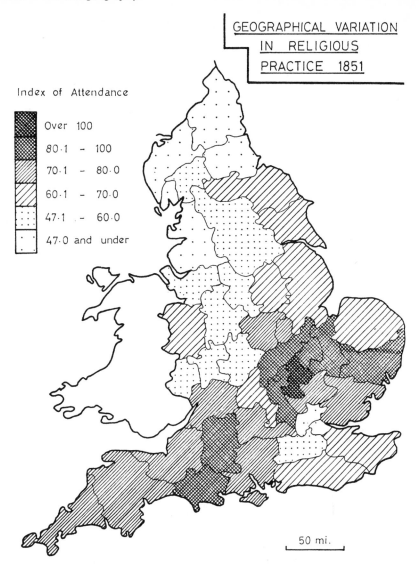

Index of Attendance

	Over 100
	80·1 – 100
	70·1 – 80·0
	60·1 – 70·0
	47·1 – 60·0
	47·0 and under

GEOGRAPHICAL VARIATION
IN RELIGIOUS
PRACTICE 1851

50 mi.

Fig. 3.8 Geographical variation in religious practice in England, 1851. The census of Religion of 1851 established, among other things, county figures of the number who attended worship: the result showed great regional variation, the metropolitan region and growing industrial areas showing low attendance. (Gay, 1971)

co-operate with the enumeration. A provincial pattern can be built up on data relating to urban and rural districts (see Fig. 3.10). Although

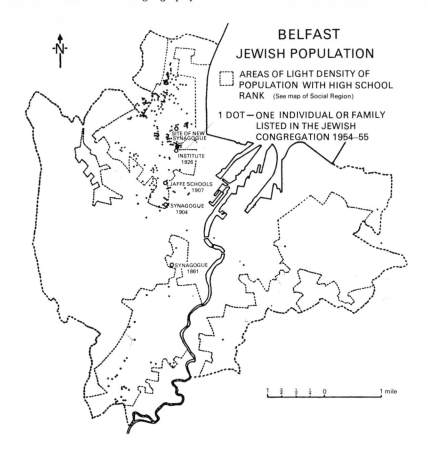

BELFAST JEWISH POPULATION

- AREAS OF LIGHT DENSITY OF POPULATION WITH HIGH SCHOOL RANK (See map of Social Region)

1 DOT — ONE INDIVIDUAL OR FAMILY LISTED IN THE JEWISH CONGREGATION 1954—55

SITE OF NEW SYNAGOGUE

INSTITUTE 1926

JAFFE SCHOOLS 1907

SYNAGOGUE 1904

SYNAGOGUE 1861

1 mile

Fig. 3.9 Belfast's Jewish population, 1954—5. From their first centre, just south of the town centre, Jews moved north into a new residential area. They have moved outward with the growth of this sector into continually higher grade residential areas. Their centre of gravity base moved northward. (Jones, 1961)

this is fairly broad-grained it clearly shows Roman Catholic dominance in much of the western rural part of the provinces. The strength of the Protestant denominations is in the east, where the Scots have had a very long history of settlement in Antrim, as have the English in north Down and north Armagh; and particularly in Belfast.[18] The census figures also enable us to examine the detailed pattern of differentiation in Belfast itself (Fig. 3.11).[19] Here the outstanding feature is the sector of Roman Catholic concentration extending south-westward from the city centre, and their concentration in the decaying areas around the

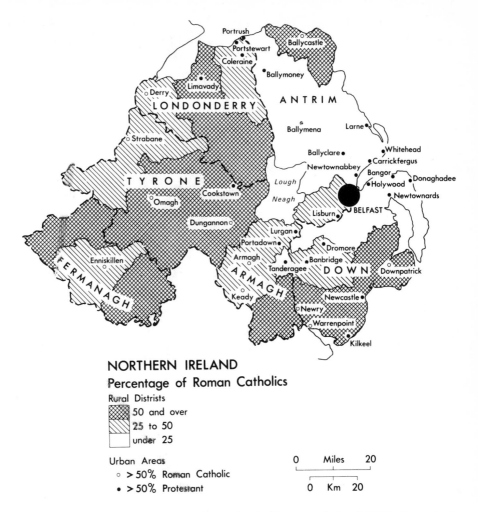

NORTHERN IRELAND
Percentage of Roman Catholics

Rural Distrists
- 50 and over
- 25 to 50
- under 25

Urban Areas
- ○ > 50% Roman Catholic
- ● > 50% Protestant

0   Miles   20

0   Km   20

Fig. 3.10 Percentage of Roman Catholics in Northern Ireland, 1971. Protestant majority is maintained because Belfast is overwhelmingly Protestant. But most districts in the three western counties, and in south Armagh and Down, have a majority of Roman Catholics. ('Northern Ireland', *Encyclopeadia Brittanica*, 1975, London)

centre. There is also a small concentration just east of the River Lagan — incidentally, hidden by ward figures which reduce this to a very low average throughout the whole sector of wards, a similar effect to that on population density noted on p. 73.

Even more detailed work can be done on religious distributions in

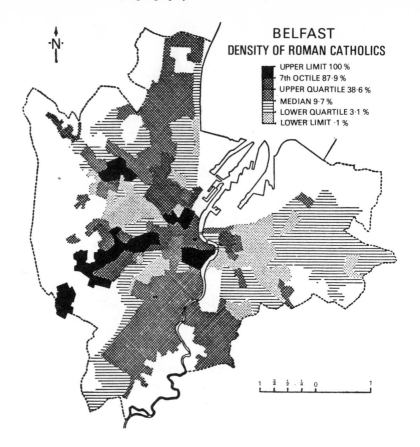

Fig. 3.11   Belfast: density of Roman Catholics, 1951. The main Roman Catholic sector lies on the axis of the Falls Road, leading into the heart of Ireland. They are also predominant in the older, often obsolescent regions immediately around the centre of the city. (Jones, 1961)

Belfast because nearly every family can be assigned to one category or the other, and the distribution of school attendance by streets shows an exact pattern of religious differences. This can be an important component in behavioural work,[20] as we shall see later, but as far as pattern is concerned the exercise becomes self-defeating because we tend to see the trees and not necessarily the wood.

More than anything else the work that has been done on language and religion underlines the difficulty in collecting and analysing data. At best the patterns are only of certain facets or of certain sections of the community. If this is kept in mind there is still much of a generalized nature which can be done, as well as specific work on certain sects within society.

CULTURAL PATTERNS

Both language and religion are major components of the culture of human groups. To what extent, then, are we overlapping cultural geography? This question does not imply that there are two well-defined fields of study — social and cultural — which are mutually exclusive. On the contrary, the data considered by both are often the same, though their methodologies and the scale of the problem may differ. Zelinsky considers the religious regions of the United States to be an integral part of the cultural geography of that country,[21] just as the language differences within the British Isles are a component of its cultural geography.[22] But the distribution of religious groups in relation to social space in Belfast,[23] or the distribution of Welsh in an American city[24] is social geography. There is clearly a contrast in scale in these examples, and in others an emphasis on the material as opposed to non-material aspects of man's culture, as we referred to in the first chapter, seems relevant. But to categorize the two branches of study too formally would be to distort a situation which is also partly a reflection of different usage of terms in Britain and in the United States. Cultural geography is a much more familiar field in the latter, particularly under the leadership of geographers like Sauer and Zelinsky. They have been particularly concerned with analysing the so-called 'cultural landscape'.[25] The spatial aspects of man's culture are seen mainly in terms of the cultural landscape, the influence culture has had on the land, and in the distribution of artefacts. To repeat what was said in Chapter 1, cultural geography examines the works of man, though the same methods can be applied to non-material aspects of culture, such as language, beliefs, and customs.

Cultural geography is also often concerned with large areas. Culture areas — though they can be sub-divided — are normally major divisions of mankind. Zelinsky uses a continental scale. The United States, he says, is his 'laboratory'. The questions he asks as a cultural geographer, are: In what ways has a particular configuration of the American cultural system shaped special processes and structures? How has it moulded the visible and invisible features of the landscape, or the way in which the American has evolved his behaviour over space and his perception of an interaction with other people, his habitat, and with ideas both near and far?[26]

Our interests are on a far lesser scale; the social geographer is more interested in looking at social structure within any culture, at the groups that are created by similarities and dissimilarities, such as castes and classes, occupation and interest groups, and the way in which people behave at the micro-level. He does not disdain the visible elements, which are indeed often the main indicators of group differences. Geographers have often used housing types as surrogates for social classes, the distribution of churches as an indication of the distribution of belief, and so on. Even language — seemingly non-material though it is — becomes visually important because we are bombarded with signs wherever we turn. Nothing is more reassuring in a foreign country than the recognition of a sign which tells us what a shop sells, or what services are provided: nothing is more frightening than being unable to recognize any of the symbols. The Westerner has at least some rapport with the people of Tokyo because so many of their signs are duplicated in English. Bilingual signs in Quebec or Brussels are an immediate indicator of social frontiers, and even the fact that one language is above the other is a symbol of group ascendancy. Physical signs, the church or mosque, type of housing, clothing— are all cultural elements which are relevant to the social geographer. On the other hand, many studies of social problems range from continental scale to local, as, for example, in the geography of social well-being, or the geography of crime; but in both cases we are dealing with a certain kind of behaviour or problem within one generally accepted broad cultural pattern.

But, unlike cultural geography, the most distinctive contributions of social geographers are concerned with urban phenomena at a micro-level. This is where most empirical work has been done, most concepts developed and methodologies improved, and this also explains why most of this book deals with society in the city.

NOTES AND REFERENCES

[1] B.E. Coates and E.M. Rawstron (1971), *Regional Variations in Britain*, London, pp. 284–5.

[2] J. Shepherd, J. Westaway, and T. Lee (1974), *A Social Atlas of London*, Oxford, p. 50.

[3] E. Jones (1961), 'Social Aspects of Population Mapping in Urban Areas', *Geography* 46, Figs. 1 and 3.

[4] Portsmouth Polytechnic (1976), *Atlas of Portsmouth*, Portsmouth; E. Jones and D.J. Sinclair (1968–70), *An Atlas of London and the London Region*, Oxford.

[5] B.T. Robson (1969), *Urban Analysis: A Study of City Structure*, London.

[6] D.O. Cowgill and M.S. Cowgill (1957), 'An Index of Segregation based on Block Statistics', *Am. Soc. Rev.* 16.

[7] Jones and Sinclair (1968–70), op. cit., Maps of income, land use and transport; K.E. Rosing and P.A. Wood (1971), *Character of a Conurbation: A Computer Atlas of Birmingham and the Black Country*, London.

[8] I.M.L. Robertson (1969), 'The Census, Research Ideals and Reality', *Trans. Inst. Brit. Geogs.*, 48, pp. 173–87.

[9] K.D. Harries (1974), *The Geography of Crime and Justice*, New York, Ch. 1.

[10] *Census of England and Wales* and *Census of Scotland*, London, Decennial Reports.

[11] *Census of Ireland* (1946), Dublin.

[12] W.T.R. Price (1975), 'Migration and the Evolution of Culture Areas: Cultural and Linguistic Frontiers in North-East Wales, 1750–1851', *Trans. Inst. Brit. Geogs.* 65.

[13] D.E. Sopher (1967), *Geography of Religion*, New Jersey.

[14] *Census of Northern Ireland*, 1926, 1951, 1961, Belfast.

[15] J.D. Gay (1971), *The Geography of Religion in England,* London. pp. 73-4, Figs. 3 and 4.

[16] E. Jones (1967), 'Religious Distributions in England and Wales', *Reader's Digest Complete Atlas of Britain*, London.

[17] E. Jones (1961), *Social Geography of Belfast*, Oxford, pp. 172–4, Fig. 42.

[18] E. Jones (1960), 'Problems of Partition and Segregation in Northern Ireland', *Conflict Resolution* 4, pp. 96–105.

[19] E. Jones (1956), 'Distribution and Segregation of Roman Catholics in Belfast', *Soc. Rev.* 4, 2 (N.S.).

[20] F.W. Boal (1969), 'Territoriality on the Shankill–Falls Divide', *Irish Geog.* 6, pp. 30–50.

[21] W. Zelinksy (1973), *The Cultural Geography of the United States*, New Jersey, pp. 94ff Fig. 3.3.

[22] E. Jones (1964), 'Cultural Geography' in T.W. Watson and J.B. Sissons (eds.), *The British Isles*, Edinburgh, pp. 407–13.

[23] F.W. Boal (1970), 'Social Space in the Belfast Urban Area' in N. Stephens and R. Glasscock (eds.), *Northern Ireland Essays*, Belfast.

[24] E. Jones (1965), *Human Geography*, London, Fig. 9.10.

[25] C.O. Sauer (1925), 'The Morphology of Landscape', *Univ. California Pubs. in Geog.* 2. (1931), 'Cultural Geography', *Encyclopaedia of the Social Services* 6, pp. 621–3.

[26] Zelinsky (1973), op. cit., p. 1.

4   The significance of patterns

Patterns demand explanation: the regularity of one pattern and its cultural repetition, e.g. the inner city distribution of migrants, or the seemingly randomness of another, e.g. the scatter of homesteads in rural Ireland, suggest a significance which the geographer must investigate. Or it may be that the pattern confirms a significance which observation had merely suggested. In either case, when a pattern is thought to be significant, i.e. the result of some interaction or process, then we are moving towards an explanation. The pattern is still a static one, so although we may not be mainly interested in process, our explanation may suggest a process. We can take a simple example from the history of medicine and the distribution of disease.

In 1854 a London physician, John Snow, carried out a classic spatial exercise in Soho. He suspected that an outbreak of cholera, which seemed to be limited to a comparatively small area, was linked with drinking impure water. He made a distribution map of all the cases and at the centre was a single water pump in Broad Street (Fig. 4.1). Within this small field of an eighth of a square mile, 500 people had died in ten days. There were eight peripheral water pumps, but none of them seemed to have a similar 'field'. Snow removed the handle of the Golden Square pump, and although by now the number of cholera cases was declining, in doing so he undoubtedly cut off the source of infection.[1]

The relationship between water and cholera was suspected before this exercise took place, but often concomitant distributions may suggest relationships which previously were not known or guessed at. This does not mean to say that concomitance is proof of relationship — the latter must be shown to exist or at least to have a high statistical probability. In medical geography, as in most other kinds of geography, singling out specific and single causal factors is probably a dangerous pastime. According to Jacques May, 'disease is a multiple phenomenon which occurs only if various factors coincide in place and time'.[2] It sometimes seems promising to link the distribution of certain diseases with environment, because of the way in which diseases respond to environmental conditions, e.g. influenza virus develops and spreads in conditions of low relative humidity and no winds, bronchitis is aggravated by fog conditions. This is because the micro-organisms involved in human disease have their own reactions to the physical environment.

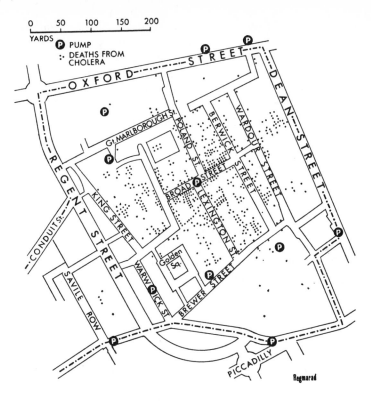

Fig. 4.1 Dr. John Snow's map of cholera deaths in the Soho district of London, 1854. Notice the affected pump in Broad Street. (Stamp, 1964)

On the other hand, some diseases have a very high correlation with certain blood groups. Liability to duodenal ulcers is 40 per cent higher in blood group D, bubonic plague is more associated with group PA, paralytic poliomyelitis with group B, and so on. The distribution of these blood groups are the result of man's migrations and have very little to do with the environment. And again, many diseases are 'environmental' in a social sense, linked to the way man lives, responding to physical conditions in houses and streets such as overcrowding, dirt, and insanitary conditions. In Belfast in the middle of the last century, a medical officer of health could show, by distribution maps, that cholera and typhus were mainly 'lower-class' diseases because they flourished in slums and crowded courts where water was polluted and sewerage non-existent. In 1852, 259 households in Belfast suffered from fevers, but none was in a 'first-class' street, and 156 were in

courts and alleyways.[3] In Western countries many such social diseases
are now under control. But in many societies cultural habits are still
potent factors — the sharing of bowls in Buddhist temples, the
communal bathing of Muslims in water which is probably polluted,
the diet constraints of so many people which affects vitamin intake.
To quote May again, 'Man is pathologically tied to his culture.'[4]

All-important to the social geographer is the way in which patterns
of ill-health become components of more general patterns of social
conditions, often part of the regional differentiation of the country.
Prof. Howe's work on mapping mortality is primarily concerned
with patterns of various diseases in the United Kingdom.[5] In the
example shown (Fig. 4.2), the pattern — whatever its eventual explanation may be — calls for investigation, and gives a new dimension to what was previously considered an exclusively medical problem.
Equally intriguing are Howe's maps of regional variations in absence
from work due to sickness and of the annual average number of visits
to the doctor (Fig. 4.3). Apparently men and women in Scotland and

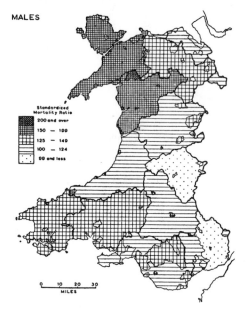

Fig. 4.2 Cancer of the stomach in males in Wales: standardized mortality rate
1947–53. The north-west of the Principality has ratios in excess of 150 and in
some instances over 200. Only Radnorshire and rural Monmouthshire have ratios
below the national average. Elsewhere there is considerable local variation with a
general excess in the rural areas. (G.M. Howe (1960), 'The Geographical Distribution
of Cancer Mortality in Wales, 1947–53', *Trans. Inst. Brit. Geogs.*)

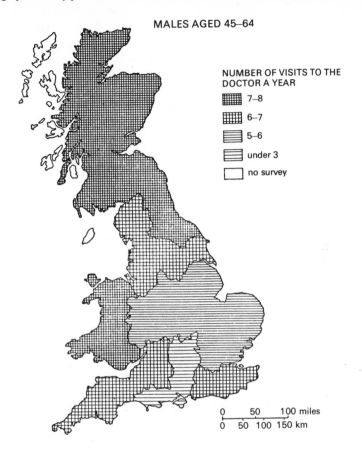

MALES AGED 45–64

NUMBER OF VISITS TO THE
DOCTOR A YEAR

⬛ 7–8

⬛ 6–7

⬛ 5–6

⬛ under 3

⬜ no survey

Fig. 4.3 Annual average number of visits to the doctor: males, aged 45–64 years.
(G. M. Howe, 1967).

Wales visit their doctors much more frequently than do most English
people.[6] But the regional characterization is important, as is the way
the information helps to define the characteristics of different groups
of people. There is a rich field for the social geographer in examining
these regional variations. Patterns of behaviour are inextricably mixed
in their reaction to certain ills and with their methods of coping with
them. Disease may be the outcome of our being a part of a biological
system, but we may change this system by technological means or by
changing our habits, and in either case this is a readjustment in a group
situation. During the potato famines of the 1840s in Ireland, the
imported grain was sometimes refused by the starving people of that

country because it did not conform to their eating habits. The consequences of such actions is eloquent of the force of social controls.

THE APPLICATION OF SIMPLE MODELS

Sometimes a distribution will suggest a simple model which will help in its interpretation. Examples may be found in the distributions of religious sects which were mentioned in the last chapter. Assuming that the distribution by counties is a fair expression of spatial differences in England and Wales, we can look further at the example of Methodism (see Fig. 4.4). Even a cursory glance shows that there are relatively few Methodists in the south-east (less than 5 per cent), but many more in the north (over 10 per cent) and south-west (over 20 per cent in Cornwall). Wesley's revival in the mid-eighteenth century was never concerned with setting up a rival organization separate from the established episcopalian church, of which he remained a member; and in many ways his movement can be seen as complementary to the latter in those areas where the Church of England failed to meet the demands of industrial and population growth. In the new manufacturing and mining areas in particular, the Methodist church took over tasks for which the established church was not prepared, particularly in the 'mining frontiers' of upland Britain. In a sense the influence of Methodism grew as metropolitan establishment influence waned. A simple core-periphery model helps in showing the significance of the distribution, in understanding how increasing distance from the metropolitan area led to increasing influence towards north and west.

Fig. 4.5 is a further example, this time showing Catholic adherence in rural France.[7] It is clear that in rural areas active participation is on the whole peripheral, while those areas near Paris in particular show substantial defection. This again suggests metropolitan influence declining with distance away from the capital and peripheral residual behaviour patterns maintaining their strength.

An example from language distribution, referred to previously, underlines the usefulness of a core-periphery model on this macro-scale. A study by Carter and Thomas examines attitudes in Wales to the opening of public houses on Sunday.[8] Traditionally, Wales was 'dry' on Sunday, a fact closely bound up with the strict sabbatarianism of the dominant Presbyterian church. A referendum in 1961 showed that in five of the thirteen counties a majority wanted to go wet (Fig. 4.6). These counties were the most anglicized and industrialized, and four were contiguous with England. The core of high resistance — over 70 per cent against Sunday opening — was made up of the

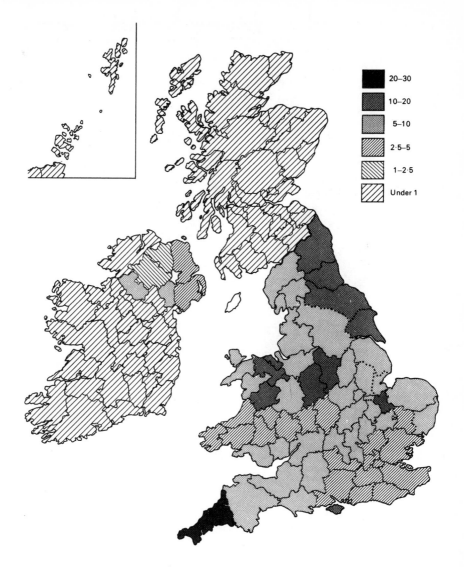

Fig. 4.4 Percentage of marriages solemnized in Methodist churches. (Based upon material taken from the *Complete Atlas of The British Isles*, Reader's Digest Association Limited 1967)

four most westerly counties. In between were four counties which voted between 50 and 70 per cent against.

Carter and Thomas related this distribution to Meinig's model of a cultural region, with core, domain and sphere. The core, i.e. over

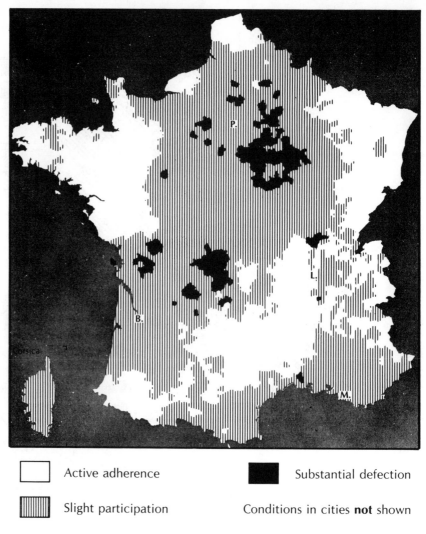

Active adherence   Substantial defection

Slight participation   Conditions in cities **not** shown

Fig. 4.5 Catholic adherence in rural France, c. 1950 (Sopher, 1967)

70 per cent, was the bastion of Welsh culture, strongly presbyterian and — most important — the area where Welsh speaking was dominant. The middle counties were the intermediate domain, and the outer anglicized counties which went wet were the sphere. Culture change from outside, i.e. from England, first comes into the sphere. It could be foreseen that the domain would succumb next to this influence,

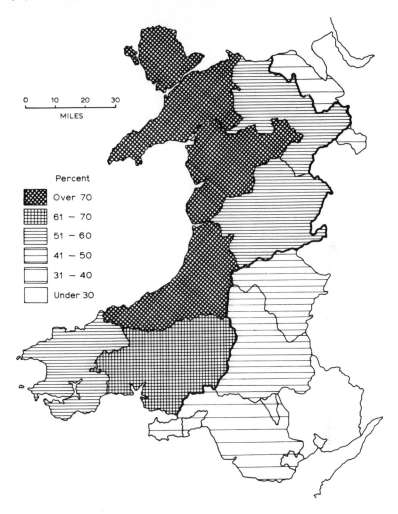

Fig. 4.6 The percentage of votes in favour of Sunday closing of licensed premises in Wales, November 1961 (Carter and Thomas, 1969)

and in the 1968 referendum only one county in the domain remained dry (Fig. 4.7). Since then a further referendum (1975) has seen even this county becoming wet, and changes are taking place on the edge of the core. The situation is dynamic, but the core is still stubbornly maintaining its cultural characteristics, the domain is experiencing changes, and the sphere is becoming stabilized as a very anglicized part of the country. The model helps us to understand the resistance to

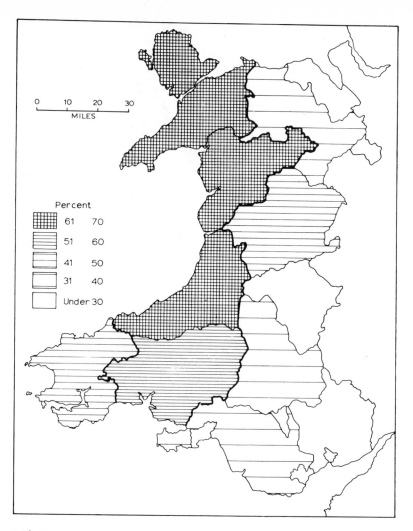

Fig. 4.7' The percentage of votes in favour of Sunday closing of licensed premises in Wales, November 1968 (Carter and Thomas, 1969)

change by the area still dominated by the Welsh language, as well as the spatial characteristics of the changes which have come from England.

The changing distribution of speakers of Irish shows the process of cultural change in its last stage. English dominates all but the merest Atlantic fringe (see Fig. 4.8). It has spread from what was its own core around Dublin into what was first a sphere, then a domain. The territorial loss of ground of Irish speaking is related to the strength of

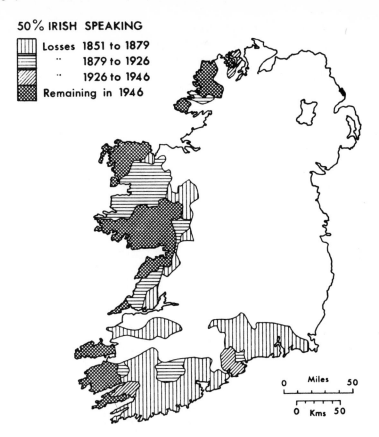

50% IRISH SPEAKING

Losses 1851 to 1879
  "   1879 to 1926
  "   1926 to 1946
Remaining in 1946

Miles   50
0

0   Kms   50

Fig. 4.8 Changes in the distribution of Irish-speaking in Ireland, 1851–1946
(E. Jones (1968) 'The Changing Distribution of the Celtic Languages, *Trans. Hon.
Soc. Cymmrodorion*, 1967)

English, though it has not yet completely overtaken the distal
promontories.

SOCIAL PATTERNS IN CITIES

It was stated in the last chapter that most things are mappable. It
is certainly true to say that mapping is extensively used as a first stage
of analysis in many of the social problems our society presents, partly
because patterns are the outcome of process and associations. Almost
every aspect of human behaviour has been approached in this way,
and some examples of such patterns in cities will emphasize the point.

At the most superficial level, a city police headquarters will have

maps of the distribution of criminal activites. These catch fleeting
spatial associations which may help to solve an immediate sequence of
crimes, or suggest a pattern of activites related to one particular centre
(Fig. 4.9). At a deeper level, an accumulation of such information over

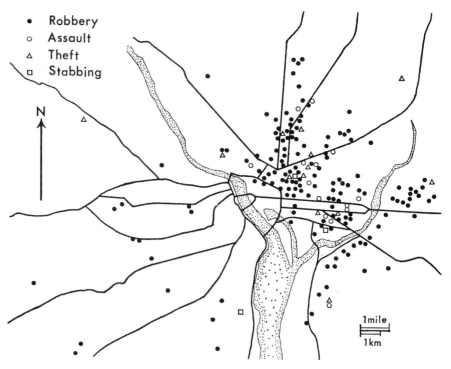

Fig. 4.9 Crime patterns in Washington, D.C.. Crimes committed in Washington
during one week in 1971 display a familiar ecological pattern. (Data from *The
Sunday Times* Magazine, June 1971.) (Herbert, 1972)

time may yield a very obvious general pattern which can be a basis of
much more fundamental studies of spatial aspects of criminal activities
and their relationship to all kinds of behaviour and environmental
factors. The first major study of this kind was made in Chicago in the
1920s, and this made two things clear. The first that there was a pronounced variation in delinquency in various parts of the city, i.e. there
was a distinctive pattern. Secondly, delinquency was location-specific
as well as characteristic of certain sections of society. In other words,
location must be a starting-point in tackling the problem of understanding delinquency.[9]

The spatial variation gave rise to very pronounced but very simple general patterns which become part and parcel of the ecological theories of the sociologists of Chicago.[10] It was found that the intensity of delinquency was inversely related to distance from the city centre. In other words, in Chicago most delinquency took place in or near the centre, and this kind of activity gradually diminished outwards until it was comparatively absent in the outer suburbs. Much more recently a study of London has tended to confirm a similar pattern by showing that the number of crimes of violence are much higher in the inner city and tend to diminish rapidly as one moves out into the suburbs (Fig. 4.10).[11] In other words, these — and other studies — suggest a

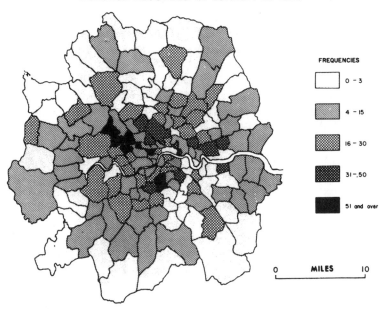

DISTRIBUTION OF THE THREE MAIN CLASSES OF CRIMES OF VIOLENCE RECORDED IN LONDON IN 1960

FREQUENCIES

0 – 3

4 – 15

16 – 30

31 –,50

51 and over

0   MILES   10

Fig. 4.10 Distribution of the three main classes of crimes of violence recorded in London in 1960 (K. D. Harris (1975) *The Geography of Crime and Justice*)

general pattern which could be applied to all major Western cities and which is closely correlated with patterns of other aspects of social well-being, like deprivation and segregation, and with patterns of environmental characteristics, like age of buildings, obsolescence, and overcrowding.[12]

Rather than expecting to see immediate linkages, or pursue arguments about causal relationships, at this stage the only emphasis we wish to stress is on the way in which these components add up to our appreciation of the total environment of a particular part of the city and to the differentiating of social groups. Many distribution studies of environmental elements in the city confirm the recurring pattern. Areas of obsolescent housing, or shared housing, or shared household facilities, or overcrowding, or pollution, are often concentrated in the inner city, pin-pointed by slum properties of the worst kind (Fig. 4.11). Distribution of low socio-economic groups, high unemployment, and deprivation confirm the linkages which we expect to find, and, together with low educational attainment and higher delinquency rates, define areas of acute social problems, some of which will be dealt with in the last two chapters (Fig. 4.12). It is not surprising that even voting behaviour will form predictable patterns. Distribution maps of social indices in London[13] confirm that most environmental and social problems are concentrated in the inner city, contrasting sharply with the suburbs. It is, therefore, predictable that, in the example shown, the Conservative votes are concentrated in the suburbs (Fig. 4.13). With the notable exception of the West End, inner London registers low or very low Conservative votes.

In other words, the characteristics of various segments of society have a strong spatial component which is related to the spatial variation in environmental features which are no less the outcome of social forces. We shall examine this relationship below, but for the moment we will deal with the kind of divisions in society which we would expect to have spatial components, and which may be the basis of sharply differentiated communities within the city.

THE DISTRIBUTION OF SOCIAL GROUPS

Many cities' populations are made up of two or more major social groups which may also be racially distinct. Such ethnic groups are easily distinguished by social traits and also sometimes by physical traits. Strangely enough, the major category of such people in the cities of the United States are not culturally distinct at all. American negroes, the descendants of African slaves, have long ago lost almost every vestige of their own culture, and consequently they are, with few exceptions, culturally indistinguishable from other Americans. Their colour and their other physical characteristics, however, are clearly recognizable, though some people are classed as negro who, though white themselves, are known to have black forbears. Much

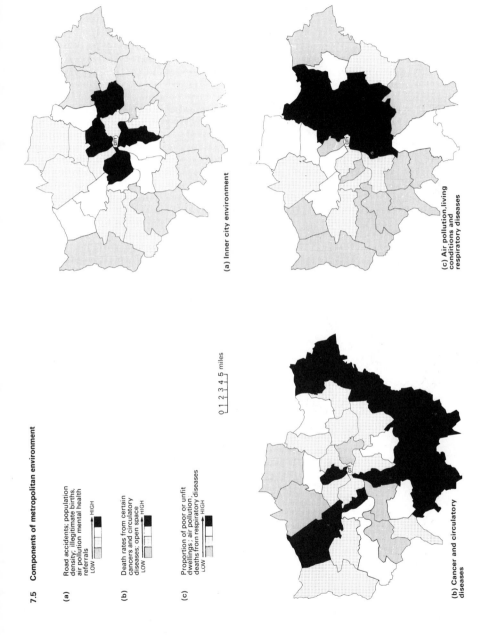

7.5   Components of metropolitan environment

(a)   Road accidents; population density; illegitimate births, air pollution mental health referrals

LOW ⟶ HIGH

(b)   Death rates from certain cancers and circulatory diseases; open space

LOW ⟶ HIGH

(c)   Proportion of poor or unfit dwellings; air pollution, deaths from respiratory diseases

LOW ⟶ HIGH

0 1 2 3 4 5 miles

(a) Inner city environment

(b) Cancer and circulatory diseases

(c) Air pollution, living conditions and respiratory diseases

Fig. 4.11   London: Components of metropolitan environment (Shepherd *et al.*, 1974) (a) Inner city environment (b) Cancer and circulatory diseases (c) Air pollution, living conditions, and respiratory diseases

Unemployment, April 1971

Number of persons
out of employment
during the week
before the census as
a percentage of the
total economically
active population

6·0 or more

5·0 – 5·9

4·0 – 4·9

3·0 – 3·9

Less than 3·0

0   1   2   3 miles

CITY

Fig. 4.12 London Unemployment, April 1971 by wards (Shepherd *et al.*, 1974)

Conservative share of the vote, borough elections, 1971

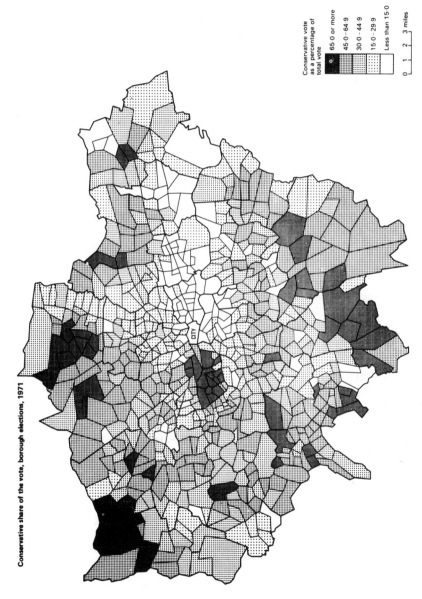

Conservative vote
as a percentage of
total vote

▉	65·0 or more
▨	45·0 – 64·9
▦	30·0 – 44·9
⋮	15·0 – 29·9
☐	Less than 15·0

0 1 2 3 miles

Fig. 4.13 London: Conservative share of the vote, borough elections, 1971 (Shepherd et al., 1974)

sociological work has been done on the distribution of black populations, particularly in cities where there has been a tendency to ghetto-formation: and the recurrent pattern — both its strong concentration and the relationships of such concentrations to inner city locations — is a familiar feature of most major cities in the United States. Harlem in New York and the black belt in Chicago (Fig. 4.14) are familiar examples. More will be said later about the segregation aspects of this pattern (p. 170).

American studies are also concerned with other ethnic groups, reflecting the great variety of peoples who came into the country from Europe, particularly in the nineteenth century and up to the first World War. When migrants first arrive in a city they are usually easily distinguishable and choose to live, if they can, in closely knit and physically distinct neighbourhoods, partly because it gives them a feeling of psychological security in a strange land. These 'urban villages' often cushion the next wave of migrants, whose introduction into city life in a strange country is made easier because they first live in familiar social surroundings, in the sound of their own language, and living in a traditional way. Usually second and third generation ethnic migrants have a very different pattern of residence, because they have been largely assimilated (see p. 167) and become Americans; they have so improved their economic lot that they can choose better places in which to live.

Rigid demarcation — more like the negro belts of the United States — is a common feature of non-Western cities, many of which formerly had their 'quarters' and in which the several social components were very strictly separated. In the Middle Eastern city, for example, the three major religious groups were kept totally separate. The old city of Jerusalem was sharply divided into four quarters — Christian, Jewish, Armenian, and Muslim. The map of distribution of religions in 1947 shows the Jews to be confined to a very restricted area in the old walled city, though the new city beyond the walls had a very large Jewish element in the west (Fig. 4.15). Muslims were more scattered at that date, but were also very dominant in the east around the mosque, while outside the old city they were very few and they were in the eastern part. Christians were more highly concentrated in the south-west quarter of the old city, and in the south-west sector of the new one. Due to constant tension and to war, these differences have been accentuated and simplified by 1967 (Fig. 4.16). In the second map there is a very sharp divide in the old city between Muslim and Christian, but no sharper than the general division between Muslim and Jew in the much greater area of the new city.[14]

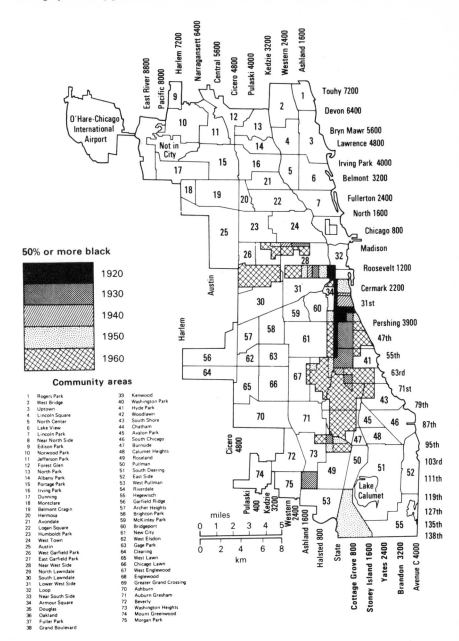

50% or more black

▓ (black)	1920
▓ (dark)	1930
▨ (hatched)	1940
▒ (dotted)	1950
▨ (cross-hatched)	1960

Community areas

1	Rogers Park	39	Kenwood
2	West Bridge	40	Washington Park
3	Uptown	41	Hyde Park
4	Lincoln Square	42	Woodlawn
5	North Center	43	South Shore
6	Lake View	44	Chatham
7	Lincoln Park	45	Avalon Park
8	Near North Side	46	South Chicago
9	Edison Park	47	Burnside
10	Norwood Park	48	Calumet Heights
11	Jefferson Park	49	Roseland
12	Forest Glen	50	Pullman
13	North Park	51	South Deering
14	Albany Park	52	East Side
15	Portage Park	53	West Pullman
16	Irving Park	54	Riverdale
17	Dunning	55	Hegewisch
18	Montclare	56	Garfield Ridge
19	Belmont Cragin	57	Archer Heights
20	Hermosa	58	Brighton Park
21	Avondale	59	McKinley Park
22	Logan Square	60	Bridgeport
23	Humboldt Park	61	New City
24	West Town	62	West Elsdon
25	Austin	63	Gage Park
26	West Garfield Park	64	Clearing
27	East Garfield Park	65	West Lawn
28	Near West Side	66	Chicago Lawn
29	North Lawndale	67	West Englewood
30	South Lawndale	68	Englewood
31	Lower West Side	69	Greater Grand Crossing
32	Loop	70	Ashburn
33	Near South Side	71	Auburn Gresham
34	Armour Square	72	Beverly
35	Douglas	73	Washington Heights
36	Oakland	74	Mount Greenwood
37	Fuller Park	75	Morgan Park
38	Grand Boulevard		

Fig. 4.14   The Chicago black belt: growth of black residential areas, 1920–60 (C. Peach (1975), *Urban Social Segregation*, Oxford)

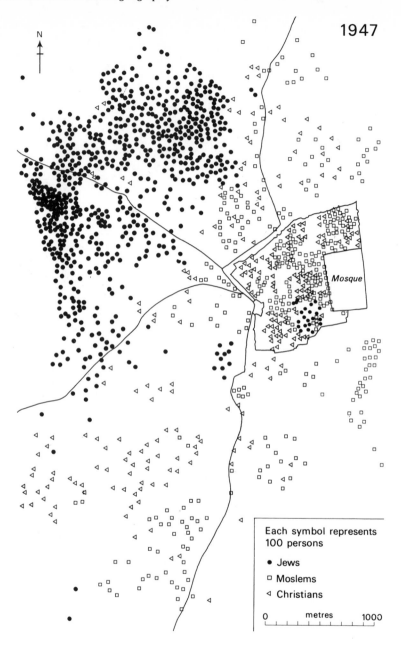

Fig. 4.15   Distribution of religious groups in Jerusalem, 1947 (*Atlas of Jerusalem*, 1973)

Fig. 4.16 Distribution of religious groups in Jerusalem, 1967 (*Atlas of Jerusalem*, 1973)

Even within the Jewish areas of Jerusalem, there is a tradition of secluded and distinctive neighbourhoods, many erected as far back as the 1880s, and so constructed that they could be locked at night. They were as socially distinct as they were physically inward-looking, for Jewish immigrants came from very different parts of Eastern Europe, and the names of their quarters often indicated their origin, e.g. Warsaw houses or Bukharian quarter.[15]

This kind of pattern is repeated time and time again in the non-Western city: from Timbuktu,[16] with its ethnic quarters and distinctive communities of Badawin and slaves living outside the built-up area of the town (Fig. 4.17), to nineteenth century Shanghai, with its British and French quarters lying outside the old walled city. The pattern was etched indelibly on many Indian towns, with the British 'civil lines' and

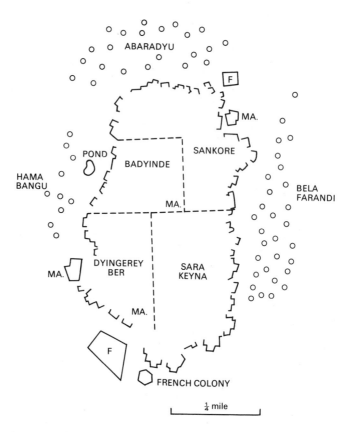

Fig. 4.17 Timbuktu: the city quarters and 'suburbs', each of which has its ethnic characteristic (Miner, 1965)

'military lines' appended to, but utterly distinct from, the indigenous Indian town and community (Fig. 4.18)

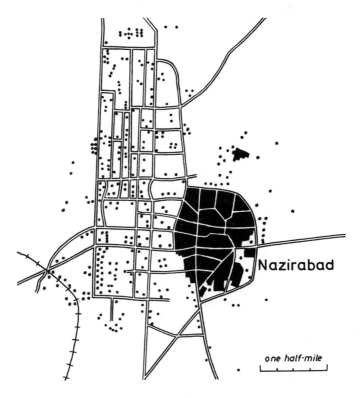

Fig. 4.18 Nazirabad. India. There are marked contrasts between the regular pattern and very light density of the European 'lines' of Indian towns and the densely peopled 'native' centres to which they are attached (E. Jones (1964), *Human Geography*, London)

Such sharp differentiation is rarely seen in Britain, mainly because of the relative homogeneity of its population, and because of the lesser differences that exist between the major groups of migrants which make up its metropolitan peoples. London and Birmingham can be said to have major ethnic problems, but these are very small compared with those of cities in the United States. There was a time when even non-coloured groups were felt to be very distinctive elements in London's composition. In the middle of the last century the Irish, driven to this and many other cities in tens of thousands by the potato famine, were 'visible' migrants, that is their language, their religion, and their poverty made them obvious in the city streets.[17] Today they are indistinguishable from others — they are 'invisible' — though the distribution of Irish-born still makes a pattern which is of great interest to the social geographer, because they tend to be concentrated in inner city areas (Fig. 4.19).[18] At the end of the last century the number and concentration of Jews in the East End of London certainly approached ghetto conditions. Their subsequent dispersal and partial assimilation has made them less 'visible', although their relative strength in some parts of north-west London is still a very distinctive aspect of the social geography of that part of the city (see p. 179).

Today, attention is sharply focused on coloured migrants in London — the most 'visible' of all; more particularly on the West Indians because they considerably outnumber Africans and Asians. Again, their number and their nucleation in no way compares with that of black people in the United States cities, nor is there anything approaching a ghetto; indeed there are only a few wards (e.g. in Southall) in which they account for over 10 per cent of the population. But they are the centre of social and political debate. Their distribution is an interesting one, because they are concentrated in areas within the inner city which are traditionally the home of migrants in the Western metropolis. The relationship of such groups to areas of deprivation and physical deterioration is a field of much research in urban sociology and in social geography.

But the relative segregation of coloured migrants is not the only evidence of social patterns in a city. Equally striking is the way in which the population is differentiated by class: wealthy suburbs contrast with working-class estates, middle-class neighbourhoods with slums. The spatial differentiation of classes is also the basis of much urban research.[19] A class is basically a group consisting of people with broadly similar economic standing (see Chapter 6), but it also has important social connotations. Economic positions tend to be socially graded, and there is no complete correspondence between social and economic grades. Wealth is a prime determinant of a person's position in the spatial structure. This issue will be discussed more fully later (p. 145). The emphasis here is on the fact that class divisions in society are reflected in the spatial pattern of the city.[20] For example, the poorer people in Western cities — like migrants — are found in the inner city, in the areas of decay and deprivation, and there is some evidence that this separation based on wealth is increasing. There was a time when the physical separation among the classes was much less. A social map of London in the eighteenth or nineteenth century, like one of modern South Africa and Rhodesia, would show a mixture of people in the best

Residential pattern of Irish

People born in the
Republic of Ireland
as a percentage of
the total population

8·0 or more
6·0–7·9
4·0–5·9
2·0–3·9
Less than 2·0

0   1   2   3 miles

Fig. 4.19 London: Residential pattern of Irish, 1971, by wards (Shepherd *et al.*, 1974)

residential areas, simply because many servants 'lived in'. There was an immense social distance between classes — 'upstairs' and 'downstairs' were two different worlds — but at least there was propinquity. They lived in the same square but moved in different circles! The later nineteenth century witnessed a greater degree of separation, as the growing middle classes, and later the white collar workers moved away from the dirt and noise of the city centre to quieter, new suburbs, leaving those less able to move to form great 'working-class' areas in the centre of the city, in addition to the extensive slums that had been there for a long time (Fig. 4.20). In this century a vast increase in local authority housing has tended to increase the segregation, because they cater for a segment of the population with similar social and economic status. Many new local authority housing areas are on the outskirts of the city; they are adding a new outer segment which socially contrasts markedly with the richer suburbs.

FACTORIAL ECOLOGY

During the last decade or so the increasing complexities of analysing the relationships between various spatial patterns has been greatly aided by multivariate techniques — factor analysis and principal component analysis. They have been immensely helpful in revealing urban residential differentiation, a field of study that has become known as factorial ecology. As Timms has said,

> The typical study in factorial ecology consists of the application of extensive factor analytical techniques to a wide range of demographic, socio-economic and housing data, generated on a sub-area framework. The analysis is founded on the belief that it will be possible to account for the manifold variation in neighbourhood characteristics in terms of a much smaller number of underlying constructs.[21]

The factors provide summaries of common patterns of variability within the data, making possible more concise statements about the urban population. Instead of dealing with a large number of variables separately — e.g. mapping each one and trying to compare the maps — the technique, taking into account the degree of correlation between each variable, reduces the number of variables into a few factors which can be said to account for certain amounts of variance.

For example, Rees's analysis of the Chicago Metropolitan Statistical Area dealt with 222 sub-areas and 57 variables.[22] The latter were reduced to 10 factors which explained 77·3 per cent of the variance in the sub-areas. The first factor, accounting for 17·8 per cent of the variance, was called 'socio-economic status' because sub-areas scored highly on this factor if they had a high proportion of college-educated

Number of people in
semi-skilled and
unskilled manual
occupations as a
percentage of the
total economically
active population

25·0 or more
20·0 – 24·9
15·0 – 19·9
10·0 – 14·9
Less than 10·0

0 1 2 3 miles

CITY

Fig. 4.20 London: Residential pattern of semi-skilled and unskilled workers, 1971, by wards (Shepherd *et al.*, 1974)

people, high proportions in white collar occupations with higher income levels, and the ability to live in sound housing with high rents (Fig. 4.21). Conversely, people in sub-areas with low scores on this factor tend to be poorly educated, to be blue collar workers earning less than $3000 p.a., and to live in low-rent housing. Factor 2 is an index of stages in the family life cycle (Fig. 4.22). High scores on this factor indicate sub-areas with fairly large families with many children and few grand-parents. Wives tend not to work outside the home and houses are recently built family houses which are either owned or are being bought. Lower scores indicate small families, few children, working wives, and families living in rented multi-unit structures close to place of work. The third factor combines racial and socio-economic factors (Fig. 4.23). Low-scoring sub-areas have many black residents who are either in service occupations, labouring, or unemployed: these low-income indices also mean poor housing and few cars. Conversely, high-scoring sub-areas have white, native-born Protestant populations, in high income brackets and living in spacious houses. Using the first two variables as axes creates a fourfold classification in which the census tracts of the city can be placed. Subsequently the tracts can be mapped, and this gives the spatial variation of four kinds of social areas, simplified in the diagram (Fig. 4.24).

Table 4.1 *Factors and variance in Chicago*

Factor	Variance %
1. Socio-economic status	17·8
2. Stage in life cycle	14·2
3. Race and resources	13·1
4. Immigrant/Catholic status	10·8
5. Population size and density	7·5
6. Jewish/Russian population	3·8
7. Housing built in 1940s Commuting by car	3·0
8. Irish/Swedish population	2·6
9. Mobility	2·4
10. Other non-whites/Italians	2·1

Source: Rees, Table 10.14, p. 355

We have spent some time listing the variables that make up the first three factors which Rees identifies because they tend to appear in many factorial ecologies. The first two factors are virtually universal in studies of the Western city.[23] The application of these variables is not only held to explain the social patterns of cities, but also to demonstrate the

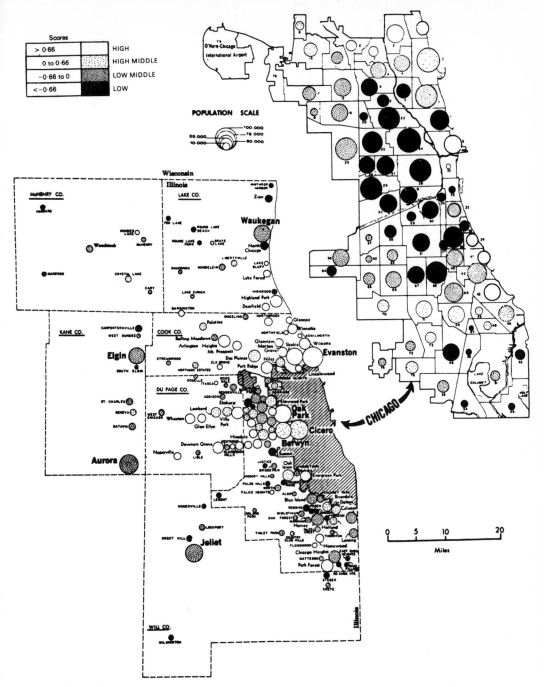

Fig. 4.21 Factor I: Socio-economic status of population in metropolitan Chicago, 1960 (Berry and Horton, 1970)

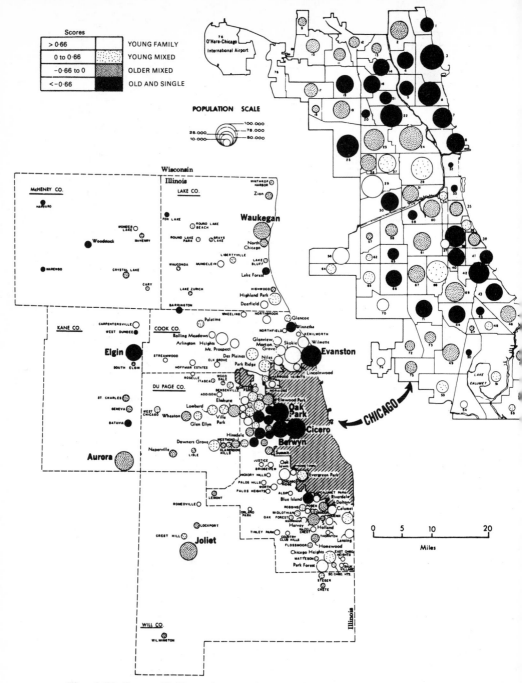

Fig. 4.22 Factor II: Stage in the life-cycle of population in metropolitan Chicago, 1960 (Berry and Horton, 1970)

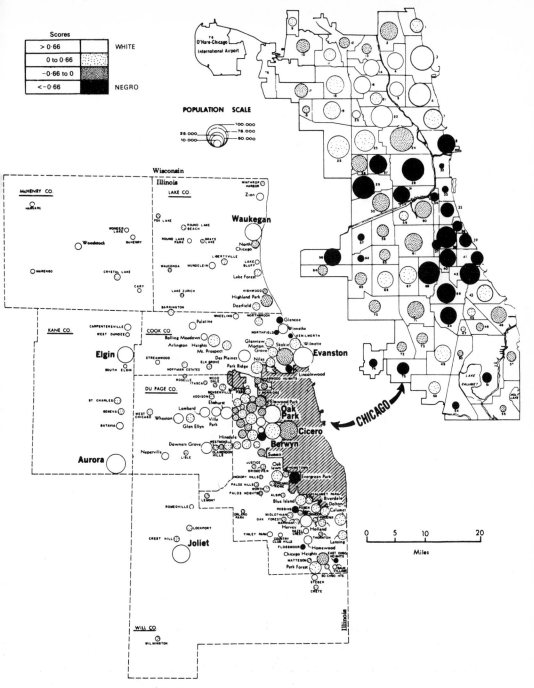

Fig. 4.23 Factor III: Race and resources in metropolitan Chicago, 1960 (Berry and Horton, 1970)

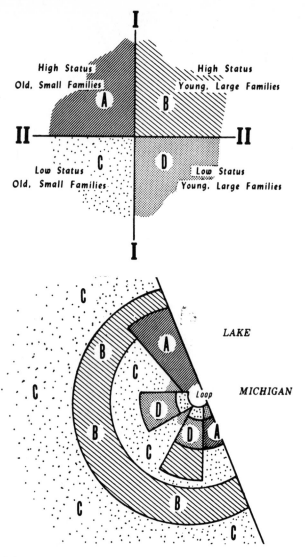

Fig. 4.24 Social areas of the Chicago metropolis (Berry and Horton, 1970)

compatability of two classic city models — those of Burgess and Hoyt.[24] Burgess's model of the North American industrial city was one of concentric zones, corresponding to growth and also to density of population and housing type. Hoyt's alternative was based on rents and house values, and these, he showed, expanded outward from the city centre in sector which tended to maintain their status irrespective of distance from the centre. It seemed that zones and sectors contradicted one another. But if the complex variables are separated scholars point out that socio-economic status is a sectoral variable and family life cycle is a zonal one.[25] The difficulty of either model by itself is that it oversimplifies the city, tending to relate a general pattern to one set of variables. Even the combined model is an oversimplification and there is no agreement that they are compatible. But accepting their combination we can also add significance of racial and ethnic characteristics for American cities to show that these have a clustering effect, and this produces a more reasonable model of the social patterning of Western cities (Fig. 4.25).[26] (See also Chapter 6.)

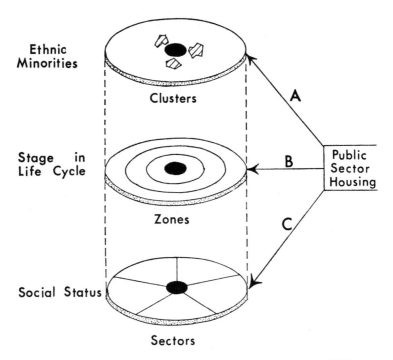

Fig. 4.25 A spatial model for the British city (Herbert, 1972)

For non-Western cities the pattern is somewhat different, and other factors become predominant. In Calcutta, for example, socio-economic status is linked with such variables as minority group membership and literacy, while traditional commercial distributions become an important element.[27] Here and in Cairo there is little factorial separation between socio-economic status and family cycle stages.[28] The findings of the factorial ecologists, therefore, are by no means universal: indeed, they tend to become culture-specific, as do the axes of their methodological forbears, the social area analysts (see p. 28).

Our examination of the implications of factor analysis has taken us a little way from its significance in this chapter, namely that the end product is a pattern, and no more than a descriptive one, albeit one based on the much more sophisticated technique of multivariate analysis. It is a pattern dictated by the nature of the data and the way they are controlled, but if care is taken with data inputs on the one hand, e.g. if a choice is made of diagnostic variables rather than bundling in anything which is available, and over the interpretation of results on the other, then factorial ecology can provide a basis for important insights into the social patterning of cities. These studies confirm or refute our intuitive judgments about the significance of individual variables and they provide a statistical basis from which we can seek explanations of the patterns.

SOCIAL SIGNIFICANCE OF PATTERNS

The patterns described above not only become the starting-point of our analysis of various facets of social behaviour, but together these distributions suggest the areas of cohesion, of relative homogeneity, where these facets of behaviour are seen as so many aspects of a particular way of life, possibly characteristic of a specific group of people, often typical of certain kinds of environment. We shall see later that for a long time social geographers have been interested in defining, describing, and accounting for such 'social areas', and the assumption is that where there is cohesion, it is an expression of 'community'.

Community is almost impossible to define to everyone's satisfaction. Considering how commonly we use the word, it is surprising how difficult it is to pin down the concept. When planners drew the outlines of our first towns in Britain in 1947, they assumed that the community was a basic unit of society, and gave some expression of it in the neighbourhood concept (Fig. 4.26). In a way the new town neighbourhood — a physical framework of houses, shopping centre, schools, playing fields, and social amenities — was meant to foster sociological community. Because people would focus their shopping and their social and recreational activities, and more than anything the school activities of their children, on the centre of the neighbourhood, it was thought that this would beget communities. This is highly unlikely. In fact individual perception of neighbourhoods varies greatly. There is not

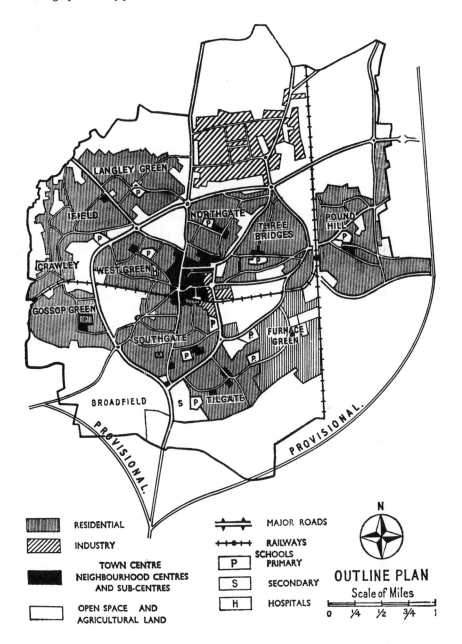

Fig. 4.26 Crawley, Surrey. Neighbourhoods, focusing on centres of shopping and provided with schools, are a feature of the first post-war planned towns of Britain.

likely to be one social outcome of such a spatial arrangement. On the other hand, social interaction is increased, space is intensified, and this confirms certain homogeneities within social groups. Some of the difficulties of defining communities are equally intractible in the countryside, and although this book is expressly concerned with urban studies, it is not amiss briefly to extend the argument into the rural world, because we may well be seeking in the town an idealized concept of what is 'right' based on our attachment to a long history of rural communities. Traditionally, we think of the nucleated village as an outcome of a sense of community, both economic and social: the interrelatedness and interdependence of groups is there clearly expressed in the cohesion of the physical form of the settlement. In a 'typical' English village, houses were grouped around a village green, which was both communal land and a centrally protected area: the pond, the church — and later the community hall — all symbolize the inward-looking social unit (Fig. 4.27). It was not necessarily homogeneous, for the social group included a squire as well as farmers and labourers, parson and doctor as well as craftsmen and shopkeepers: but they once shared common land, they had a sense of belonging, and they often felt themselves socially very closely knit.

That a village in New England had many similar features is not merely evidence of the diffusion of a settlement pattern across the Atlantic, but demonstrates that the village is the outcome of the communal bonds which so closely held together the inhabitants of the first settlements — further emphasized perhaps by the more acute need for physical protection in an alien environment.

The physical entity, the symbolism of church and green, have all given a very strong 'romantic' slant to our ideas of 'community'; though we tend to underestimate the economic interdependence of such villages and their former self-sufficiency, elements which have by now more or less disappeared. It is also necessary to remind ourselves that the link between settlement form and social structure was often found in land tenure and the extent to which those who worked on the land identified themselves with specific parcels of it. A two-field or a three-field system is often associated with strongly nucleated settlements, but consolidation of strips into separate farm units often led to a scattering of steads.[29] Even those villages which are found in England are now interspersed with single farms, the result of enclosure and consolidation. In Wales, the extended family unit dispersed as soon as the land which they farmed was divided, by inheritance laws, between descendants of the original owner, and consequently no villages in the English sense of the word are found in Wales.[30]

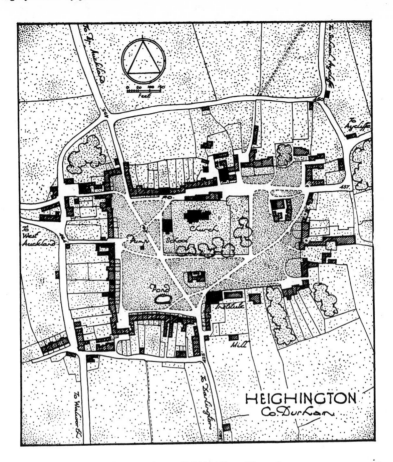

Fig. 4.27 Heighington, Co. Durham (800). The village is a very compact, inward-looking settlement around a common green and the communal services such as church, school, pump, and pond. It reflects a former social and economic unit with a slight 'defensive' element.

But it would be wrong to suggest that when morphology changes and the village disperses, then the sense of community disappears. This can be refuted most strongly where dispersal is complete, and has been so for many centuries, as in Wales. The settlement gives no clue, either to the extent of social relationships or to the strength of family and social ties. To a stranger, delimiting a community area may well seem impossible, for the church is as isolated as any farm, and there is no focus on either pub or pond. But a pattern begins to emerge as soon as one begins to plot the family ties between farms, the congregations of those solitary churches, the membership of the Women's Institute, and so on (Fig. 4.28). There soon becomes apparent a series of distinct territories within which social interaction is intensive and the sense of community extremely strong.[31] This extends to economic interdependence. A study of a remote rural parish in the Lleyn Peninsula in North Wales showed intensive 'neighbouring', i.e. a borrowing of tools and equipment, sometimes in exchange for labour (Fig. 4.29).[32] In this way, a smallholder would exchange his own labour during harvesting in return for the use of a plough. Small farms and larger were, in many ways, economically interdependent. In the same way the sheep farmers of central Wales help one another within a specific territory with demanding tasks like shearing and dipping. These areas of co-operation and of neighbourliness have remained stable for centuries. The social cohesion in what appears to be a physically fragmented settlement is rarely matched in the most nucleated villages. Propinquity is not a necessary condition of community.

But nor is propinquity necessarily an expression of community. The nucleated village today need not express any kind of social cohesion. The society that produced them has long disappeared. We have inherited the shells of social units, and we probably cherish and value these much more highly than the social order which produced them. The English village is no longer an economic unit, is never self-sufficient. Much of our countryside is filled with an adventitious population. Farm houses have been taken over by business men, and cottages by week-enders. Village growth is an outcome of commuter traffic. Pahl's study of north Hertfordshire villages showed how deceptive appearances can be, how different, socially, one village can be from the next, and how many of them are no more than metropolitan adjuncts.[33]

This does not mean that 'community' is something in the past. It means that there is no simple equation between community and the built environment, and that life and technology today ensure that community in the aspatial sense — community of interest — is more significant than relationships arising out of mere propinquity. And it also means that community cannot be built into a town. It can arise. People wishing to give rise to a community may well do so in a city. There are endless arguments about the extent to which 'community' is brought into a city by migrants, how far it persists, or even if it can be reborn. We will see later than 'urban villages' are well-recognized features, that they have a distinct function (p. 181). But, normally, unless there is continued immigration, these villages disappear as individuals leave them to become absorbed in the larger urban society. Some sociologists argue that the city functions in such a way as to

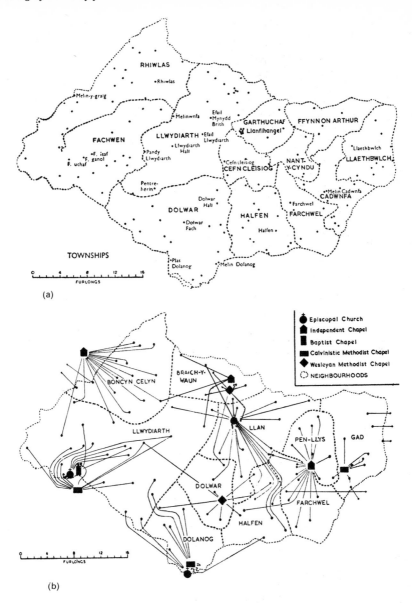

Fig. 4.28 In the mid-nineteenth century 'townships' indicated territorial units which originated in medieval times. Many of these are still apparent in the community grouping of neighbourhoods, based on attendance at places of worship (Rees, 1950) (a) Townships with the dwellings inhabited in 1842 (b) Neighbourhoods and Places of Worship. The continuous lines indicate the places of worship attended by members of each household

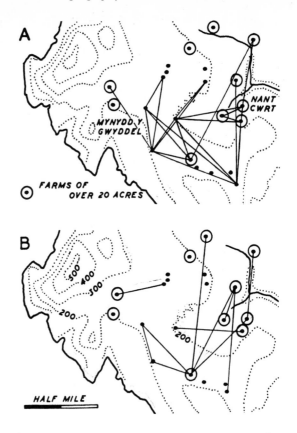

Fig. 4.29 A Neighbourhood: Co-operation in Field Task-Work, Lleyn, North Wales (Jenkins, Jones, Hughes & Owen, 1960) (a) Sheep-shearing and root crops (b) Hay and corn harvest

destroy territorial communities, presenting the alternative of aspatial interest groups, and making the sense of 'place' irrelevant. In the words of an old American song:

> Any old place I hang my hat
> Is home sweet home for me.

Territorial identity has largely gone. Indeed, the suburb has often been condemned as the antithesis of community. 'Living nowhere' according to one writer; 'a collective attempt to live a private life'[34] according to another, where a postal address becomes N.W.6 or S.E.13, entities known only to post office officials. The amorphous social as well as physical attributes of the suburb are only sometimes relieved by former village centres caught up by village expansion, and the way in which these acquire status, linked to their name, is eloqquent of the attraction of the romantic ideal and of identity with a location.

On the other hand, it has been shown that in the inner city, in East London at least, community feeling may be very strong. In Bethnal Green there is a close identity with the place, a focus on local corner shops and pubs, a closely knit family network based on frequent visits.[35] Significantly, this is an area which a century and a half ago was described as having no sense of community, much in the terms which are used today for many suburban estates, which suggests that communities may be re-formed as well as maintained. Perhaps the need for local identity is more important than has been appreciated, but it is certainly too simplistic to break down a city into a number of neatly labelled communities, as was done in the L.C.C. plan of 1944,[36] and it was certainly naive of post-war planners to think that they could be created by building neighbourhoods. People's behaviour is complex, and the network of relationships in an age of mobility makes spatial limitations hazardous. Nevertheless, this elusive concept challenges study, at a point where group identification is expressed in terms of place and becomes part of the distinctive spatial pattern.

In this chapter and the last we have dealt with the basic distributional aspects of social geography. The mapping of data, the seemingly simplest of preliminaries, itself introduced several problems of the kind which reflect the nature of the data; which, centring as they do on human behaviour, and even belief, is often open to nuances of meaning which are difficult to pin down. It needs stressing that the patterns which emerge are first and foremost purely descriptive; even when multivariate techniques produce intricate factors we can do no more than map these and then try to interpet them. But patterns can expose spatial relationships, both within one set of data and between two sets of data. Sometimes they verify a theoretically derived relationship, sometimes they suggest a relationship previously unsuspected. The significance of pattern is in beginning to relate it in this way to concepts, to see the way in which processes arise. We have already said that pattern and process are inextricably interwoven — the first often leads to or illumines the second.

NOTES AND REFERENCES

[1] L.D. Stamp (1964), *Some Aspects of Medical Geography*, Oxford, p. 16, Fig. 10.
[2] J. May (1950), 'Medical Geography, Methods and Objectives', *Geog. Rev.* 40, p. 10.

[3] A.G. Malcolm (1852), 'The Sanitary State of Belfast', *Belfast Social Inquiry Society*, Belfast.

[4] May (1950), op. cit., p. 22.

[5] G.M. Howe (1963), *National Atlas of Disease and Mortality in the United Kingdom*, London.

[6] G.M. Howe (1967), 'Characteristics of Population', *Reader's Digest Complete Atlas of the British Isles*, London.

[7] D.E. Sopher (1967), *Geography of Religions*, New Jersey, p. 161, Fig. 12.

[8] H. Carter and J.G. Thomas (1969), 'The Referendum on the Sunday Opening of Licenced Premises in Wales as a Criterion of a Culture Region', *Reg. Studies*, 3.

[9] C.R. Shaw (1929), *Delinquency Areas*, Chicago; C.R. Shaw & H.D. McKay (1942), *Juvenile Delinquency and Urban Areas*, Chicago.

[10] R.E. Park & E.W. Burgess (1967), *The City*, Chicago; E.W. Burgess & D.T. Bogue (1964), *Contributions to Urban Sociology*, Chicago.

[11] See also F.H. Peach (1963), *Crimes of Violence*, London.

[12] For further discussion of crime and social geography, see D. Herbert (1972), *Urban Geography, A Social Perspective*, Newton Abbott, pp. 199–221; T. Morris (1957), *The Criminal Area*, London; S.L. Boggs (1966), 'Urban Crime Patterns', *Am. Soc. Rev.* 30, pp. 899–908; C.F. Schmidt (1960), 'Urban Crime Areas', *Am. Soc. Rev.*, 25; and K.D. Harries (1974), *The Geography of Crime and Justice*, New York.

[13] E. Jones and D.J. Sinclair, (1968–70), *Atlas of London and the London Region*, Oxford; J. Shepherd, J. Westaway and T. Lee (1974), *A Social Atlas of London*, Oxford.

[14] *Atlas of Jerusalem* (1973), Jerusalem, Maps 8.1 and 8.2.

[15] D.H.K. Amiran (1973), 'The Development of Jerusalem, 1860–1970', *Urban Geography of Jerusalem*, Jerusalem, p. 31.

[16] H. Miner (1965), *The Primitive City of Timbuctoo*, New York, Chapter 3.

[17] J.A. Jackson (1964), 'The Irish', in R. Glass (ed.), *London: Aspects of Change*, London.

[18] Jones and Sinclair (1968–70), op. cit.

[19] P. Collinson and J. Mogey (1959), 'Residence and Social Class in Oxford', *Am. J. Soc.*, 54, pp. 599–605. B.J. Heraud (1968), 'Social Class and the New Towns', *Urban Studies* 5.

[20] P. Willmott and M. Young (1973), 'Social Class and Geography', in D. Donnison and D. Eversley (eds.), *London: Urban Patterns, Problems and Policies*, London.

[21] D.W.C. Timms (1971), *The Urban Mosaic*, Cambridge, pp. 54–5.

[22] P.H. Rees (1970), 'Concepts of Social Space', in B.T.L. Berry and F.E. Horton (eds.), *Geographic Perspectives on Urban Systems*, Chicago.

[23] See Table 2.3, pp. 56–8 in Timms (1971), op. cit.

[24] For a full discussion of these models, see R.J. Johnston (1969), *Urban Residential Patterns*, London, Chapter 3.

[25] T.R. Anderson and J. Egeland (1961), 'Spatial Aspects of Social Area Analysis', *Am. Soc. Rev.*, 26, pp. 392–7. B.J.L. Berry (1965), 'Internal Structure of the City', *Law and Contemporary Problems*, 3, pp. 111–9.

[26] Herbert (1972), op. cit., p. 183, Fig. 54.

[27] B.J.L. Berry and P.H. Rees (1969), 'The Factorial Ecology of Calcutta', *Am. J. Soc.*, 74, pp. 447–91.

[28] In J. Abu Lughod (1969), 'Testing the Theory of Social Analysis', *Am. Soc. Rev.*, 34, pp. 189–212.

[29] J.M. Houston (1953), *A Social Geography of Europe*, Oxford.

[30] E.G. Bowen (1971), 'The Dispersed Habitat of Wales' in R.H. Buchanan, E. Jones and D. McCourt (eds.), *Man and His Habitat*, London.

[31] A.D. Rees (1950), *Life in a Welsh Countryside*, Cardiff.

[32] T.J. Hughes (1960), 'Aberdaron' in D. Jenkins, E. Jones, T.J. Hughes and T.M. Owen, *Welsh Rural Communities*, Cardiff.

[33] R.E. Pahl (1964), *Urbs in Rure*, London.

[34] L. Mumford (1940), *The Culture of Cities*, London, p. 215.

[35] M. Young and P. Willmott (1957), *Family and Kinship in East London*. London.

[36] P. Abercrombie (1945), *Greater London Plan, 1944*, London, p. 111.

III · PROCESSES

5   The behavioural approach

The last chapters were concerned primarily with pattern, but it is clear that pattern does not mean much unless it is seen as the outcome of process. Process is much more difficult to analyse than pattern, particularly in spatial terms, because relatively speaking the data are more elusive. Most social patterns are based on information taken at a certain specific time, and the information must be taken again at another time if we are to see the dynamic aspect of a problem. A map of the distribution of population in a city like London is no more than a snapshot of the situation on, say, one particular night in April 1971. It is almost literally a sleeping population, because the picture has been 'frozen' at this moment and registers merely where people live. What really happens is that the following morning that same population re-distributes itself and the pattern is radically altered. The empty hub of the city — for the city of London has only a very small permanent population of 4,000 — becomes crowded with people. The population of inner London — that is, the City and the West End — becomes augmented by a million people, drawn from all parts of London and effectively half emptying many suburbs. Outside the inner city a million children leave their homes and congregate in schools scattered throughout the suburbs: housewives are shopping in every high street: traffic moves incessantly. A 'still' of London at noon would give a very different picture from that of twelve hours previously. The city has become alive to vast pulsating movements as the population expands and contracts. The 'still' — rather like the frames outside a cinema — gives us no indication of the plot.

Over a longer period of time we can cope much better with the dynamics of population in the city because census data are available at five-year and ten-year intervals, and mapping these shows how the city centre has gradually become emptier of permanent population, how pressure has built up around the core, how the edge of the city has been pushed into the countryside as new suburbs are added over each period of time. All this reveals process, and ultimately it is in process that we begin to see explanations emerging.

This chapter will be dealing mainly with micro-processes, where individual decisions can be seen operating. The behaviour of human beings can vary enormously in scale, between, for example, an individual decision to travel into town to see a play, and the mass movement of about thirty million people from Europe to North America in the hundred years before the First World War. It is obviously convenient to introduce points along such a scale, and there must be a difference in approach and in level of explanation between, for instance, the study of processes of societies as a whole, or of any large segment of them, and the description of the behaviour of individuals. Most geographic work is done at the aggregate level — the stage at which individual behaviour is smoothed over and may even disappear from view. It is essential sometimes to simplify the assumptions in order to make generalizations about society as a whole. For example, as we shall see in Chapter 8, in order to explain migration from, say, the uplands of Wales to London, one could apply a simple push–pull model based on the assumption that people move in order to better their economic lot. People are 'pushed' out of the poor areas by the threat of unemployment, low standard of living, and lack of amenities; they are attracted to London by an increase in work opportunities, higher wages, better housing, and more recreational facilities. Such a model introduces a 'normative' framework, which means we are making simple assumptions about objectives, and that the human response is a 'rational' one, that this is the way we would expect the goals to be achieved, and that the individual has all the information at his disposal to make the decision which seems so clear and obvious in the model. This is an explanation at the macro-level. It does explain in general terms a large part of the reason for the process, and it can also serve as 'standard behaviour' against which other behaviour can be measured.

Even at this level of explanation there can be different interpretations. Studies of shopping behaviour show that the economically rational man — the consumer who responds automatically to changes in price and quantity of goods — illustrates only one type of standard behaviour. It has been described as the behaviour of 'Marshallian man'. If other traits are emphasized other standards can be evoked, and scholars talk about 'Pavlovian man', conditioned to respond to advertising; or 'Freudian man', the psycho-analytically oriented consumer, whose choice of places to buy goods depends on such stimuli as the packaging of goods or the methods of advertising. These are standard responses which are meant to explain behaviour throughout society, at the macro-scale. Perhaps another model of man we should be investigating could be called 'Veblerian man', whose behaviour depends on his group member-ship, or his levels of aspiration. What he buys and where he buys it are influenced by the behaviour of his peer-group, his neighbours, family, work-mates.[1] This marks the beginning of disaggregation, breaking down the wide generalization and linking behaviour with smaller groups in society.

This goes some way towards the very complicated happenings at the level of the individual, whether he is a migrant or a shopper. He is not entirely a hapless, purposeless individual in the grip of certain forces. People do not act 'rationally' in automatic reaction to economic conditions, for example. Though large numbers do move from the economically impoverished areas of upland Wales to the prosperous south-east and London, there are some who move in the opposite direction. They value aspects of life outside the economic parameter; peace and quiet, clean air, or even speaking the Welsh language may be considered more important than a 'better standard of living' when that term is equated with more money and better access to goods, sources, and amenities.

Even those who leave permanently may not be motivated as simply and uniformly as the model suggests. Lewis's study suggested that the many reasons given for leaving central Wales could be grouped into five categories: (a) occupational, accounting for 32 per cent of the migrants; (b) income – 29 per cent; (c) social – 19 per cent; (d) community – 12 per cent; and (e) personal – 8 per cent.[2] It is extremely difficult to say what a 'rational' decision amounts to, or whether a migrant has sufficient information to come to such a decision. Family links may far outweigh job opportunities. It is precisely these family ties which appear to be so important in determining the route of West Indian and African migration to Britain (p. 53).

We have discussed, in the first chapter, the difficulties implicit in linking the behavioural level of explanation with macro-models about aggregate activities. It would be fruitless to explore unique explanations, though these can often throw light on aggregate behaviour, but we can certainly work towards a subtler breakdown of the aggregate which would link with the idea of 'Veblerian man' described above.

This means we must reduce the aggregates to relatively homogeneous segments of society. The core of social geography is concerned with such groups: these are socially defined rather than statistically defined. For example, in our aggregate study of migration, generalizations are necessarily crude if we refer to all those who move. Even a statistical breakdown will reveal many more aspects. An analysis of age-groups will show that most migrants are between the ages of fifteen and forty-five: further, there may be more men than women. These facts will suggest a refinement of the original model and give us a more accurate picture of the kind of person who moves. But we are still very little nearer to understanding *why* they move. Behavioural geographers begin at the other end: they examine the behaviour and motives of a sample of people. The exercise is by no means an easy one. In one sense there are as many reasons as persons, and constructing questionnaires is fraught with difficulties. Most people have more than one reason for moving and may find great difficulty in giving a priority which enables the questioner to 'pigeonhole' the answer. Indeed, some people may not be able to express or communicate their reasons. But there would be agreement about a range of reasons out of which may emerge generalizations. Without delving deeper into the psychological antecedants, the next stage is the assumption that the reasons are based broadly on common values, common goals and aspirations, which have been acquired by learning processes. We talk about the aspirations of the 'working-class' or of the 'middle class', the hopes of 'slum dwellers', the values of 'suburbanites'. Very often, therefore, we can expect responses to fall into a pattern corresponding to social groups, and this helps to bridge the gap between individual behaviour and the aggregate model.[3] Some of the implications of the group structure of our society have already been mentioned in Chapter 1 and will be dealt with in more detail in the next chapter.

THE TIME ELEMENT

Processes are temporal. Any change in spatial pattern must involve time. This is a dimension which no geographer can ignore but which we tend to assume, and which is very inadequately explored outside the context of historical geography. Demographers sometimes think of a person's life as represented by a straight line from birth to death, ignoring entirely the space element: whereas geographers think of people in two-dimensional space, tending to ignore the time element. Either approach, temporal or spatial, is deficient in itself because life is acted in a space–time dimension which we have to explore as such if we are to appreciate the processes of behaviour on a micro-level. Pioneer work on this aspect has been done in the University of Lund, particularly by Hägerstrand and his colleagues,[4] and a simple diagram will illustrate his concept of the space–time dimension very well Geographers' two-dimensionsal space is the surface of the earth or the surface of a map. A line on this surface indicates movement in space but not in time. Hägerstrand suggests that we use a third dimension to signify time (Fig. 5.1(a)). On the spatial surface movement is represented by broken lines connecting the 'stations', that is the locations visited during a day — these are three simple movements and four 'stations'. The line rising vertically from each station represents

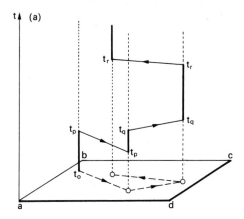

Fig. 5.1(a) Part of the time—space path of an individual. Dotted vertical lines represent stations. Movements taken place between stations at times t_p, t_q, and t_r. Dashed lines project movements on the landscape. (Hägerstrand, 1969).

time and along this we can mark the duration of our individual's stay at that station. So the continuous heavy line represents the individual's movements in space—time. Another simple diagram can show the paths of three members of a family during a single day: the father leaving home first for a long stint at the office, the child leaving for school but returning for a midday meal, the mother leaving, rather later, for her destination — the local shopping centre — but returning before lunch, and eventually the child coming home, followed by the father returning from his office (Fig. 5.1(b)). The third diagram (Fig. 5.1(c)) reminds

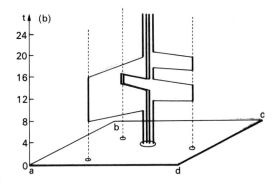

Fig. 5.1(b) A household. (Hägerstrand, 1969).

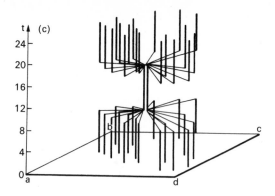

Fig. 5.1(c) A School. (Hägerstrand, 1969).

us that some stations act as a cluster point for a certain time during the day: in this case a large number of children from many stations spend some time travelling to school, where they are assembled together for a given number of hours before they scatter again.

Hägerstrand has used similar diagrams to illustrate a life cycle of movements on a slightly larger scale, e.g. a person may move out of the locality in which he was born when he is eighteen, to a college, a station where the next three or four years may be spent. His next move is to a new station where he finds his first job, followed by more movements during his life cycle, and possibly a return to the first station for retirement. This space–time path could easily link up with another, if he marries a woman he met at the college 'station', for example, and both individuals would share the remainder of that path. At some point new lines will appear on the diagram as children are born and subsequently depart to form new paths of their own.

So far most of the work on space–time has been descriptive, but as in certain other forms of behaviour patterns appear for the simple reason that certain groups of people tend to respond in the same way to certain circumstances during their life cycle. These patterns reveal another interesting fact: that individuals are constantly grouping or re-grouping and finding themselves components of different groups at different times, as well as at different places. A simple example of this is the college teacher, who begins his day by being a member of a family group. When he changes 'station' he is one of a group of academics in a college staff room, or a member of a discussion group composed entirely of geographers. If he decides to go to a theatre, he is a member of yet another group — a common interest group. The great numbers of groups we study are, to some degree, made up of the same individuals. As far as location, or the use of space, is concerned, groups are not necessarily fixed units whose identity persists in time, but merely the temporary coming together of individuals who then disperse and become members of another group.

An important aspect of this study is the way in which it looks upon time as a commodity, i.e. it is limited and to some extent it can be chopped up into pieces. In our society, unlike others in this respect, we are very aware of the segmentation of time, and our minds tend to be dominated by clocks and time-tables and calendars.[5] Work is arranged in shift systems, schools are run on regular time-tables, holidays are fixed, and so on. This rather mechanical view is relatively recent historically. Much older, and common to all societies, is a sort of biological timing machine of day and night which has its own rhythm, and another of seasons which produces the rhythm of work in a pre-industrial society. These have an element of flexibility, whereas our own categories of time are demanding and to some extent cut across the biological ones. For example, a shift system in a factory ignores 'day' and 'night', but rigidly adheres to certain hours. It is surprising how time-regulated Western society has become, not perhaps because of the machine, but certainly in time with it. Even our recreations are rationed by time. Some of the great novels of the nineteenth century were produced in regular weekly parts, as are our own soap operas on radio and television, doled out in small identical doses at exactly the same time every day, interrupted by 'commercial' time which has a price. In other words, we 'buy' time, we 'use' it, and 'spend' it — indeed, nineteenth-century preachers were adamant that it was a sin to 'waste' it. 'Time is money' — it is a commodity. These ideas have produced clearly discernable time-patterns of behaviour which makes investigation simpler.

The practical issues involved in studying the time element are very difficult.[6] Behavioural geography is concerned in the first instance with people's overt spatial behaviour, and our first task is to record this in such a way that it can be analysed subsequently. Information-gathering is done by questionnaires which take the form of space-time budgets. In these the individual is asked to record activities over a specified time — sometimes a day, sometimes a longer period. The diaries have the advantage of recording behaviour which, although overt, is not observable in the usual sense because it is over such a long period and involves many locations, some of which may be very far apart. A space-time budget demands that the individual records his activity and the location of that activity at specified intervals, say fifteen minutes, during the day. To simplify the data activities are grouped into a number of rather generalized classes, e.g. formal work, non-formal work, travel, shopping, leisure, eating, social, domestic, personal.[7] Locations may be limited if the study is, for example, interested in linkages between firms in the city.[8]

Subsequent analysis may be focused on the cyclic pattern of certain behaviour, such as the fact that most people eat at the same time or do their formal work during the same hours (Fig. 5.2). Or it may distinguish between activities which are fixed in space, e.g. office activities

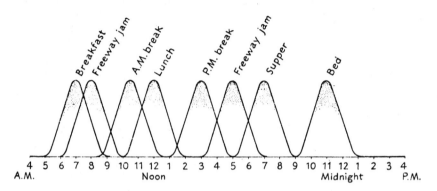

Fig. 5.2 Human activities tend to form peaks because they are often conducted in unison rather like the 'cicadian' rhythm of those insects (G. Danzig & T. Seatz (1973) *Compact City: A Plan for a Liveable Urban Environment*, Reading)

in a specific office block, from those which are fixed in time. Most activities are a mix of these, but it may be possible to distinguish a difference in structuring of the two elements at different times of the day.[9] Other studies are more concerned with movement between locations and its behavioural component.[10]

CONSTRAINTS OF TIME

Two things emerge from such studies. The first is that we are much less free in the way we organize our movement and our time than we may think. We live within very considerable constraints. Because of the difficulty of grouping and re-grouping students and staff at a college, for example, a very rigid and complicated time-table must be invented, which consists of a given number of slots for locations and for times, and if these were ignored there would be chaos. Everyone lunches at 12.30 or 1 o'clock because that is the time that lunch is available, just as we take coffee at eleven; if you wish to shop after work, it must be done before six o'clock because the shops close at that time; similarly, theatre groups must get together at a set hour, and so on. Access and communications — means of moving from one station to another — are all geared to a pattern. There are 'rush-hour' trains and 'last' trains, and 'workmen's' trains. Our behaviour is structured both in time and space. This may suggest a kind of determinism, but of course the strict pattern is itself the outcome of a consensus decision of what is desirable, and this is often a compromise between conflicting interests. Shops close at a certain time by consensus — expressed by by-laws — and they vary: in London late-night shopping may be introduced, or a compulsory half closing day is removed. Sunday, by consensus, is a rest day. The pattern is an outcome of agreed behaviour, but at any one time there are many considerable constraints to complete freedom of access and a full use of one's time.

The second point is that space-time considerations give a new meaning to land-use.[11] When a geographer constructs a land-use map he may seem to attribute definite characteristics to a specific area of land. Yet an activity may normally occupy only *part* of the time available at that location. An office block is used for eight or nine hours in twenty-four, but it is permanently an office block. We have become very used to separating activities spatially in two dimensions, mainly because of the need for particularizing a use, i.e. constructing something specific which can be used only in one way and is therefore linked permanently to the time during which it is used. For example, the battle between pedestrians and non-pedestrians in our streets, which became particularly acute in the seventeenth and eighteenth centuries with the vast increased number of wheeled vehicles, was settled by dividing the space, giving the pedestrians a small proportion — a pavement — and allowing the coaches to use the rest. This division has persisted, and the most elaborate systems involving lights and policemen are needed when these two elements cross one another's paths.

One answer to this lies in multiple land-use, which can be very easily done if an additional two-dimensional surface is introduced. Many cities have an underground transport system and some have an elevated system. But use can be made of the *same* surface — as long as it is sufficiently undifferentiated — if we introduce a time separation. For example, pedestrianization of shopping streets need not eliminate the use of vehicles entirely if it is restricted to specific times. As pedestrians normally use streets between, say, eight in the morning and six in the evening, delivery vans and service vehicles could be allowed full access during early morning and late evening. The answer lies in time separation.

There are wider implications to space-time studies if we consider their relationship with environmental perception.[12] People's behaviour is linked to the way in which they perceive space (p. 62), and in many ways these studies are beginning to reveal the inadequacies of classical location theory. Over the last two decades geographers have seen the gradual relaxation of the grip which the Euclidean approach had on their subject. The concept of distance is sometimes replaced by that of contact. City systems are being analysed in terms of linkages, and in many ways modern methods of communication have introduced the idea of discontinuous space. Whether geographers can propose an equally satisfying view of location, based on the behavioural approach, is still to be seen, because it does lead us to the complexities of human responses which are only being touched upon by workers in this field.

Time budget studies are beginning to make us more aware of the way in which our lives are parcelled into time packages, how these tend to be more or less the same for groups of people, and in particular how they are tied to specific places and specific movements in space. Peaks of social activity, guided by constraints of this kind, give the lives of most people a regular rhythmic pattern linking time and place. It is an aspect of the micro-approach which will make our future analyses of processes more comprehensive and easier to understand.

NOTES AND REFERENCES

[1] R.G. Golledge (1970), 'Some Equilibrium Models for Consumer Behaviour', *Econ. Geography* 46, pp. 417–24.

[2] G.J. Lewis (1974), *The Micro-Approach: Migration* (Open University), Milton Keynes,

[3] 'Geography and Behaviour' in W.K.D. Davies (ed.) *The Geographical Revolution in Geography.*

[4] T. Hägerstrand (1969), 'On the Definition of Migration', *Scandinavian Pop. Studies*, reprinted in E. Jones (ed.), (1975), *Readings in Social Geography*, Oxford. T. Hägerstrand (1969), 'What About People in Regional Science?', *Papers and Proc. Reg. Sci. Ass.* 24, pp. 7–24.

[5] L. Mumford (1946), *Technique and Civilisation*, London.

[6] J. Anderson (1970), 'Space Time Budgets, *L.S.E. Geog. Dept., Discussion Paper* 40. J. Anderson (1971), 'Space-Time Budgets and Activity Studies in Urban Geography and Planning', *Environment and Planning* 3, pp. 355–68. See also F.S. Chapin and T.H. Logan (1969), 'Patterns of Time-Space Use' in H.S. Perloff (ed.), *Quality of the Urban Environment*. T. MacMurray (1971), 'Aspects of Time and the Study of Activity Patterns', *Town Planning Rev.* 42.

[7] I. Cullan and V. Gordon (1972), The Structure of the Activity Patterns, *Research Paper No. 1*, Joint Unit for Planning Research, London.

[8] J.B. Goddard (1971), 'Office Communications and Office Location', *Regional Studies* 5, pp. 263–80.

[9] Joint Unit for Planning Research (1974), *The University in an Urban Environment*, London.

[10] M.E.E. Hurst (1969), 'The Structure of Movement and Household Travel Behaviour', *Urban Studies* 6.

[11] T.S. Chapin (1965), *Urban Land Use Planning*, Urbana (esp. Chapter 6).

[12] Anderson (1970), op. cit.

In this chapter we are especially concerned with the processes that result in particular residential patterns in cities. Broadly these patterns will reflect the ordering of societies either at different stages of development, as in Western cities which have become industrialized, or in different cultural contexts. Partly because our primary concern in this book is the Western city today, a reflection of the industrial capitalist world, and consequently because the reader will be familiar with the more general features of its residential pattern, it may be worthwhile first to look briefly at examples of cities outside this province to see if their residential patterns reflect other social and economic systems.

THE PRE-INDUSTRIAL CITY

Our thesis is that social stratification is reflected in patterns of residential location. It is almost impossible to generalize on the various kinds of stratification which exist — and have existed — outside Western industrial society. The simplest is despotic agrarian stratification in which the vast majority are politically controlled by a small élite, powerful and privileged and at the service of an absolute ruler. Until recently China was an example. Feudal stratification, as in medieval Europe, has intermediate classes, e.g. the clergy, and the bourgeoisie, and some societies are further complicated by intricate caste systems, though these may be reduced to four major castes — priests, warriors, commoners, and slaves. In a caste system the sub-castes are often important elements in differentiation as are migrant and ethnic groups, and they often play a very large part in creating mosaics of residential units. Middle Eastern cities provide many examples. Sjoberg, however, reduces all these to two basic strata — the élite and the lower class, a consuming sector and a producing sector.[1] Sjoberg claims that even the Indian caste system can be thought of in terms of upper and lower, with outcasts forming a third group. This two-part arrangement conveniently generalizes the situation in all pre-industrial cities — whether they be in medieval Europe, with the evidence still apparent in some cities, the Middle East, or the Far East. Sjoberg recognizes an overlap, because some elements of the élite class will be in the lower class, e.g. lower echelons in the military group or in priestly orders, merchants, and artisans. The dual nature of the pre-industrial society subsumes differences in ethnicity or occupation which give such variety to the residential mosaic of the non-Western city.

Sjoberg further equates these two strata with residential different-iation, giving us a simple two-part model. The core of the pre-industrial city is mainly made up of élite residences — palaces and large houses associated with centres of power, religion, and government. The under-privileged 'fan out towards the periphery, with the very poorest and the outcasts living in the suburbs, the farthest removed from the centre'.[2]

There are many historical examples, as well as existing examples in underdeveloped countries, which fit this model. Y.F. Tuan tells us that a fundamental type of city in China, and one which is still evident, is one in which there are 'three contrasting units: a small enclosure which was the aristocratic and administrative centre ... industrial and commerical quarters with residences in a large enclosure; farmland immediately beyond the city walls'.[3] Ecologically, a concentric pattern was usual, e.g. in the Han dynasty 'the poor lived close to the city walls ... whereas the residences of officials, the government and public buildings, occupied a central place'.[4]

The simple two-part zoning may be seen at its best perhaps in Angkor Thom at the height of the Khumer Empire. Angkor Thom is a massive complex of temples and palaces, dominated by the incredible Bayon. McGee writes: 'the enclosure, the area within the moat, was essentially the royal city — a religious, administrative and aristocratic centre, where the king, the priesthood, the army, the civil functionaries, the main artisans and merchants lived. The surrounding area was made up of a combination of densely packed villages'.[5]

The association of 'villages' — i.e. agriculturally based settlements — with monumental centres gave the impression of large towns or cities. In simple societies such primary producers do often add greatly to the number of inhabitants, though it is doubtful if they are 'urban' in any way. Many Chinese cities of the past had peasant farmers living within the walls; and in the Yoruban towns of Nigeria the majority are farmers, some of whom have land inside the wall but most of whom travel long distances to their fields.[6] In the classical Mayan cities of the Yucatan peninsula, the imperceptible merging of the city with its agricultural fringe may have inflated the massive population figures often ascribed to them. Density in these settlements was light, and not all the sites were occupied simultaneously: consequently it is impossible to tell where the city ends and the countryside begins.[7]

However, the Mayan city is interesting from another point of view, namely that its buildings suggest that there were intermediate strata in the society. The core was certainly a ceremonial centre, with its grouped pyramids, courts, plazas, and avenues, but around these were several zones suggesting a grading of the élite downwards until the residences become uniformly small and nondescript. Although the gap — in time as well as space — is great between a Mayan city like Tikal and an imperial capital of twentieth-century Europe, one cannot help thinking of a modern parallel to this ecological pattern in Stefan Zweig's description of Vienna at the turn of the century:[8]

Vienna . . . was a clearly ordered, and a wonderfully orchestrated city. The Imperial house still set the tempo. The palace was the centre, not only in a spatial sense, but also in a cultural sense, of the supernationality of the monarchy. The palaces of the Austrian, the Polish, the Czech and the Hungarian nobility formed as it were a second enclosure around the Imperial palace. Then came the 'good society', consisting of the lesser nobility, the higher officials, industry and the old families, then the petty bourgeoisie and the proletariat. Each of these social strata lived in its own circle, and even in its own district, the nobility and the palaces in the heart of the city, the diplomats in the third district, industry and the merchants in the vicinity of the Ringstrasse, the petty bourgeoisie in the inner districts, and the proletariat in the outer circle.

The applicability of such models is a striking indication of parallels in divergent social structures.

The core–peripheral dichotomy which underlies the more sophisticated examples is nowhere better seen today than in the explosively growing cities of Latin America. In these cities the core is made up of modern apartment blocks, offices, hotels, and administrative buildings; and, beyond a built-up residential area, are squatter settlements of shanty towns. Sometimes, as in Caracas (see p. 209), they almost fringe the city, and in Rio de Janeiro they line the hillsides around the city's rich core. More will be said later about shanty towns, but here they do emphasize the simple model based on Sjoberg's élite/workers dichotomy.

The ubiquity of the concentric zonal pattern need not exclude other variations. Y.F. Tuan[9] quotes a description of Ch'ang-an, the great ninth-century Chinese city, as being

divided into two great parts by a very long and very broad street. The Emperor, his chief ministers, the soldiery, the supreme judge, the eunuchs, and all those belonging to the imperial household, lived in that part of the city which is on the right hand eastward; the people had no manner of communication with them; and they were not admitted into places watered by canals . . . whose borders were planted with trees and adorned with magnificent dwellings. The part on the left hand westward is inhabited by the people and merchants, where there are also great squares and markets for all the necessities of life.

Again it is tempting to jump ten centuries and make a comparison, for this is very much a mirror image of Regency London and John

Nash's description of another very long and very broad street — Regent Street: 'The whole communication from Charing Cross to Oxford Street will be a boundary and complete separation between the streets and squares occupied by the nobility and gentry and the narrower streets and meaner houses occupied by mechanics and the trading part of the community.'[10] This ecological separation of London, from the élitist complex of government and power around Westminster and St. James's, was not christened 'The West End' until the end of the nineteenth century, but persists today as a dominant element in the social geography of inner London, and is still a very sharp contrast with the 'East End'.

Our examples of pre-industrial cities have been widely scattered territorially and temporally, because the modern Western city is characteristic of only a limited part of the world and has had a comparatively brief history. Modern residential patterns are the outcome of the industrial society of the last century, and in order to see this at its best — or worst! — we can quote one more historical example. Engels' description of Manchester in the 1840s is that of a prototypical industrial city, and itself becomes a model.[11]

Manchester contains, at its heart, a rather extended commercial district . . . Nearly the whole district is abandoned by dwellers, and is lonely and deserted at night . . . With the exception of this commercial district, all Manchester proper . . . is unmixed working people's quarters, stretching like a girdle, averaging a mile and a half in breadth, around the commercial district. Outside, beyond this girdle, lives the upper and middle bourgeoisie, the middle bourgeoisie in regularly laid out streets in the vicinity of the working quarters . . . the upper bourgeoisie in remote villas with gardens . . . in free, wholesome country air, in fine comfortable houses.

The empty core and the gradation upwards and outwards of socio-economic class is the basis on which present Western industrial models are built. It has turned the pre-industrial city inside out, though there are exceptions. Needless to say changes have continued which make the application of this model more difficult in the mid-twentieth century. We are in a post-industrial period which has changed the occupational status structure very considerably, and the exercise of social controls — the building of municipal housing — has added a new variable which demands a more culture-specific approach. But basically, any discussion of residential patterns in our own cities must start with the classic industrial model, and the significance of class in the process which gave rise to it.

CLASS STRUCTURE

For Marx a class is 'a group of people [who] share a common relationship to property, perform the same function in the organization of production, have similar relations to power in society and have a tendency to common behaviour patterns, as determined by their objective behaviour.'[12] Membership of a social class is thus economically based — it is the social position of individuals with the same type of relations to property (the means of production). In the Marxian view, there are only two such possible relationships. A person can either own and/or control the means of production (the bourgeois or capitalist) or live by selling his labour (the proletarian or worker). Marx was not, however, advocating a theory of economic determinism. There is a subjective dimension to class, i.e. class consciousness. This is not simply to know that you are working class or capitalist but it is a transformation of the objective interests of a class into subjective interests. When class consciousness develops, a class becomes not merely a class in itself but a class for itself. The bourgeoisie (ruling class) is, by definition, a class for itself; the internalization of its objective interests has led to the attainment of its goals — the domination of society.

A drawback of the Marxian model, however, is that for the modern Western world the two-class idea seems antiquated. It also ignores important cultural considerations such as status — although these have been dismissed by Harvey, who says that 'the urban space economy is replete with all manner of pseudo-hierarchical spatial orderings to reflect prestige and status in residential location. These orderings are very important to the self-respect of people, but are irrelevant to the basic economic structure of society.'[13] It is our view that it is precisely because these orderings are important to self-respect, i.e. to the individual's definition of his spatial situation, that a conception of class must include these cultural ideas (see p. 18). We prefer, therefore, to use, the ideas put forward by Weber. For Weber, power in society is not simply economically determined, although economic characteristics still form the basis of class. This 'class situation' is 'the typical chance for a supply of goods, external living conditions, and personal life experiences in so far as this chance is determined by the amount and kind of power, or lack of such, to dispose of goods or skills for the sake of income in a given economic order.'[14] For Weber, then, a class situation is a market situation — a wider conception than that of Marx as other factors can be taken into account in determining such a situation. Thus any market situation, not just the labour market, can lead to the emergence of groups with a certain market position and interests. Cultural and political phenomena — prestige, honour, political affiliation — can reinforce or differentiate economically determined interests. For example, as Weber has argued, it is possible for propertied and unpropertied men to belong to the same status group, a status situation being designated as 'every typical component of the life and fate of men that is determined by specific, positive or negative, social estimation of honour'.[15] Honour can thus become part of a market situation, and in our society, honour will be determined by such factors as education, amount of consumption, and housing space. These break down interests based solely on the labour market. Thus, for example, interests based on residence — on say, a private housing estate — can bind together those differentially placed in the labour market, e.g. a clerk or junior manager and a bricklayer or assembly-line worker. If the quality of the estate — however defined — is threatened by a proposed development, between-job-type links (clerk–bricklayer) can be forged at the expense of within-job-type links (bricklayer–assembly line worker). The private estate can unite to oppose a threat to its collective status. Honour can then be an important part of market situation.

This broader definition of class leads us to view the British class structure as being diamond-shaped. Simmie has suggested that there are three dominant market situations (and that two sub-groups can be found between the three major ones). Firstly, consider the three market situations. 'At the top just under a fifth are non-manual workers whose market situation is based on their possession of wealth, property, size and security of income. In the middle, the economically active population are skilled manual workers whose market situation depends largely on the size of their incomes and organized collective action usually based in the trade union movement . . . At the bottom . . . and usually in the weakest market situation, are nearly one-third of the work-force who are semi- or unskilled manual workers.'[16] As we have said, there exist two other groupings between these three major ones. Simmie thus produced a five-group social class structure (Fig. 6.1). Broadly speaking, at the top there is less than 10 per cent of the population with over half the total wealth; then the upper middle class, made up mainly of non-manual workers on salaries; some 50 per cent of the population who sell their skilled labour in the market and who, through increases in home ownership, pension funds, etc. do own some capital; the lower middle class, made up mainly of semi-skilled manual workers; and at the bottom about 20 per cent of the population who lack capital and who, to a large extent, depend on state support, e.g. the old, unemployed, and the sick. The ownership and control of capital decreases from the top to the bottom. It is also true to say that

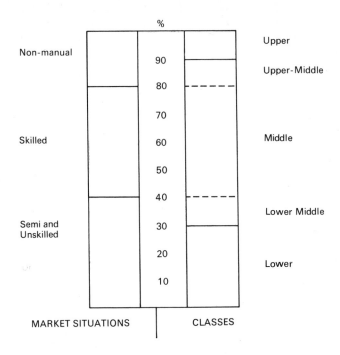

Fig. 6.1   Occupation and Class Structure

the amount of housing space and access to facilities usually decrease down the hierarchy. Status considerations make even this group structure more complex. For example, teachers are economically on the same level as the semi-skilled group, whereas socially they tend to be regarded as middle class. Such cases do have important spatial ramifications. Access to housing via mortgage facilities depends primarily on basic income and the security of this income and not on total wage (basic and overtime). The teacher can be seen to benefit to a greater extent than the skilled worker on piecework or overtime.

The Weberian notion of class — market situation and status situation — seems then to fit the facts. Market situation can help us assess the life-chances of groups in different competitive circumstances. It focuses attention on the criteria that determine 'success' in different markets. Market situation constrains our ability to choose scarce and desirable resources such as housing. Our class membership restricts our range of choice, although it is important to remember that this range can be broadened by the suppliers of houses and of finance: by builders constructing cheaper houses for sale to bring more people into the private housing market and by finance made more available to a larger number of people (see p. 151). The range of choice can also be increased by incomes rising faster than the cost of goods. If the supply of this good is not increased rapidly, however, the relative increase in incomes can lead to a large short-term unsatisfiable demand and consequent price increases. This happened during the 1970s in the private housing sector in Great Britain, when construction was static or declining and the average price of houses doubling between 1969 and 1973.

We are primarily interested here in class as a constraint on choice. An outstanding example of a study of this kind is that by Rex and Moore.[17] They saw the conflict over housing space as the central process of the city as a social unit. Their major aim was the examination of the problems underlying Burgess's social differentiation of the city. In this, use was made of the Weberian notion of market situation. In their relationship to the means of production, those who share the same position in the labour market can be further divided into smaller groups because of differences in access to housing space. This, of course, includes correspondence between the position in the labour market and the position in the housing market, but the former cannot explain all the nuances of the latter.

To particularize, it can be said that there are three ways of gaining access to housing: by having access to capital or credit, by obtaining a council tenancy, and in the free market in housing. An individual's chances of obtaining a mortgage or a council tenancy places him, in Rex's view, in one of seven housing classes. These are listed as follows:
1. Outright owners of large houses in desirable areas.
2. Mortgage-payers who 'own' whole houses in desirable areas.
3. Council tenants in council-built houses.
4. Council tenants in slum properties awaiting demolition.
5. Tenants of private house-owners, usually in the inner ring.
6. House-owners who must take lodgers to meet loan repayments.
7. Lodgers in rooms.

In this scheme, the amount of choice a person has over where he lives, i.e. the degree to which his class membership acts as a constraint, decreases from 1 to 7. For the majority the problem is either (a) to obtain a mortgage or (b) to acquire council tenancy, and it is in this that we can see the link between class and tenure, between attributes of households and attributes of stock. There is, of course, no clear-cut correspondence between a particular class and a particular type of tenure. This is especially true today when, in Britain, home ownership has become more widespread and more socially dispersed so that by

1974, 52 per cent of all dwellings were in owner-occupation. A recent study has shown though that professional workers are still more likely to own their own houses, to live in detached or semi-detached houses, and to have larger houses than manual workers.[18] They are, however, more likely to be paying for their houses. Fig. 6.2 shows that over 80 per cent of professional workers own their own houses, compared with

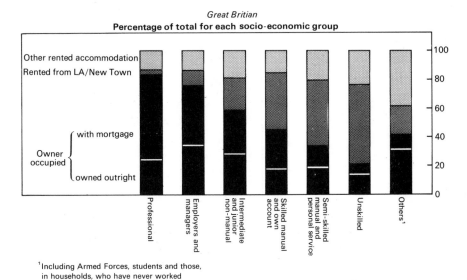

Great Britian
Percentage of total for each socio-economic group

Fig. 6.2 Tenure of dwellings by socio-economic group of head of household, 1971/72 (*Social Trends*, 1975)

only 20 per cent of unskilled workers. As Table 6.1 shows, 77 per cent of professional workers live in detached or semi-detached houses, while 70 per cent of unskilled workers live in terrace houses or flats. The spread of owner-occupation down the social hierarchy may have its limits. Security of income as well as its size is an important consideration in applying for a mortgage. Barbolet has shown that for manual and clerical workers earning similar incomes, the latter obtain higher mortgages because of greater job security.[19] Those who provide credit can be viewed as 'gate-keepers' to scarce and desirable houses. Individuals who qualify by the rules of credit-giving institutions have the gate opened for them: for the rest it is firmly closed. In Britain, building societies' values of caution and least risk are shown in their identification of 'good payers', and are strengthened by control procedures

Table 6.1 *Type of accommodation of household, 1971 and 1972 combined*

| | Great Britain | | | Flat | | Percentages Total sample size (=100%) |
	Detached	Semi-detached	Terraced	Purpose-built	Converted	
Socio-economic grouping of head of household.						
Professional	46	31	11	6	6	907
Employers and managers	33	34	15	8	5	3,209
Intermediate	23	35	20	11	10	1,503
Junior non-manual	14	35	25	16	9	3,186
Skilled manual	10	34	36	12	5	7,591
Semi-skilled manual	8	30	37	17	7	4,288
Unskilled manual	4	26	40	23	7	1,526
All groupings	15	33	30	13	6	22,197

Source: Social Trends (1975), p.19.

relating to mortgage approvals and defaulting operations. Lending policy is a mix of factors, some reflecting head-office policy, some local market conditions, and some the attitudes and influence of local professionals in housing policy and allocation.[20]

These 'local professionals' include surveyors, solicitors, insurance officials and estate agents. The last are also thought to act as 'gate-keepers'. There is some evidence to suggest that in Britain some agents try to guide coloured buyers into some districts and away from others. There is more evidence of such practice in the United States, where the realtor influences the housing situation according to white preferences. Consequent overcrowding and ghettoization of black neighbourhoods (p. 169) do not enter the decision. 'The practitioners of exclusion see as the outcome for themselves a clear conscience, peace of mind, and personal satisfaction in knowing that they are not hurting people by lowering the value of their property, giving them unwanted neighbours, or starting their neighbourhood on the downgrade, and knowing that their reputation, their status in the community and their business itself will not be harmed.'[21] Realtors hold a key position in the private housing market in the United States. They wield great social power in influencing who lives where.

Of course gate-keepers only operate on housing stock ready for occupation or stock available in a short period. They are controlling a fixed gate. Other institutions decide the size of the gate, i.e. the amount of housing available, or to put it another way, the range of choice (p. 147). These institutions include landowners, builders and developers, and politicians and planners. These forces are largely interdependent, the actions of one constraining the other. For example, legislation enacted by politicians and implemented by planners, like development control, influences the decision of landowners and builders.[22] Together their actions constrain the range of choice.

A different set of constraints operates in public authority housing. Morris and Mogey showed that council tenancies are based on 'housing need'.[23] Large families or those affected by slum clearance are given priority, while length of residence and degree of affiliation to politically powerful groups may sometimes be considered. There does, however, seem to be a grading of tenants in terms of rent-paying habits, and hygiene standards.[24] This has led to the creation of 'problem estates' of council-defined 'bad' families. Such estates often become self-fulfilling prophecies after a time.

There are households who fail to qualify for a mortgage or to amass enough points to obtain a council tenancy. These live in the ever-shrinking private rented sector, which controlled only 17 per cent of all dwellings in the United Kingdom in 1974, compared with 45 per cent in 1950. With low incomes and often several dependants, many families can become condemned to a life of multi-occupation or even to temporary squatting. There are, again, in this sector, constraints on individuals and groups that reinforce those of low income. Landlords have considerable, if informal, influence over the kind of person to whom they let their property. Estate agents can act as gate-keepers when they act for landlords in letting or in collecting rents. Government legislation must also be mentioned. The various rent control acts have had the effect not only of limiting rent increases, but also of leading to the sale of properties and their transfer from the rented to the owner-occupied sector.

There is a close link between class and tenure which leads to social segregation, which must be mentioned here, although segregation will be discussed more fully in Chapter 7. Class is vitally important in determining the social position of individuals, and as we have also said, social position strongly influences location. This influence is greatly reinforced by psychological attributes. Individuals perceive themselves to be of a certain social standing and often feel that this standing is threatened by the presence of others of lower social position. This view is catered for by those who build houses. Fairly uniform estates, both private and public, are built with a small range of prices. Attempts to create socially mixed areas have usually failed, as the evidence of Crawley new town shows.[25] A mix of house types was provided in the neighbourhoods of this new town so that individuals of different social standing could live in close proximity. Social mix was thought to be desirable by planners. It has been argued that the absence of a full social spectrum is the cause of many social stresses and that social mix promotes the tolerance of cultural and social differences, and even enriches residents' lives. Political conflicts can also be reduced by social links and an exposure to an alternative way of life makes it easier to get along with different people. These advantages are thought to accrue in socially mixed areas. Conversely, socially homogeneous areas are thought to be lopsided, lacking in social solidarity and without respect for different kinds of people.[26] But in Crawley it was found that as people moved from their initial residence, a pattern of social segregation emerged, with areas becoming dominated by one group or another. Here, then, it appears that the psychological process outweighed attempts to create a socially mixed community. This is consistent with the finding that it is the perceived similarity of fellow residents that is a very important aspect of residential satisfaction (see p. 157).

STAGES IN THE LIFE-CYCLE

Life-cycle stages present social geographers with more problems than does class. 'While it is possible to suggest ideal types of steps in the life cycle of *families*, it is difficult to aggregate this to a spatial pattern and argue about ideal types of *areal* life cycle.'[27] Not all individuals, of course, pass through the life-cycle stages in the way suggested below. Dobriner suggested that familism, basic to the life cycle argument, is only one of three kinds of life style found in the city.[28] The other life styles are 'consumerism', in which people opt for the 'good life', and 'careerism', in which the main aim is the improvement of socio-economic status — people in this category are sometimes referred to as spiralist because they move up and also move out. In both these categories there are many who do not marry and many who do not have children. The three life-styles are not mutually exclusive — one can start as a spiralist and then change one's life-style to familism. This last — and by far the most common — life-style, is central to our theme. It focuses on the bearing of children, although it does not imply extended family relationships. It is a life-style which has great influence on mobility, tending to gear movements to phases in the life-cycle of the family. Most researchers agree that the life-cycle includes several distinct stages: (a) a pre-child stage; (b) child-bearing; (c) child-rearing and child-launching; (d) a post-child stage; and finally (e) a stage of widowhood. At each stage requirements are very different. During the first stage, space demands are very small, and possibly a newly-married couple is more adaptable and less demanding, and both partners are probably working: accessibility is considered important, and income is probably modest; and all these factors suggest a central location in cheap rented accommodation. Child-bearing brings an increasing awareness of the quality of environment as well as a demand for more space, but income constraints may still prevent the move that comes later, in the child-rearing stage. This is often a move to home ownership and to the suburbs. Here the emphasis is on comparative stability, school considerations often curtailing movement. Another move may come when the children leave home, and when peak income is sometimes reflected in the ability to buy a better and bigger house, but still in the suburbs. In the post-child stage space demands may drop dramatically, and although many couples maintain their bigger houses, some may well move to smaller houses and even back into the city to less but more expensive space accessible to central amenities. In later life, or after the death of one partner, the remaining person will often move, first into very limited accommodation, and finally into the house of a son or a daughter, or into a residential home.

Robson has tried to relate the life-cycles of households to the age-profiles of areas.[29] Fig. 6.3 shows alternative routes through a household life-cycle. The dotted lines point to the notion that older households can move to join households formed by their children. The right-hand side shows schematic profiles of the age structures corresponding to each major life-cycle stage. The actual age profile of any district might best be gauged against one or more of these curves. This demonstrates that these models present only idealized pictures of the age structure of areas.

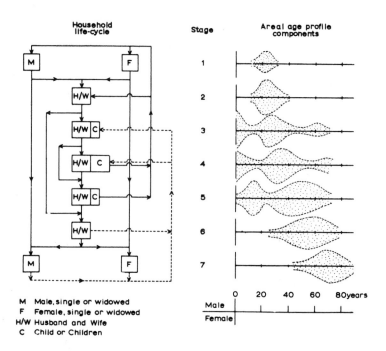

Household life-cycle | Stage | Areal age profile components

1
2
3
4
5
6
7

0   20   40   60   80 years

M   Male, single or widowed   Male
F   Female, single or widowed   Female
H/W Husband and Wife
C   Child or Children

Fig. 6.3 Household life cycles and the age profiles of areas (Robson 1973)

Age structure can of course vary greatly within communities, as Jones's study of the age-sex distribution within different religious groups in Belfast shows (Fig. 6.4).[30] The pyramids of industrial Protestant population (areas H, I, R, S on Fig. 6.4) lack the high proportions in the younger age groups that are present in Catholic areas (C, D, E). The differences between groups of the same religion can be seen by comparing the industrial Protestant districts with those Protestant areas in the

Fig. 6.4 Age/sex pyramids for selected enumeration districts in Belfast, 1960 (Jones (1961) *Social Geography of Belfast*, London)

wealthier suburbs (P, U, V).

    These age-sex distributions are a surrogate for life-cycle stages, and provide only a generalized view. Few people, however, will move through all the stages listed on p. 153. A Chicago study suggests that perhaps one in three of all moves to suburbs are based purely on familism, although it played some part in 83 per cent of the decisions to move.[31] It is, therefore, an important factor in determining the pattern of residential location and in intra-urban mobility.

INTRA-URBAN MOBILITY

What we have attempted to do so far is to examine two factors — class and life-cycle stage — that are important in explaining the social patterning in cities. Put another way, we have tried to begin answering the question of who lives where and why by looking at the constraints placed upon the housing desires of individuals. We now want to loosen these constraints and examine urban mobility, for to be mobile requires a certain freedom of action and of choice. The residential mobility process is complex, involving such questions as who moves, why, where to, when, and how. That these are important questions is indicated by the fact that about 10 per cent of the households in the United Kingdom move every year, while in the United States this figure is nearer 20 per cent.

If we look at why people move we also have some idea of who moves as well. As with residential location *per se*, two of the major determinants of intra-urban mobility are in fact class and life-cycle stage, or more correctly in this case, changes in status and changes in life-cycle stage. The Nationwide Building Society recently found that about 36 per cent of the people moved for life-cycle reasons, 33 per cent for career or income, i.e. status reasons, and about 30 per cent for other reasons. So it is those who are getting married (33 per cent) or changing jobs (12 per cent) or moving to larger accommodation for a variety of reasons (16 per cent) who are the main movers.[32] There are obvious parallels here with the three-fold typology of life-styles which we mentioned earlier.

But status and life-cycle considerations are only part of the story. In fact Rossi found it necessary to evaluate complaints about dwellings as well as these other factors in order to predict mobility.[33] It seems likely that virtually everyone tries to achieve as satisfactory a residential environment as possible. They must, however, work within the particular constraints which we have already discussed above. Little satisfaction comes from a house that is too costly for the family budget or too small for family requirements. Within these broad limits of income and family life-cycle stage, however, there are several factors that increase or decrease residential satisfaction, especially if the discussion is widened to include the neighbourhood. Generally, in order to satisfy, a residential environment must symbolize desirable aspects of our wider social world. There must be a 'fit' between social desires and environmental provision. In our own society this 'fit' is best illustrated by the desire to bring up children in a spacious environment and the attempt to live in suburbs, in single family houses with gardens.

There is, however, more to residential satisfaction than family requirements. We endow our living space with social meaning (p. 32) until
it becomes our home territory (p. 40). We identify with our residential
location, and part of this identification will depend on whether our
living space meets our social needs and symbolizes and maintains our
status. As social animals most people need the controlled presence of
others in their environment: the need is for potential interaction, the
control for the sake of privacy. These ideas have been investigated in
the context of Marina Towers, Chicago, a vast lake-side apartment
block.[34] Here the degree of social interaction was found to be a
function of independence (the desire to develop as one wants), privacy
(the desire to seal off pressures from the outside world), and control
(the desire to choose one's own friends). Different residential environments provide these three needs to different degrees. If there is great
physical proximity, privacy is difficult to achieve. But satisfaction can
be increased and privacy maintained by substituting social distance
for physical distance by, for example, not inviting people into your
home.[35] The three factors, independence, privacy, and control are
certainly best achieved in suburban locations.

But there is still a need for social interaction. The presence of *any*
people is not enough. Satisfaction depends on who is available for
social interaction. It seems as if all social groups wish to live with
people like themselves, i.e., there is an implicit desire for social
segregation (p. 152). Perceived similarities with neighbours are more
important in residential satisfaction than the total amount of contact
or interaction.[36] So we can have a state of virtually no interaction but
considerable satisfaction based on shared views on how alike people in
the neighbourhood are. People want their neighbourhood and their
neighbours to reflect their own status. They want similar behavioural
standards and patterns, and quite often different patterns of behaviour
will produce conflict. West Enders in Boston were attached to their
slum district because of their informal interlocking ties, whereas the
middle class residents of Woodford were satisfied because of its many
clubs and associations.[37]

Another aspect of residential satisfaction is the symbolic importance
of living space. Much depends on design. Estate satisfaction in working-
class districts seem to be determined mainly by its appearance, standard
of maintenance, quality of dwelling, and feelings about living above
ground level.[38] The social factors are certainly not irrelevant: proximity
is important, though density itself is largely a design feature. But
monotonous, drab, and closed-in living spaces are disliked, while light,
spacious, and flexible ones — i.e. spaces which can be used in alternative

ways — are all liked.[39]

Residential satisfaction is a complex phenomenon, a mix of constraints and requirements that vary from group to group. Wolpert, in discussing mobility, has referred to these satisfactions as 'place utilities'. This is the measure of attractiveness or unattractiveness of an area relative to other alternative locations, as perceived by the individual decision-maker in relation to his particular needs.[40] Later, Wolpert enlarged his idea into a 'stress model', in which mobility is a form of adaption to stresses in the environment.[41] Stress can arise in several ways: the home may become too small for the family, the neighbourhood become inconducive to a desired life-style. The result of stress is the decision to look for a new home. This does not necessarily mean that a move will be made. The stress can be met by reducing one's demand, i.e. being satisfied with less, or by improving one's existing living space. In recent years in Britain this has been a very popular solution, the number of dwellings receiving improvement grants increasing from 46,000 in 1961 to 375,000 in 1973 (p. 244).

The decision to move depends on economic considerations, in that a family must be able to afford a move. Within this constraint, any move will depend on the information available to the family. This search process involves considering the types of available information and the knowledge of alternative locations. Rossi found informal channels to be far more important and effective than formal ones like estate agents (See Table 6.2).[42]

Table 6.2. *Source of Information Used by Movers*

Information source	Cover: percentage of migrants using that information source	The Impact: the percentage of migrants using the source effectively	Index of effectiveness to coverage
Newspapers	63	18	·29
Real estate agents	50	14	·28
Personal contacts	62	47	·76
Walking or driving around	57	19	·33
Windfall	31	25	·81

(Rossi (1955), p.161)

Similar results were produced in a study of Swansea.[43] The use of information sources for high-cost and low-cost areas respectively was newspapers, 11 per cent and 13 per cent; estate agents, 17 per cent and

8 per cent; family and friends, 25 per cent and 15 per cent; looking around, 39 per cent and 21 per cent. Herbert comments that such figures suggest a very limited search and a minimum of information.

This is important in considering the actual location of the new residence. In examining where people have moved to we need to return to the idea of place utility and its twin concepts of awareness and action spaces. To be able to move into a particular locality you must be aware of the housing possibilities there. You must also be able to rank a number of localities in some perceived order of preference (see p. 55). Thus in Horton and Reynolds' terms, action spaces are 'the collection of all urban locations about which the individual has information, and the subjective utility or preference he associates with these locations.'[44] It has been argued that the action spaces of individuals bias the search pattern of movers. Adams, for example, argues that the general sectoral movement of householders from their homes to the city centre produces sectoral mental maps of the city, and that this influences any relocation decision, i.e. the search for a new residence takes place mainly within the known sector.[45]

Horton and Reynolds's study of Cedar Rapids tends to substantiate this, especially for suburban dwellers. Herbert's findings in Swansea lend support to the idea of directional bias and also a distance-decay function. For low-cost respondents the search was usually restricted to one residential area, often the district of previous residence, while high-cost respondents had followed the new housing market as it had expanded into the established high socio-economic status sector.

All this points to the limitations set on choice by the very immensity of the complete range. But operating at each stage in the process are constraints, and by way of summarizing our discussion so far we can examine the work of Murie, who stresses the way in which many decisions are taken out of the hands of incipient movers and are taken instead by managers or controllers within the market, whether this be the bureaucratic process of local authority or of privately run agencies.[46] The key to movement may lie, not in the impetus — that is, why people want to move — but in their *eligibility* within the controlling system — that is, how they are *allowed* to move. For example, with the exception of a small minority who can afford to buy houses outright, or acquire them in some other way, the vast majority are very much at the mercy of building societies or any other organizations which finance the undertakings. In the public sector the rules of eligibility may be very complex indeed, including circumstances, family size, job security, and so on. Murie sums up by saying that the nature of intra-urban mobility is more consistent with explanations focusing on constraints, access, and eligibility, 'competition for space being based on eligibility determined by institutions on criteria like merit, reward and market factors, plus criteria of need.'[47]

Murie's study, rather than giving priority to any one reason for moving and having to a large extent discounted the full emphasis of a life-cycle of stages, mentions four 'trigger mechanisms' which set the process of movement in motion. They are (a) a change in the family life cycle; (b) a change in income; (c) change in employment location, and (d) a change in the environment, such as the implementation of an improvement scheme or a clearance scheme. To be completed the process must pass through a series of filters which act as a sort of test or a constraint, any one of which can affect the outcome, and indeed prevent its completion. They are (1) the life-style preference, affecting interpretation of change, and based on values and aspirations, income and occupations; (2) search and information behaviour, affecting perception; (3) access and eligibility, affecting the success of the action, i.e. the 'rules' of the institution whether in the private or in the public sector; (4) availability of the required accommodation. The ultimate success depends on the nature of the housing that is available.

Taking all these factors into account, it follows that groups by no means have equal access to houses, and are therefore constrained in their movements. Indeed, this goes a long way to explaining the distribution of groups in cities. There is a tendency for those who are entirely constrained to find themselves in the inner city, more particularly in the zone of transition, whereas the greatest amount of the movement takes place in the inner and outer suburbs. As we shall see later, other distinguishing characteristics of groups may aggravate the problem, as when, for example, ethnic differences lead to ghetto formations. But all these are closely interrelated. That racial prejudice enters as one constraint is strongly suggested by figures put forward by Deakin when he compares housing tenure groups in the G.L.C. in 1966 between English and coloured migrants.[48]

Table 6.3 *Tenure of English and Coloured Migrants*

	Owner occupier	Local authority renting	Unfurnished renting	Furnished renting
English	38·9%	22·3%	29·0%	7·3%
Coloured migrants	32·6%	4·2%	18·1%	43·6%

These figures suggest that coloured migrants find it virtually impossible to obtain local authority houses. Though owner occupation is by no means equably spread, their chances in this sector are much higher. But most significantly a vastly disproportionate percentage is forced into the private furnished renting market, which is the most vulnerable of all. This analysis is confirmed by a more recent study on the access of migrants to different kinds of accommodation.[49]

FILTERING

The space available for all this movement, that is the housing stock, is also very complex. The age, the size, the degree of obsolescence, and the general environmental characteristics of each house vary immensely, but as a result of similar growth patterns many Western cities show a general regularity of sequence of house types. The inner city will almost inevitably have a high proportion of large houses, formerly lived in by big, middle-class families, only a few of which have been modified to meet modern demands, and most of which have deteriorated physically and been sub-divided and flatted. The inner city, too, will have extensive later nineteenth-century by-law housing which may have the appropriate space for the modern family, but will almost always be obsolescent to some degree. Municipal housing often will have replaced the old residential property. Suburban housing will be environmentally much more acceptable, as well as more likely to meet modern family needs, but here, too, there is a fairly wide spectrum from the older, small semi-detached inter-war house to the newer developments which may vary greatly in size.

Ideally, there should be a 'fit' between the needs of households and the stock the city has to offer. Even if this were the case, however, the changing needs implied in the family cycle would demand constant movement: one cannot expect every family to maintain the same establishment throughout its life. However, housing stock, like people, ages, and may even be considered to go through stages, either physically as it becomes increasingly obsolescent, or in function as it outlives one use and fails to meet the requirements of another. In Britain seventy or eighty years may be considered a reasonable life for a house, but in fact there is still considerable stock which is over a hundred years old, whereas the rapidly increasing standards of living in the last half century have made many houses obsolete which were built much more recently. One concept of adaptation, however, is that in which stock 'filters' downwards with age, on the assumption that a less exacting standard of housing is expected to meet the requirements of the poorer than for those of the richer.[50] Indeed, the term was first used in the 1920s to describe a way of fulfilling the needs of lower income groups. Slum dwellers, it was suggested, could be re-housed in property vacated by those in higher income groups who had moved into new houses, and in this way social groups are thought of as 'filtering up' as houses 'filter down'. One may question whether this really meant improvement, as the property undergoing change may have deteriorated below an acceptable standard. Filtering is thought by some to extend even further, each social class tending to move into property vacated by that immediately above it in the hierarchy. This assumes that only the topmost class builds new houses, which is patently not so, for the new housing market caters for a wide spectrum of socio-economic classes. It also assumes that the richest groups can only adapt to pressure from below by moving. This is not necessarily so. Such groups have great political and economic power which can be used to resist the encroachment of other groups and activities. The idea of filtering does not adequately convey this. We should perhaps think in terms of houses filtering downward and groups being 'blown out' of their places in the urban structure. Which groups are blown out depends on where the pressure from the base of the housing market is concentrated. It has been suggested that middle-income groups are more likely to be displaced than the rich. It is they who move to suburbia while the rich often remain where they are, or 'filter in' to older property in 'good' locations.

That different life-styles characterize different parts of our cities is a familiar feature. It has arisen from a most complex relationship between the structure of society and the physical fabric of the city. The former is the outcome of social processes which have given us stratification and class, the latter the outcome of historically different responses to the need for shelter. Although there is a large measure of choice in many people's location and movement, most people are subject to many constraints, imposed not only by their social position and by the availability of housing, but by numerous institutionalized 'gateways' which tend to emphasize group differences. In the following chapter we shall see how, in certain instances, this is further heightened by innate group differences — like colour and ethnic origin — to produce even greater separation.

NOTES AND REFERENCES

[1] G. Sjoberg (1960), *The Pre-Industrial City*, Glencoe, Ill. Chapter V.
[2] Ibid., pp. 97—8.
[3] Y.F. Tuan (1968), 'A Preface to Chinese Cities', in R.P. Beckinsale and J.M. Houston (eds.), *Urbanisation and its Problems*, Oxford, p. 224.

⁴ Ibid., p. 228.

⁵ T.G. McGee (1967), *The South East Asian City*, London, p. 37.

⁶ A.L. Mabogunje (1968), *Urbanisation in Nigeria*, London, p. 124.

⁷ J.E.S. Thompson (1966), *The Rise and Fall of Waza Civilisation*, London.

⁸ S. Zweig (1942), *The World of Yesterday*.

⁹ Tuan (1968), op. cit., p. 218.

¹⁰ H. Hobhouse (1975), *A History of Regent Street*, London, p. 32.

¹¹ F. Engels (1969), *Conditions of the Working Class in England*, London.

¹² D. Marquand and I. Clegg (1969), *Class and Power*, London, p. 6.

¹³ D. Harvey (1973), *Social Justice and the City*, London, p. 281.

¹⁴ H.H. Gerth & C.W. Mills (1948), *From Max Weber*, London, p. 181.

¹⁵ Ibid., pp. 186−7.

¹⁶ J.M. Simmie (1974), *Citizens in Conflict: The Sociology of Town Planning*, London, p.88.

¹⁷ J. Rex & R. Moore (1967), *Race, Community & Conflict: A Study of Sparkbrook*, Oxford. See especially, J. Rex (1968), 'The Sociology of a Zone of Transition' in R.E. Pahl (ed.) *Readings in Urban Sociology*, Oxford pp. 211−31.

¹⁸ Central Statistical Office (1975), 'Social Commentary: Social Class', *Social Trends* 6, pp. 10−32.

¹⁹ R. Barbolet (1969), Housing Classes & The Socio-Ecological System *Centre for Environment Studies, University Working Paper* 4.

²⁰ See J. Ford (1975), 'The Role of the Building Society Manager in the Urban Stratification System', *Urban Studies* 12, pp. 295−302.

²¹ R. Helper (1969), *Racial Policies & Practices of Real Estate Brokers*, Minneapolis.

²² This supply side of the housing provision equation has been examined by, for example, some of the contributors in P. Hall *et al.* (1973), *The Containment of Urban England*, London, 2 vols. See also E.A. Craven (1969), 'Private Residential Expansion in Kent', *Urban Studies* 6, 1−16, S. Jenkins (1975), *Landlords to London*, London, examines the landowner−planner link in London.

²³ R.N. Morris & J. Mogey (1965), *The Sociology of Housing*, London.

²⁴ See J.B. Cullingworth (1973), *Problems of an Urban Society*, ii., London, 53−5.

²⁵ See B.J. Heraud (1968), 'Social Class & The New Towns', *Urban Studies* 5, 33−58.

²⁶ See the discussion of H.J. Gans (1961), 'The Balanced Community: Homogeneity or Heterogeneity in Residential Areas.', *Journal of the American Institute of Planners* 27, pp. 176−84.

²⁷ B.T. Robson (1975), *Urban Social Areas*, Oxford, p. 24.

²⁸ W.M. Dobriner (1963), *Class in Suburbia*, New Jersey.

²⁹ B.T. Robson (1973), 'A View on the Urban Scene' in M. Chisholm & B. Rodgers (eds.), *Studies in Human Geography*, London, pp. 203−41.

³⁰ A full discussion of these distributions can be found in E. Jones (1960), *A Social Geography of Belfast*, Oxford, pp. 146−51.

³¹ W. Bell (1968), The City, the Suburb and a Theory of Social Choice', in S. Greer, *et al.* (eds.), *The New Urbanisation*, New York, pp. 132−168.

³² Nationwide Building Society (1970), 'Why Do People Move?', Occasional Bulletin 99.

³³ P.H. Rossi (1955), *Why Families Move*, New York.

³⁴ See R. Blumhorst (1967), *Faithful Rebels*, Urbana.

³⁵ See, for example, the study by E. Pfeil (1968), 'The Pattern of Neighbouring Relations in Dortmund−Nordstadt'; in Pahl (ed.), op. cit., pp. 136−58.

³⁶ See S. Keller (1968), *The Urban Neighborhood*, New York.

³⁷ M. Fried & P. Gleicher (1961), 'Some Sources of Residential Satisfaction in an Urban Slum', *Journal of the American Institute of Planners* 27, pp. 305−15; and P. Willmott and M. Young (1960), *Family and Class in a London Suburb*, London, for the Boston and Woodford studies respectively.

³⁸ Department of the Environment (1969), *The Estate Outside the Dwelling*, London.

³⁹ See A. Rapoport & R. Kantor (1967), 'Complexity and Ambiguity in Environmental Design', *Journal of the American Institute of Planners* 33, pp. 210−22. The importance of

environmental design was given early and brilliant exposition in G. Cullen (1961), *Townscape*, London.

[40] J. Wolpert (1965), Behavioural Aspects of the Decision to Migrate, *Papers of the Regional Science Association* 15, pp. 159–69.

[41] J. Wolpert (1966), 'Migration as an Adjustment to Environment Stress', *Journal of Social Issues* 22, pp. 92–102. Stress also plays an important role in the intra-urban migration scheme of L.A. Brown and E.G. Moore (1970), 'The Intra-Urban Migration Process: A Perspective', *Geografiska Annaler* 52B, pp. 1–13. See also the discussion in Robson (1975), op. cit.

[42] Rossi, op. cit.

[43] D.T. Herbert (1973) 'The Residential Mobility Process: Some Empirical Observations', *Area* 5, pp. 242–51.

[44] P.E. Horton and D.R. Reynolds (1971), 'Effects of Urban Spatial Structure on Individual Behaviour', *Economic Geography* 47, pp. 36–48.

[45] J.S. Adams (1969), 'Directional Bias in Intra-Urban Migration', *Economic Geography* 45, pp. 303–23.

[46] A. Murie (1975), Household Movement and Housing, *Univ. Birmingham Centre for Urban and Regional Studies, Occ. Paper No. 28.*

[47] Murie (1975), op. cit.

[48] N. Deakin and C. Ungerson (1973), 'Beyond the Ghetto: The Illusion of Choice', in D. Donnison and D. Eversley (eds.), *London: Urban Patterns, Problems and Policies*, London.

[49] Runnymede Trust (1975), *Race and Council Housing in London*, London.

[50] J.S. Lowry (1960), 'Filtering and Housing Standards: A Conceptual Analysis', *Land Economics* 36, pp. 362–70. See also Harvey, *op. cit.*, pp. 172–3.

7   Segregation

DEGREE OF ASSIMILATION

The introduction to a recent book of readings on segregation begins by saying that it is concerned with 'the relationship between social distance and geographical space'. The assumption is that degrees of interaction between groups in society, more particularly between host and migrant groups, are reflected in the degree to which groups are spatially segregated.[1] In an earlier chapter we saw that factorial ecology studies revealed racial or ethnic status to be an important variable in accounting for residential differentiation. There are many processes in society which give rise to minority groups sharply distinguished from the 'host'. For example, the migration of Europeans to North America in the nineteenth century gave rise to many a 'little Sicily' or a 'German town' in cities, just as oriental movement gave rise to 'Chinatowns' in California. Elsewhere the 'invading' minority has been technologically superior to the 'host' and forms an élite over the majority, as in colonial cities in Africa and Asia, but the result in spatial terms is again a very distinct 'quarter'.

The interaction of migrant and host groups varies enormously.[2] If the differences are not great the minority group may well integrate with the host group in a comparatively short time. In the United States, for example, those who are nearest the earliest settlers in physical type and culture find assimilation easy. The prototype set before the migrant is that of the white Anglo-Saxon protestant, and consequently certain European migrants who are 'visible' by virtue of a darker skin (Mediterranean stock), by language (Slavonic) or because of a difference in religion do not find integration easy. Formal education through a common language, introducing new behaviour, new values to children of migrants is the recognized path to *assimilation*, which is normally accomplished in the second or third generation. It is a process which is encouraged by the migrants themselves who, after all, came to the United States in order to benefit from its resources: they have already made the cultural break with the Old World and desire nothing better for their children than that they become Americans in every sense of the word. Few people migrate in order to maintain their group identity, and even those groups who do, for religious or idealistic reasons, like the Pennsylvania Dutch, are more often than not swamped by the overwhelming processes of Americanization, and do not survive (see p. 178).

Assimilation expresses itself in the city in the freedom for most people to live anywhere within certain constraints such as income. Groups, which in the early stages of settling tend to live in one area, lose identity spatially as well as socially. Assimilation is also held to be a sound goal as national policy. For a century the melting pot concept was universally accepted in the United States. More recently, however, there has been a perceptible change, some people arguing the value of maintaining ethnic differences in order to enrich the national heritage. So an alternative to assimilation is encouraged. This we can call *accommodation*, by which groups are allowed to be different from the host, have a different life-style, express themselves as a sub-culture, though there may well be a close interdependence between groups. Traditionally, for example, Jews in Muslim cities have been accommodated because they carry out essential functions in banking and trading which are forbidden to certain strict Islamic sects. Maintaining ethnic differences can lend colour and variety to community life.

Accommodation is also a method of dealing with groups which the host society does not wish to assimilate. In the United States racial groups, as opposed to ethnic groups, are not considered assimilable. Colour alone — for the black in the States shares almost every aspect of his culture with the white population — is an insuperable barrier. But such accommodation is not based on equality and interrelatedness: and the resulting spatial segregation is often an outcome of tension and conflict. The degree of segregation which is associated with non-whites in the United States and coloured Commonwealth immigrants in Britain reflects prejudice on the part of the host community which constrains movement. If discrimination results in residential segregation, then it enters into the processes governing these patterns.

There are two ways in which the relationship between such migrants and the host can be viewed.[3] The so-called 'liberal view' assumes that there is no fundamental clash of interests between coloured migrants and their host, and that barriers, however crude, are based on prejudiced stereotyping and discrimination: these must be overcome by rational argument and education, and are indeed legislated against. Once the barrier is overcome the coloured migrant becomes either integrated, or accommodated as an equal partner in a pluralistic society. Opposing this view is a Marxian model which subsumes racial relations in a theory of class relations; that is, the fundamental social division in a city is between the haves and have-nots and the coloured migrant is merely a member of the latter. According to the first view the gradual wearing away of discrimination will lead to dispersal: according to the second, conflict will maintain the divisions until resources are equally distributed throughout society, by a radical restructuring of that society.[4]

We can see how discrimination operates by examining the migrant's role in the housing market in Britain. Rex, who takes a 'liberal' view of discrimination, sees two factors at work.[5] Firstly, the migrants are identified by both their former and present roles. In the past in Commonwealth countries they filled colonial roles, and were exploited by members of a technologically more advanced culture. Moving to metropolitan centres in Britain they found themselves at the bottom of the urban class system, doing jobs which no one else wanted. Secondly, the coloured migrant encountered the host society's deterministic value system which stressed the maintenance of the superordinate position of the host and the subordinate position of the migrant. The two factors inevitably conspired against the migrant who found himself in the worst jobs — and in the worst housing.

A study on racial discrimination in housing[6] illustrated the difficulty migrants have in obtaining housing, 71 per cent of Africans, 40 per cent of West Indians, and 24 per cent of Asians reporting such difficulties in new immigrant areas — incidentally very much greater proportions than in old immigrant areas. This led to the dependence of many on informal contacts and, in the last resort, on rented accommodation. The authors suggested three factors which affected the coloured migrants' experience:

(a) The nature of the available housing. This is summarized in Table 7.1 which suggests eight categories of housing, defined by tenure and location. But it also shows that moves are limited between these categories: some — significantly, those to the suburbs — are missed out. This limits the total housing available and also constrains its quality.

(b) Conditions of access. Houses for sale are controlled by those who wish to sell them, by estate agents, and particularly by building societies who decide who can borrow money to buy them. Rented accommodation is controlled by landlords or by council officials. Together, these controls we have referred to as 'gatekeepers' (see p. 147). Further constraints are added in the United States by local ordnances governing density and size of houses, again, by implication, excluding certain people.[7] In particular, where black pressure is high, estate agents and real estate brokers — reflecting a wider consensus — aim at black exclusion from the suburbs, and have helped to maintain and contain ghettos. Only a white man has the right to choose his neighbours.

Table 7.1. *Immigrant Housing Movement in Manchester*

Ownership	Type	Category	Location	Pattern of Movement
Private	Rented	1	Inner City	Centre
		2	Elewhere	
	Owned	3	Inner	Inner Area
		4	Intermediate	Intermediate 7 2 4
		5	Suburbs	
Local Authority	Rented	6	Inner	Suburbs 8 5
		7	Intermediate	
		8	Suburbs	Outskirts

Pattern of Movement diagram:

Inner Area: $1 \longrightarrow 3$, 6, with arrows down to Intermediate 7, 2, 4; Suburbs 8, 5; Outskirts.

Source: Barnett *et al.* (1970), pp. 78−9.

Lending agencies, too are concerned in maintaining property values in areas where they have investment, and consequently prefer to exclude the non-white. Financial institutions may even charge the non-white higher interest rates over shorter periods. Although restrictive covenants have been made unenforcible in the United States courts, like-minded people may still informally agree to limit access of non-whites to their particular neighbourhood.

(c) The social position of the migrant. This is a reflection of his income, job security and prospects, all of which affect his chances of borrowing money. It is also an outcome of the size of his family, whether he has been long-established in the city, whether he wants a temporary or permanent home. Moreover, his social ties, and whether he wishes to live near his own people or not, may be decisive in influencing where he lives. The economic position of the migrant can be very important. In a study in London, Lee was able to hold the colour factor steady, and suggest what the distribution of West Indians would be if this were the outcome of socio-economic status only. The result showed only slightly greater dispersal — that is, they were still grossly underrepresented in the outer wards of the city than a random distribution would suggest, and the three areas of concentration — south, west, and north of the city centre — still showed very conspicuous over-representation. In other words, their distribution can be explained largely by factors other than colour. The common assumption that race alone restricts certain people to certain areas must be questioned. Lee suggests that the 'issue of segregation must be broadened from race to poverty', a salutory reminder that many more indigenous

British than coloured migrants live in the poor conditions which we associate with such quarters.[8]

If all these factors work against the migrant in the housing market it is likely to lead to considerable concentration or even to the formation of ghettos.

GHETTOS

The word ghetto is probably overused and misused. It also has emotional overtones. Historically it has a fairly exact meaning, but today it is applied to many kinds and degrees of segregation.[9] The ghetto was the quarter of the medieval city exclusive to the Jews, and was familiar in Europe, the Near East, and North Africa. Social separation was partly the result of Jewish society's own exclusiveness, partly the result of other societies' attitudes towards Jews as a minority. In spite of finding themselves in diverse cultural environments, Jews were unwilling to change their religion or mode of life: they did not intermarry with other groups: their traditions were sacrosanct. And so separation was imposed — partly to protect the Jews themselves from attack by others. The ghetto first appeared in thirteenth century Muslim cities and spread to Western Europe: most were walled, and many were locked at night and during Christian festivals. Inside the ghetto the Jews were autonomous: outside they were barely tolerated. Most legalized ghettos of this kind were swept away by the last century, though they were maintained until recently in some Muslim countries. Even so, large Jewish minorities still tended to keep together, partly for protection, physical and psychological, partly as a way of maintaining their religion and culture wherever they found themselves. Today the ghetto describes an extreme degree of segregation rather than a legal separation of area. The distribution of Jews in London in 1900, for example, though in no ways constituting a legal ghetto, showed a tremendous concentration in Aldgate and Stepney, where there were dozens of streets in which they accounted for more than 90 per cent of the population. South Africa is the exception to the abolition of legal ghettos. Here black ghetto has political and legal sanction. The government decrees that in urban areas the racial groups must live apart, and this has led to the state construction of ghettos such as Soweto on the outskirts of Johannesburg.

Clearly the word ghetto should be used only in a limited sense, indicating extreme segregation, usually based on racial criteria or on very fundamental cultural differences. But segregation covers a very wide variety of situations and reflects a varying degree of social differentiation. At one end of the scale the dissimilarities between ethnic groups are often very apparent: the migrant is 'visible', i.e. obvious, to his host because of a peculiarity of colour or tongue or belief. Sometimes cultural differences bite deeply indeed, as the case of Northern Ireland shows. At the other end of the scale segregation — sometimes more and sometimes less transitory — can also be an expression of class or status differences within one culture. Local authority tenants and middle-class owner occupiers in Britain are often segregated, simply because residential areas are developed in parcels which are exclusively one or the other, and all connotations of class and status are enshrined in 'estates' of this kind. As a resident in a fast growing 'village' in London's metropolitan area put it: 'Expensive houses and cheap houses are never built in the same area, therefore social divisions are created.'[10]

THE BLACK BELT

In the United States the word ghetto is applied to the concentration of the non-whites in many cities, and it is an indication both of their segregation and exclusiveness, and of the intractability of the problems which they pose.[11] Segregation is acute, spatially and socially, and because most of the black belts cannot easily expand into surrounding white territory, there is a build-up of the population and problems (see Fig. 4.14). The black belt is a city within a city. This was dramatically shown in an early study of Chicago.[12] The negro belt was then (1931) about five miles long and a mile wide, extending directly southward from 12th Street, near the Loop, to 71st Street. For the purpose of analysis, the belt was divided into seven zones, the first next to the Loop, the last between 63rd and 71st Streets, i.e. each was eight or nine blocks long. Plotting several social characteristics along the axis, zone by zone, showed a persistent continuum from north to south which corresponded with the way in which these same characteristics varied in the successive concentric zones which Burgess analysed for the city as a whole. For example, newer migrants tended to be nearer the north, that is near the centre of Chiacgo because migrants came in at this point. Professional and white collar workers increased in proportion from north to south (from 5·8 per cent in zone 1 to 34·2 per cent in zone 7), and illiteracy decreased fairly consistently in the same direction from 13·4 per cent to 2·7 per cent. Home ownership increased from 0 to 6·7 per cent in zone 3, 11·4 per cent in zone 6 and to 29·8 per cent in the last zone: and juvenile delinquency decreased gradually from 42·8 per cent to 1·4 per cent, as did other forms of 'disorganization' like adult delinquency and family desertion. It was as if a small city were contained within the larger, but reflected the zonal ecological pattern of the latter.

Movement from such a ghetto is extremely difficult, and yet population growth sets up pressure that makes expansion inevitable. Its shape suggests that it can expand in one direction only, southward from the point of origin near the city centre; lateral movement is constrained by forbidding the sale of property to black people. This process has been analysed in some detail by Morrill, who shows that the role of proximity is vital.[13] He concluded therefore that the expansion is a process of spatial diffusion, and set up a model of the process incorporating population increase, the nature of resistance and its relation to distance, the character and population of the destination blocks, and so on. He was able to simulate the expansion of the black ghetto in Seattle for two ten-year periods, 1940–60, and the results of the first simulation accorded very well with the actual situation in 1950. Morrill suggests that about 10 per cent blacks can be tolerated, but the blacks themselves prefer to belong to larger groups, and any city with high proportions of blacks may find it extremely unlikely that there will be radical changes in the ghetto situation in the near future.

MEASURING AND MAPPING SEGREGATION

Measuring segregation is difficult, though sociologists and social geographers have devised several methods. In the United States the major concern for some time was comparing the degrees of segregation between one city and another and inventing indices which would make this possible. The relationship between two groups e.g. white and non-white in a city can be shown on a graph. If the X and Y co-ordinates respectively show the cumulative percentage of the two groups in sub-areas of a city, a diagonal line indicates no segregation; that is, the percentages within each sub-area are absolutely consonant with the percentage in the city as a whole. Complete segregation of the two groups would merely give two lines, one along the X and one along the Y axis. Normally, the segregation line is a curve, and the maximum distance between this and the diagonal indicates the minimum percentage of one group which would have to move to other sub-areas in order to produce an unsegregated situation. Figure 7.1 shows such curves for several ethnic groups in Melbourne in 1961, and incidentally shows quite clearly the marked differences between groups which reflect their degree of acceptance by the host.[14] Various other measures

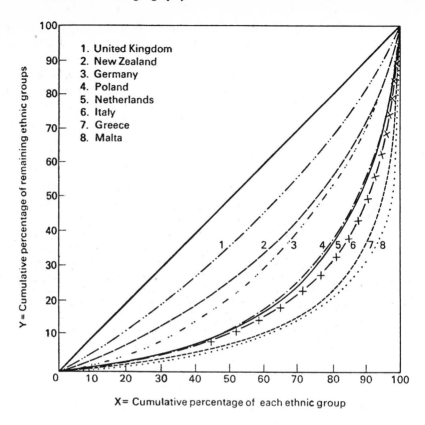

Fig. 7.1 Concentration curves of the residential distribution of ethnic groups in 611 ACDS, Melbourne, 1961 (F.L. Jones, 1967)

have been devised, but all of them relate the curve to the diagonal; the method used here is the simplest and it can be expressed as a dissimilarity index. In this index 100 means complete segregation and 0 means no segregation.

The dissimilarity index tells us nothing about the distribution of the segregated quarter within a city, but is a useful, easily calculated index which is applicable to all cities. Taueber and Taueber[15] applied it to 207 cities in the United States — all those with over 1000 non-white households in 1960 — and found the index varied between 60·4 in San Jose and 98·1 in Fort Lauderdale in Florida. By applying the index to 1940 data as well as to 1960, they were able to show that segregation seemed to be decreasing a little in the north-east (New York from 86·8 to 79·3), less so in some cities in the mid-west (Detroit 89·9 to

84·5), and that it was actually increasing in the south (Dallas 80·2 to 94·6), possibly an indication of late and continuing urbanization in that area.

British minority studies are less interested in variations between cities and more in segregation within cities. A simple distribution map will give some idea of the concentration of a group merely by relative location, but it will not indicate the degree of concentration. A proportion by wards or enumeration districts will also give a visual impression of a simple measure, but even this is open to misinterpretation, because it is unrelated to the numbers in the city as a whole, e.g. the proportion of a small minority in a city will not compare with the proportion of a large foreign group. An easily calculated index is the *location quotient* which indicates the deviation of any proportion from what one would expect if the group were evenly distributed throughout the city. In other words, it compares the proportional expectation of numbers with the actual numbers in any sub-division. A ward which has 3 per cent of London's total population and also 3 per cent of the city's West Indian population, will have a location quotient of 1. If 10 per cent of that ward population are West Indian, then the quotient will be 10/3 = 3·3.

Lee mapped wards in London with similar location quotients and this gives an excellent visual impression of concentrations (Fig. 7.2).[16] The same quotient, incidentally, can be used to compare the relative concentration of two groups.

Table 7.2. *Percentage of Wards with a given Quotient (1966 Census)*

Location Quotient	West Indians %	Irish %
over 2	64·6	26·9
1—2	18·8	36
·51—·99	7·9	27
0—·5	8·6	9·7

In the above table, for example, 64·6 per cent of the wards containing West Indians are shown as having a quotient of 2 or more, and only 16·5 per cent of the wards have low quotients (under 1). On the other hand, 36 per cent of the wards with Irish born migrants have quotients between 1 and 2 — not a heavy concentration — and only 26·9 per cent above 2. In other words the Irish are less concentrated than the West Indians.

Most of the work on indices has been done on borough and ward data in Britain and on census tract material in the United States. We have already seen how the size of the unit can influence the very thing you are measuring (Chapter 3). This was demonstrated by Poole and

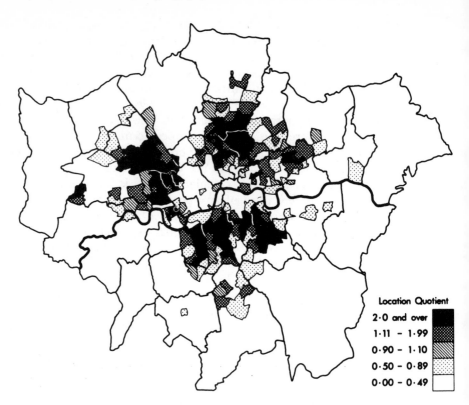

Fig. 7.2 (a) London: The distribution and concentration of the West Indian-born population in 1966, by location quotient (T.R. Lee, 1973)

Boal in Belfast by applying the dissimilarity index (which can be applied to a part of a city as well as to a whole) to an area, but with a diminishing number of sub-sets. Eighty-five sub-sets (in this instance grid squares) gave a dissimilarity index of 84·8; 22 sub-sets over the same area gave a dissimilarity index of 81·6; and 5·5 sub-sets gave a dissimilarity index of 71·4.[17]

In a large city such as London wards give a fine enough grain, but in a smaller city local variations can be hidden by wards — as the Belfast example showed (p. 73). In that city enumeration districts were used to show the segregation between Roman Catholics and Protestants, using an index slightly different from the above (Fig. 7.3).[18] This index assumed that if the distribution of those two elements were random, any sub-set, i.e. any enumeration district, would have the same proportions as the city as a whole. Any departure from this indicated some degree of segregation. The proportion of Roman Catholics

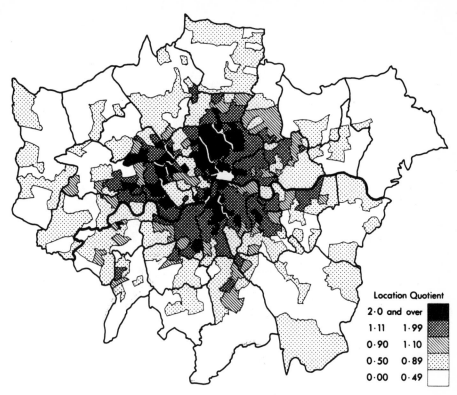

Fig. 7.2 (b)   London: The socio-economic distribution and concentration of the West Indian-born population in 1966 (T.R. Lee, 1973)

in the city was 25·9 per cent. Any enumeration district with 25·9 per cent Roman Catholics had no segregation, and an index of 0. On the other hand, if the proportion was 100 per cent or 0 per cent, then segregation was complete and this gave an index of 1. When the percentage fell between 25·9 and 0 in one direction and 25·9 and 100 per cent in the other, the index was calculated as a ratio of that distance, e.g. 12·99 per cent and 62·59 per cent, both half-way, and both have an index of ·5 — i.e. the departure from non-segregation is identical. These indices were then mapped. (It is still possible even on this scale for an enumeration district to straddle two completed segregated areas and give an impression of mix. But with so small a sub-set this was found very rarely and the total picture was both fine-grained and accurate.)

Later work on Belfast has been done on street data.[19] But this has introduced a new concept of segregation. Whereas all the above indices

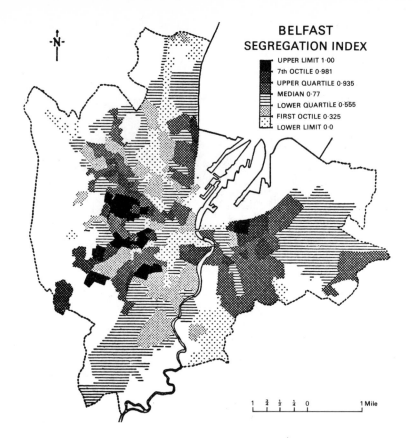

Fig. 7.3 Belfast Segregation Index, 1951 (E. Jones 1961)

are useful tools of measurement, they may become meaningless to the people who are actually segregated, and therefore bear little relation to the social problems arising from segregation. For example, few people in Belfast can be expected to know the proportion of Roman Catholics in the city, nor the degree to which their neighbourhood departs from it. They become acutely aware of segregation as a problem when the neighbourhood is on or near the balance of majority or minority. That is, one is more likely to get awareness — and tensions — where the two groups are not dissimilar in numbers, when each may feel itself to be threatened by the other. This means that streets or neighbourhoods with between 40 and 60 per cent of one group or the other may well be better indices of problem areas than those with very high extremes.

PROCESSES AND MODELS

Measuring segregation is a means to an end. We need to know much more about process, both about changes in patterns of segregation and the social process which usually gives rise to them, and whether it is possible to suggest general models. Indices over time may show two spatial processes: building up — that is, increasing segregation, and breaking down — that is, decreasing segregation. In addition there could be change in the location of a segregated area with or without a change in the degree of segregation. We have already dealt with some of the underlying social processes, like assimilation. Here we are concerned with the spatial aspects.

Increasing segregation may come about by a minority being augmented by additional migrants from elsewhere. Where immigration is considerable, as in the United States between the mid-nineteenth century and the First World War, incipient ghettos — small concentrations of ethnic groups or urban villages — inevitably attract the newcomers. These tend to cushion the migrants in a new city, by providing the first accommodation, because the inhabitants are known to the migrants, or because they are the same kin groups. Italians arriving in Boston in 1910, for example, tended to go to North Boston; blacks choosing Chicago as a home went to the black belt.

On the other hand, segregation may increase because of tensions arising from sharper social divisions. In Belfast, for example, the periodic rioting between the two religious factions has resulted in 'increasing exclusiveness'. In a period between widespread disturbances there is a lessening of tension and more mixture, but the almost immediate reaction to trouble is a movement from mixed areas to highly concentrated areas — a sorting-out process. In August 1971 at least 2,000 households are recorded as having moved,[20] and in each case Protestants moved from a predominantly Roman Catholic district to be replaced by Roman Catholic families who had fled from Protestant areas. Sometimes the move is very short, even to the next street, or in some cases merely further up the same street, and it is rarely that people move outside the same city sector. In all cases it leads to a clear definition and increasing homogeneity of separate religious areas. One can understand the desire for protection, or even for peace of mind.

Spatial segregation is rarely static. Where ethnic or racial differences are sharp, the pattern of residential differentiation may be stable over a long period: where differences are less and there is a process of assimilation, spatial concentrations can disappear. Where periodic tensions are common, segregation can intensify and then relax. But fundamentally we can think in terms of ethnic segregated areas which move easily or disappear, and of ghetto areas which sometimes move but do not disappear.

These have been summarized in two sets of models by Johnston,[21] relating ethnic segregation to the growth of the city (Fig. 7.4). The first is a set of ghetto models:

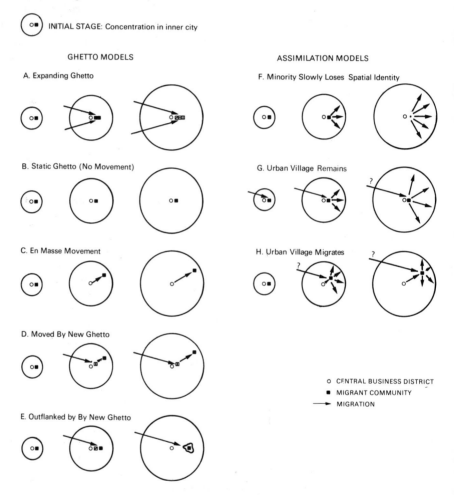

Fig. 7.4   Models of Minority Group location. Schematic diagrams of a growing city, showing the various hypothesized distribution of migrant groups. (Johnston, 1971)

(A) In the first the ghetto retains its original site near the centre, but grows outward from this with the growth of the city. An example of this is the black belt of Chicago which was described above (p. 170), where incoming migrants force an elongation of the original sector.

(B) The ghetto might remain static, both in size and in relation to the centre, if there is no feeding of new migrants.

(C) The ghetto might move entirely to a new site as the city itself grows and as the group's economic position improves.

(D) The ghetto may move to give way to a new ghetto which takes up a central position. This might also describe the offshoots of the ghetto which are found in more peripheral areas in Chicago.

(E) Lastly, Johnston envisages a new ghetto outflanking an older one which proves resistant to change.

These are some possibilities in what is usually a most complex process, and are sometimes more difficult to identify if the cohesion of the group is not quite as positive as the word ghetto implies. The movement of black migrants in Chicago shows more than one model. A good example of (c) is the Russian group in Chicago. Originally, this was a compact ghetto on the West Side, but between 1910 and 1920 moved as a body several miles west, but still in a very concentrated group.[22] By 1960 there was much greater dispersion but with a heavier concentration along the lake-side, particularly in North Chicago.[23]

The Russian element in Chicago is also Jewish, and a very similar movement, with some loosening of ghetto bonds, is found in the history of their settlement in London. Starting with a ghetto in the East End[24] they gradually moved west and north, although retaining their high proportion in the original ghetto (see Fig. 7.5). This reflects (i) the partial assimilation of Jews and their acceptance into English society; (ii) their climb up the social and economic ladder; and (iii) the subsequent identification of social strata among the Jews themselves. The diagram shows that even during the build-up of the East End concentration, some economically better-off families were moving into Bloomsbury, then the nearest of the desirable residential areas of London.

Subsequently, a considerable jump was achieved by rich families into the West End, and this became a focus from which there was a gradual growth outwards, along the north-west axis, following the prosperous suburbanization movement. The most considerable of these moves was to Golders Green, when that area was first built after the First World War, and subsequently this has consolidated into a considerable area extending into Hendon, which can now be regarded as the main concentration. Meanwhile, less prosperous Jews were moving from the East End into Finsbury and the region to the north.[25] It should be kept in mind that the maps and figures on which the segregated areas are based

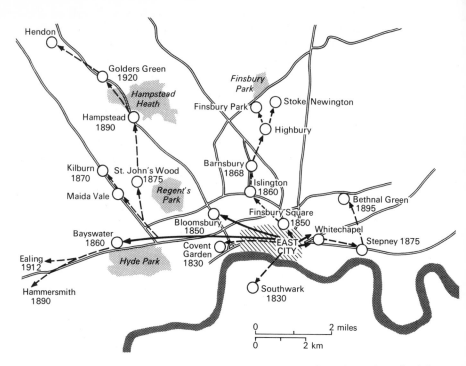

Fig. 7.5 The spread of London's Jewish population from its point of origin east of the city

represent Orthodox Jewry and do not include liberal and unorthodox Jews who have now become assimilated. There is a sense in which the former can never be assimilated, but remain self-identified because they maintain their group solidarity based on religious observances and their associated customs. All these facets of life have a spatial component because Orthodox Jews must live within walking distance of a synagogue. Such institutions, the need for schools, Kosher butchers, etc. mean that in spite of movement, a degree of cohesion and segregation is maintained because of these localized factors.

Johnston suggests three assimilation models:

(F) The first is loss of spatial identity. Rapid assimilation will absorb a migrant group so that the second generation may be indistinguishable from the hosts. In London, the majority of the quarter million Irish, once very visible by language, religion, and poverty, stereotyped and discriminated against, are now lost in the population as a whole. Only those born in Ireland are recorded by the census and exemplify the usual inner city residential patterns (see Fig. 4.19). The majority are dispersed over the whole of north London, and there is no sign of their first concentration in Holborn and St. Giles.

(G) The second model shows an urban village remaining, in spite of assimilation. This was once a very common ethnic situation in the United States, when incoming migrants fed the original 'village', balancing in numbers those who dispersed. Many studies show how these 'villages' (seen as a valuable function area) cushioned migrants to a new city, providing the first accommodation to newcomers by kin or friends, and making the cultural change easier.[26]

(H) The third assimilation model is that of a migrating village — i.e. where cohesion is maintained and even strengthened by new migrants, but where social status has improved very considerably, resulting in the movement to newer residential areas. One stage in the history of a Welsh community in Utica, N.Y. illustrates this. Figure 7.6 shows that in the middle of the nineteenth century the Welsh formed a very compact community in this town, near the Erie Canal. By 1915,

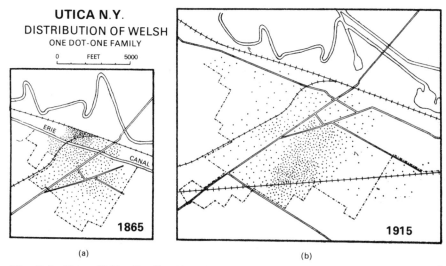

(a)   (b)

Fig. 7.6   Utica, N.Y.: distribution of Welsh, 1865 and 1915. In the first map the concentration between canal and railway shows the hub of community activities. By 1915 this had virtually disappeared and the Welsh occupied a middle-class ward in the newer section of the growing city

however, very few Welsh people were found here: they had moved almost in their entirety to a new residential area, this time on the right side of the tracks. The move, which included rebuilding three churches, was sudden and dramatic, having been triggered off by the newly arrived and rapidly increasing numbers of Poles, who set up their own 'village' in this now rather obsolescent part of the town.

The chapter began by describing some of the group relationships — in particular between host and migrant — which give rise to social distance. Sometimes the social distance is maintained by the migrant group's own desire to retain its identity and to foster its own institutions. At other times it is reinforced by the host society whose ability to absorb migrants varies according to the way in which they regard racial or cultural differences. The degrees of assimilation are spatially apparent, and are one of the main variables in the residential differentiation of the city. Wirth's emphasis on heterogeneity is justified in many cities, arising as it does from a social and spatial structuring which reflects an intricate process of adjustment and accommodation.

NOTES AND REFERENCES

[1] C. Peach (ed.) (1975), *Urban Social Segregation*, Oxford, p. 1.

[2] N. Glazer and D.P. Moynihan (1963), *Beyond the Melting Pot*, Cambridge, Mass., is a good introduction to ethnic minority problems in New York.

[3] J. Doherty (1969), 'The Distribution of Immigrants in London', *Race Today* 1, pp. 227–31.

[4] N. Deakin and B.C. Cohen (1970), 'Dispersal and Choice: Towards a Strategy for Ethnic Minorities in Britain', *Environment and Planning* 2, pp. 193–207.

[5] J. Rex (1970), 'The Concept of Race in Sociological Theory', in S. Zubaida (ed.), *Race and Racialism*, London, pp. 35–56.

[6] A.S. Barnett, C.G. Pickvance, and R.H. Ward (1970), 'Some Factors underlying Racial Discrimination in Housing', *Race* 2.

[7] R.E. Forman (1971), *Black Ghetto, White Ghetto and Slum*, New Jersey.

[8] T.R. Lee (1973), 'Ethnic and Social Class Factors in Residential Segregation', *Environment and Planning* 5.

[9] L. Wirth (1928), *The Ghetto*, Chicago.

[10] P. Ambrose (1974), *The Quiet Revolution*, London, p. 153.

[11] H.M. Rose (1971) *The Black Ghetto*, London. For a vivid description of ghetto life, see L. Rainwater (1970), *Behind Ghetto Walls*, London.

[12] E.F. Frasier (1964), 'The Negro Family in Chicago' in E.W. Burgess and D.J. Bogue (eds.), *Contributions to Urban Sociology*, Chicago.

[13] R.M. Morrill (1965), 'The Negro Ghetto: Problems and Alternatives', *Geog. Rev.* 55. See also H.M. Rose, (1970), 'The Development of an Urban Sub-system: the Case of the Negro Ghetto', *Ann. Assoc. Am. Geogs.* 60, pp. 1–17.

[14] F.L. Jones (1967), 'Ethnic Concentration and Assimilation: an Australian Case Study', *Social Forces* 45.

[15] K.E. Taeuber and A.F.T. Taeuber (1965), *Negroes in Cities*, Chicago. See also S. Lieberson (1963), *Ethnic Patterns in American Cities*, New York.

[16] Lee (1973), op. cit.

[17] M.A. Poole and F. Boal (1973), 'Segregation in Belfast', in B.D. Clarke and M.B. Cleave, *Social Patterns in Cities*, Inst. Brit. Geogrs. Publi., London.

[18] E. Jones (1956), 'Distribution and Segregation of Roman Catholics in Belfast', *Soc. Rev.* 4.

[19] Poole and Boal (1973), op. cit.

[20] Community Relations Research Unit (1971), *Flight*, Belfast.

[21] R.J. Johnston, (1971), *Urban Residential Patterns*, London, pp. 110–14.

[22] P.T. Cressey (1938), 'Population Succession in Chicago, 1898–1930', *Am. J. Soc.* 44.

[23] B.J.L. Berry and F.E. Horton, (1970), *Geographic Perspectives on Urban Systems*, Chicago, p. 346.

[24] L. Gartner, (1960), *The Jewish Immigrant in London, 1810–1914*, London.

[25] V.D. Lipman, (1954), *Social History of the Jews in England, 1850–1950*, London.

[26] See especially H.J. Gans (1962), *The Urban Village*, New York. This is in part a study of the functions performed by the urban village for the Italians of Boston.

8 Macro-processes

Macro-processes are those which involve entire societies or large groups within societies, and for which explanation is derived in general terms rather than in individual or small-group behaviour. Even when behaviour and decision-making operate on the individual level, these are subsumed under generalizations which are put forward to account for seeming commonly shared motivation. The way in which the change of scale involves different kinds of explanations for micro- and macro-processes is discussed elsewhere (p. 11); but traditionally the geographer has been more interested in macro-processes, trying to understand the components of major changes of universal interest which can be applied throughout the world.

MIGRATION

One of the most familiar geographical phenomena which have been related to macro-processes is migration. Terrestially, at least, man is ubiquitous, the widest ranging and most adaptive of all the animal kingdom. If we assume a discrete point of origin — or even several — man's present distribution illustrates the extent of his movements. Even in historical times, the extent and variety of people's movements is quite bewildering, and it is legitimate to doubt whether we are asking the right question. Rather than ask what are the processes which lead to movement, we should perhaps try and discover what makes man sedentary. Movement is universal. Nevertheless, the complexity of processes which result in movement warrant investigation as they are so relevant to spatial redistribution.

Before we try to impose an order on this bewildering variety of movements, we should remind ourselves that they must be measured. Although many primitive wanderings can be effectively described non-quantitatively, to deal with problems effectively movements must be recorded; and this can be done only if a person crosses from one administrative unit to another. Migration is change of residence across an administrative boundary — e.g. intercontinental or international, inter-regional, rural to urban, inter-ward, and so on. This can lead to anomalies, as a very small movement from one unit to a contiguous one is taken note of, but not a possibly much larger movement within a unit. To some extent the scale of the 'net' has an effect on the number of movements. But it must be remembered that the problems we pose are also scaled and usually relate to one magnitude at a time.

One other point must be kept in mind which is also referred to elsewhere. That is, care must be taken to distinguish between *gross* and *net* figures of movement. If region A, over a period, has gained a population of a thousand from region B, this is a net figure which may tell only part of the story. The figure *could* be the result of a thousand people simply moving in one direction. But it could also hide the fact that two thousand went from B to A and one thousand from A to B, or that fifteen hundred went from B to A and five hundred of these returned. The gross movements in these examples would be three thousand and two thousand respectively, but these are hidden in the 'accounting' processes of many censuses. There are times when gross movements are very important, but generally speaking, net movements are simpler starting-points for explanations involving processes on the macro-scale.

A TYPOLOGY OF MIGRATION

There are various ways of classifying migrations. Some refer to the extent of movement or to the change in culture involved, e.g. inter-continental, international, rural–urban. Others refer to the primary distinction between voluntary and forced movements. Richmond links different kinds of migration with different types of society i.e. migration in traditional society is largely forced and is a response to push factors, whereas in industrial societies it is largely voluntary, responds to pull factors, and is mainly to towns and cities. In post-industrial society it is transient, a two-way movement and mainly inter-urban.[1] In all cases it is assumed that movement is 'permanent', and these typologies do not refer to temporary movements.

Space forbids an extended discussion of temporary movements, but their relevance to some aspects of social geography warrants some examples. Transhumance, the seasonal movement of herds and herders to summer pastures, though not affecting the permanent pattern of occupation, is central to the lives of many pastoral peoples. This is a movement from winter homestead to pasture and back, to the alps of central Europe, the *saeters* of Norway, the *shielings* of Scotland or the *booleys* of Ireland.[2] Economic necessity may also dictate seasonal movement of labour.[3] The labour-intensive fruit- and vegetable-cropping industry in the United States attracted a large mainly mobile population who moved with the seasonal demands of their trade. We are more accustomed to the daily rhythm of movements in and out of our own cities, each having its own commuter country from which it draws its daily force (see Fig. 8.1). Equally firmly established is the seasonal movement of holiday-makers.[4] These movements have tended to increase with the use of cars and of fast public transport. The attraction of coasts in Britain or in France means a metropolitan exodus in summer of no mean proportions, and increasingly the search for warmer climate or remoteness is involving millions of people in long annual treks. Finally we should not forget that the oldest and strongest motive for periodic movement is religious — the visit to holy places. In medieval Europe it accounted for very long journeys, whether to Canterbury or to Jerusalem. The illustration of the extent of modern movement to Mecca, the heart of Islam, shows how important this motive remains (Fig. 8.2). All these are important facets of life which would be missed by the 'official net' which supplies us with data concerning migration — i.e. a permanent change of domicile.

Table 8.1 *A Typology of Migration*

Relationship	Migratory Force	Class of Migration	Type of Migration	
			(a) Conserving	(b) Innovating
Nature & Man	Ecological Push	Primitive	Wandering Ranging	Flight from the land
State & Man	Migration Policy	Forced	Displacement	Slave Trade
		Impelled	Flight	Coolie Trade
Man and his Norms	Higher Aspirations	Free	Group	Pioneering
Collective Behaviour	Social Momentum	Mass	Repeated Settlement	Urbanisation

Source: W. Peterson (1970). p. 65.

In order to clarify the great complexities of permanent movements it is best to use some kind of typology, and the one which is illustrated distinguishes some of the main classes.[5] In this typology the distinction between 'voluntary' and 'involuntary' movements, though not the primary means of differentiation, fairly clear in the non-primitive classes. It would be academic to argue the pros and cons of freedom of movement in primitive wanderings, but it is worth reminding ourselves that even in more sophisticated societies the distinction is not always clear cut. Mass movements in particular — e.g. the trek of the Mormons from Illinois to the Great Salt Lake — has elements of both.

This typology, in addition to classifying kinds of migration, relates them to the social processes which produce them. The simplest kind of movement can be related to man's reaction to physical environmental conditions. Where he is incapable of adaptation or of overcoming environmental forces, then the latter are thought of as 'pushing' him from one location to another. On the most primitive level, the hunter and food-gatherer must of necessity search for food, and in doing so they are continually moving. On a more sophisticated level, a sudden ecological change can uproot a normally sedentary population and cause extensive migration. Examples of this are the dust bowl of the American interior in the 1930s, or the failure of the potato crop in Ireland in the 1840s. This has been labelled 'innovating' because the displaced persons, more often than not, were also forced to abandon their old way of life entirely and turn to new modes of life and livelihood, e.g. from peasant farmers to factory operatives.

The second category involves involuntary or forced movement. The interaction is between social groups and politically organized society which will decide the destiny of those groups. Very often the sanction will arise from consensus, as when some groups are held as slaves by others, sometimes from direct government intervention, e.g. the expulsion of Jews by Nazi Germany. The best-known and largest movement of this kind was the slave trade, the organized displacement of millions of Africans to the Caribbean and North America. Estimates of the numbers involved vary enormously, but between 5 and 15 million reached the New World, and considering the great toll on life, at least 50 per cent more must have been forcibly uprooted from their homeland.

War leads to enormous displacement — about six million people in the First World War I, and possibly sixty million in the Second World War. Much of this was forced displacement, some impelled flight. Movements of boundaries, changes in political 'regions', almost inevitably lead to forced and impelled movements, and large-scale transference of population has more than once been used as a solution to minority problems. Examples of these are the repatriation of 300,000 Turks and 1,200,000 Greeks after the war of 1921, or the movement of six million Muslims and six million Hindus to their respective areas in the partition of India in 1947. State policy also works in the other direction, i.e. by preventing movement. Until a century or so ago, most European countries prevented what they thought of as loss of manpower, and there are still severe limitations to movements in, for example, the U.S.S.R. Even more dramatic is the way in which receiving

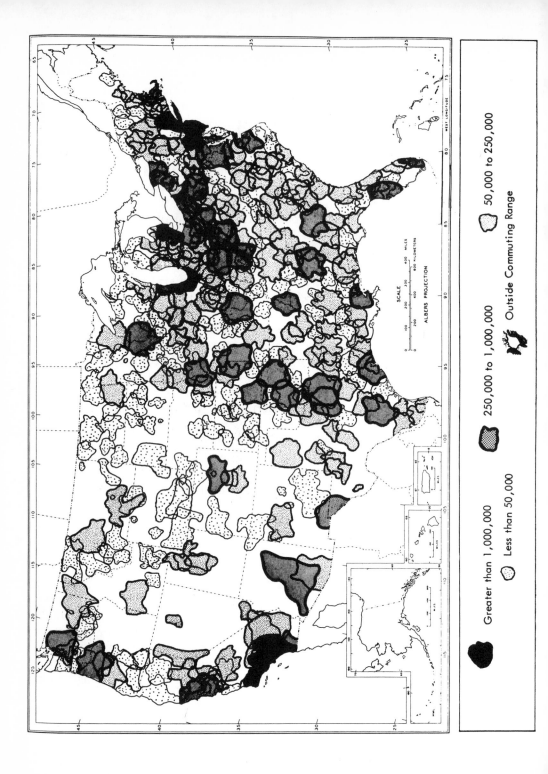

SCALE

200 100 0 100 200 300 400 MILES
0 200 400 600 KILOMETERS

ALBERS PROJECTION

Greater than 1,000,000

250,000 to 1,000,000

50,000 to 250,000

Less than 50,000

Outside Commuting Range

Fig. 8.1 (opposite) Extent of commuting fields in 1960 in the U.S. Areas in daily contact with metropolitan and smaller urban centres are shaded to indicate the size of the centre. The extensiveness of the areas whence there is commuting to more than one metropolis reveals the complexity of urbanization. (Berry & Horton, 1970)

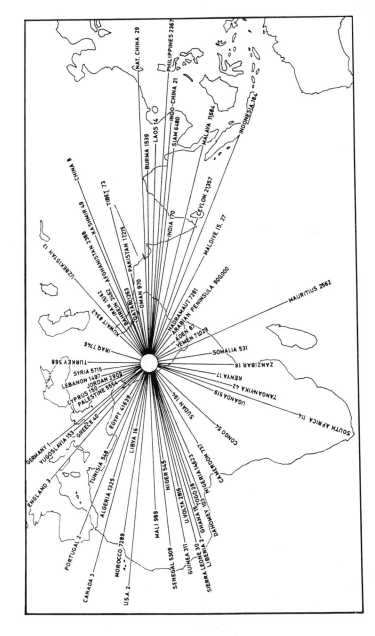

Fig. 8.2 The convergence of pilgrims on Mecca and Medina. (Based on a map prepared by the World Health Organization.) (Prothero, 1965)

countries can control movement. Over a century until the First World War, about thirty-six million people entered the United States, but the door was then virtually shut by quota laws (Immigration Act of 1924) which reduced the total intake to about 150,000 a year. Even more important, the quotas discriminated against certain people. This was brought about simply by restricting immigration to 2 per cent of the number in any ethnic group living in the United States in 1890, i.e. before the main stream of movement shifted from northern and western Europe to southern and eastern. Anglo-Saxons were still welcome and rarely filled their quota, but southern and eastern Europeans were not. The White Australian Policy (Immigration Restriction Act, 1901) successfully excluded all but a few Asians and relatively small numbers who are not Anglo-Saxon. And in Britain it was felt necessary in 1962 (Commonwealth Immigration Act) to cut the increasing numbers of migrants from the Commonwealth from an average of 98,000 for the preceding five years to 10,000 workers and their families.

Voluntary movement is either on a small scale or is swallowed in mass movements which can more easily be related to large-scale economic and social change. But the smaller-scale movement, often of tightly knit groups, has an important part to play in the story for several reasons. The first is that movement is occasioned by questioning the norms of society. Where these seem to stifle initiative or when they endanger the expression of new ideas, then groups — and individuals — will often move to 'new' lands, i.e. lands which present no real cultural challenge, in order to be left in peace and live their lives according to their own ideas. Groups with utopian ideals are a case in point. The Mormons left the 'settled' areas of the United States in order to set up a new social and economic order, which could best be tried out well beyond the existing frontier. Individuals and families wishing to free themselves from the constraints of society are also found on and beyond frontiers. These are the pioneers. In a similar way, some groups are formed to protect values which they feel are threatened by change in their own society, and migrate in order to preserve these values. There are many examples of such groups, perhaps the most famous being the Pilgrim Fathers. But most are small and are eventually swamped by the larger society which overtakes them. Few are 'allowed' to survive, like the Amish, or Pennsylvanian Dutch; but where they do they are very conservative in their view and fight innovations.

One rather special kind of movement is related to work. Migrants sometimes travel very great distances, often seasonally, to find work. It is not unusual for such movements to involve men only, and they return to their families either periodically or after a prolonged absence.

In Britain the potato harvests of the last century saw a regular migration from the west of Ireland. The Chinese element in South East Asia is explained by migrant labour. Figures 8.3 and 8.4 show how extensive these movements are in Africa.

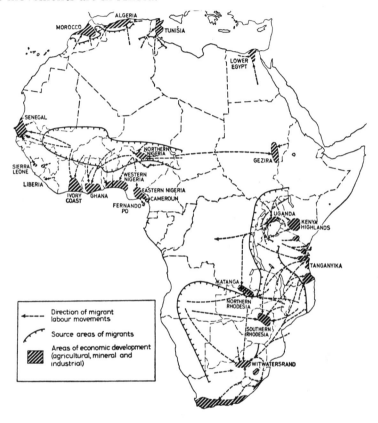

Fig. 8.3 Main movement of migrant labour in Africa. (Prothero, 1965)

Individual motivations are often submerged in what are called mass movements. Petersen uses the term 'social momentum' to suggest that individuals are often caught up in such movements almost in spite of themselves. The free movement from Europe to North America is the most striking historical example (see Fig. 8.5). Paradoxically, the movement was by individuals and families, lacking the social solidarity of the utopian groups; but nevertheless, all the individual decisions it seems can be subsumed under one vast generalization:

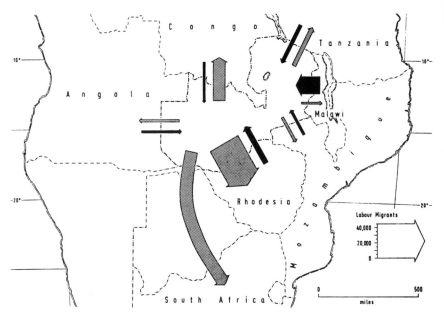

Fig. 8.4 International exchanges of labour, 1962. Arrows indicate the number and distribution of Zambian males at work or seeking work in foreign countries and the number and origin of alien males at work or seeking work in Zambia. Arrows do not indicate the migration routes (G. Kay (1967), *Social Geography of Zambia*, London)

these people were all seeking to better themselves, and establish a new milieu for their children.

Normally this kind of movement did not result in radical innovation: people in Europe were often tempted to a particular part of America because they thought it was like their homeland, and all they wanted was to reproduce a familiar pattern of life in more rewarding surroundings. The farming areas of north-eastern America were not very different from farming lands in England or Scandinavia or Germany. Even today, the field patterns, the homesteads and barns, are not unlike those which the migrants had known in their homeland. On the other hand, later migrants to the United States found themselves entering an increasingly industrial society in which cities were growing at an unprecedented rate. Former smallholders and farm labourers from Ireland were happy to stay in New York and Chicago, Italians and Poles swelled every industrial city in the north-east: the transformation of peasants to urbanites seemed all too easy. In a sense, these migrants were taking part in a much wider social change which for many people did not

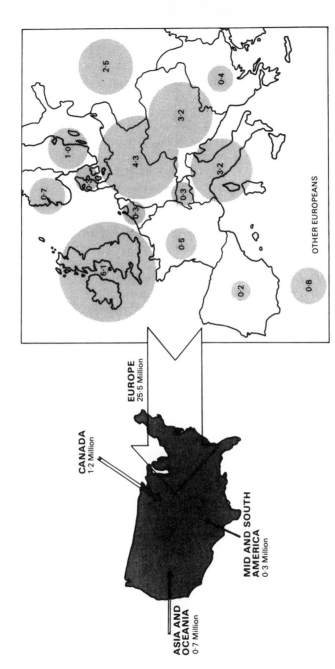

Fig. 8.5   United States: Immigrants, 1831–1910 (J.O.M. Broeck and J.W. Webb (1968), *Geography of Mankind*, N.Y.

involve change of country. Urbanization was a movement from the country to the town, but for some Irish people it meant from Co. Donegal to Brooklyn. This will be dealt with in more detail later: here we are merely concerned with a massive displacement of people, which reached a peak in nineteenth-century Britain and north-west Europe and in the early twentieth century, southern and eastern Europe. It is a movement which is now affecting the rest of the world; indeed the rate of urbanization and the number of people involved is greater in the tropical world today than it is in Europe.

MODELS OF MIGRATION

Models of migration are concerned mainly with collective behaviour, and with large numbers of people. Although forces prompting movement are very much related to individual circumstances and individual responses to change in the milieu, they have been generalized and simplified here because we are dealing with an aggregate of people and consequently personal motivation is often hidden. The simplest is the push–pull model to describe movement between origin and destination. The push elements include economic and social factors, such as decline in natural resources, loss of employment, or discriminatory treatment and alienation. Pull factors are the opposite — the attraction will be greater and the flow of migrants will be greater and more conducive social environment or an increase in opportunities.

In the event of two cities vying with each other, it is unlikely that they will offer equal opportunities; in terms of the model their pull will be unequal. One will be larger, richer, more desirable, and so on: its attraction will be greater and the peon of migrants will be greater and have a wider region. Population size is often taken as a measure of different pulls, and the extent of the difference can be gauged by a gravity model whose equation is[6]

$$Mij = K \frac{P_i P_j}{dij}$$

where Mij = number of migrants between places i and j
Pi = population of place i dij = distance between i and j
Pj = population of place j K = constant

In addition there can be intervening obstacles and intervening opportunities which affect the expected flow from one to the other. Distance itself can be an obstacle, either absolutely or in terms of costs. For example, although North America, with many pulls, seemed a desirable destination to the starving Irish of the 1840s, only those who could afford the passage actually made the move. There may be other barriers.

It may be that the Berlin Wall physically prevents a considerable movement, but less tangible barriers are equally strong — frontiers, legal restrictions like the United States' quota, and others based on cultural differences which are difficult to surmount — e.g. language, religion, and customs. Intervening opportunities mean that the line of movement which seems a direct one between area of origin and centre of attraction may not always be direct. Many migrants may be absorbed on the way when they meet conditions which seem to satisfy their needs. It is extremely difficult to measure 'opportunities' in a way which can be expressed as a model, though this has been attempted. Stouffer postulated that the number of migrants going from A to B is a function of the number of opportunities at B and an inverse function of the number of opportunities intervening between A and B, as well as the number of migrants competing for opportunities at B.[7]

Few have attempted to take the generalizations further than this, but a nineteenth-century statistician, Ravenstein, in a famous study of migration in England and Wales in the 1880s, proposed a series of 'laws' which he held were more or less universal.[8] Periodically, people have tested one or more of these laws and some of them certainly stand the test of time. The main propositions are as follows:

1. The majority of migrants move only a short distance, and consequently there is a general displacement of persons producing 'currents of migration' in the direction of the great centres of commerce and industry.
2. The process of absorption is created by movement from immediately around a great city, creating gaps which are filled from more remote areas. This also means that few migrants will be found in cities from areas progressively further away.
3. Dispersion has similar features and is the inverse of absorption.
4. Each main current of migration produces a compensating counter-current. This reminds us that gross figures of movement are hidden by the net movements with which we usually deal. One in six European migrants to the United States returned to Europe; many urbanites retire to the countryside; southern states black people move to northern cities in America, but there is a counter-current of retired whites to Florida.
5. Long-distance migrants generally go to large cities — as did so many Irish smallholders and, later, Italians.
6. Town dwellers are less migratory than country dwellers.
7. Females are more migratory than males.

The values of these 'laws' is that they go deeper than the simple demographic book-keeping which produces net figures. They relate very much to the England of the 1880s, but no one has since attempted so comprehensive a model, although individual aspects have been dealt with in a more sophisticated manner.

H.R. Jones's study of upland Wales was one which tested some of the 'laws'.[9] He was able to show that numbers of migrants decreased with distance, that there was a counter-movement, and that cities attracted irrespective of distance. The distance-decay effect has been substantiated frequently.[10] But macro-processes are only the summation of the micro-processes which are now attracting more behavioural studies. Migration is one of the best topics for demonstrating the application of both these approaches, but the latter has been most rewarding in intra-urban studies. However, with large-scale migration, Kant has explained the Hungarian Szkler migration from Romania to Budapest in terms of a linguistic component of place utility.[11] The idea of chain migration has also been put forward as the 'continual movement of people who perform the sequential functions of emigrant, information provider for following migrants and agent of locational adaptation for following migrants'. Both Hägerstrand,[12] referring to international migrations, and Pinkey,[13] referring to migrations to Paris, have used such ideas.

URBANIZATION

The implications of movements of great numbers of people from one location to another are immense, and vary according to the type of process involved. There is a redistribution of population and, almost certainly in the earlier stages of movement, a change in demographic structure. For example, most movements spurred by the search for better living conditions have a high proportion of men in the working age groups, and an equilibrium between sexes and a 'normal' age structure will take a long time to achieve. Sometimes migrants groups lose their identity before it is achieved by intermingling with the host group, something which is facilitated by the degree of acceptance and the speed of assimilation, if this is thought to be desirable. To a large extent the 'melting pot' policy of the United States and its free acceptance of migrants until after the First World War, together with the motivation of the vast majority of migrants who were consciously aspiring to assimilation, led to a tremendous increase in the number of people in the United States without disturbing its fundamental social structure or the bases of its society such as the central place of the family in society, democratic principles in government, latitudinarianism in religion.[14] Economically, a parallel transformation may take place, as it did in the United States when so many people were 'translated' from an impoverished peasantry to become an essential part of a growing industrialization. Migrants to America in the nineteenth century were 'hands' to provide the essential labour for an expanding country — canals, roads, railways, and cities transformed the landscape — and to tend the machinery which was to produce the wealth of the nation.

In this way the people involved in the trans-Atlantic movement were part of — and contributed to — a process in which they consciously set aside one culture and adopted another. An Irish-speaking smallholder from Co. Clare became a navvy in New York, or an Italian-speaking peasant became a mill hand in Pittsburg. And in this change was involved one other process of overwhelming importance — the country dweller became a city dweller: though this urbanization was small compared with the massive move into cities which was going on in Europe at the same time. Before discussing its implications, it would be as well first of all to appreciate the magnitude of this process throughout the world, and its growth in the relatively recent history of mankind.

THE GROWTH OF CITIES

First let us consider urbanization as the physical movement and migration of people, the process by which populations become concentrated in urban places. This begs some questions about what is an urban place, but for the moment we can accept a commonsense approach to what is meant by urban, and for the sake of simplicity and for world comparisons, use the United Nations' definition of urban places as those with population of 20,000 or more (see Fig. 8.6).

The following table is a simple guide to the way in which world urbanization has increased during this century and last.

Table 8.2. *World urbanization 1800 — 1970*

	Total World Population	Pop. living in Towns over 20,000	% Urban	% increases of Urban
1800	907 m.	22 m.	2·4	
1900	1,610 m.	148 m.	9·2	673
1950	2,509 m.	525 m.	20·9	355
1970	3,650 m.	1,022 m.	28·0	194

The percentage increases are impressive, but the significance of the figures lies in the absolute numbers of those who are living in towns and cities.

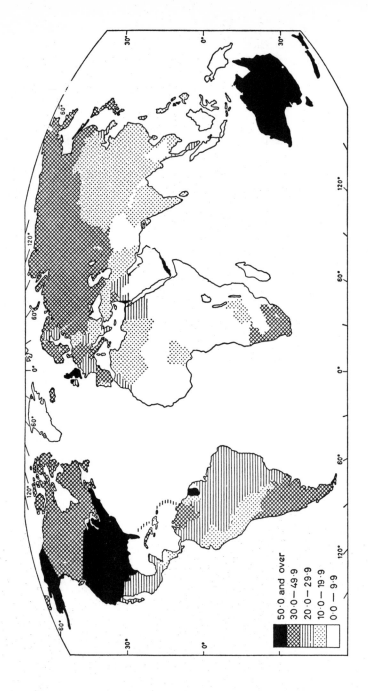

Fig. 8.6 Percentages of population living in towns of over 20,000 inhabitants by countries (E. Jones 1965, *Towns and Cities*, Oxford.)

50·0 and over
30·0 — 49·9
20·0 — 29·9
10·0 — 19·9
0·0 — 9·9

The global figures hide an even more significant feature — the shift of high rates of increase from the developed to the underdeveloped world. The nineteenth-century figures refer mainly to the former. The link with industrialization in the last century was very close, and the first industrialized countries became the highly urbanized. The majority of people in England and Wales lived in towns and cities by 1850. Germany's population was over 50 per cent urban by 1900, France by 1930, and the United States by 1920. Compared with these proportions, urbanization in developing countries is still low, but by 1950 two-thirds of the world's urban population was in such countries, and the recent growth of their major cities is much more rapid than anything experienced by the Western world. The absolute increases are staggering. Between 1950 and 1960, the number of million cities in the tropics increased from 4 to 14. In that decade, whereas mid-latitude cities doubled or trebled, cities in or near the tropics increased by three or four times, and those nearest the equator, five times. There are now more city inhabitants in the underdeveloped countries than there were in the whole world in 1950.[15]

Most of this recent phenomenal increase in the tropics reflects movements of people. Hauser and Schnore sum it up by saying that 'the emergence of the large industrial and commercial city, the conditions of life producing relatively high mortality and relatively low fertility, in part a result of selective male in-migration, must have made natural increase a relatively minor factor in urban growth.'[16] They point to the fact that in six of the ten Latin American countries, immigration accounted for half the urban growth between 1930 and 1950.

URBANIZATION AS A SOCIAL PROCESS

But all this is mere accounting. We must stress that the calculations of additions and subtractions are no more than a starting-point to the understanding of what is one of the major social processes through which mankind has passed. The demographic changes outlined above are the effect of other processes. At a simple mechanical, ecological level such changes can be seen as an environmental adaptation which relates to a shift in resources and in the way they are exploited. Assuming that technology and social organization, themselves very important variables, allow for an adjustment, this could be seen as a response to population pressure on the land and the means of absorbing work by other and non-primary activities. This presupposes the ability of the food producers to produce more than is necessary for their own consumption, and an organization which translates this into a social surplus which is a basis of other activities, i.e. manufacturing, trade, and so on. The pressure on the land and the surplus manpower so produced gives the push element, and the newly-created activity and wealth of the city, the pull element.

In advanced societies, the number of persons needed to produce food has dropped dramatically in the last century and a half, and labour has been absorbed in secondary and tertiary activities, thus transforming the way of life of millions of people. To many this is the essence of urbanization, the actual concentration of population in discrete settlements being almost incidental. According to Louis Wirth, 'as long as we identify urbanism with the physical form of the city, we are not likely to arrive at an adequate concept of urbanization.'[17] Wirth did not disregard the former, for in his well-known definition of the city he includes population, i.e. size and density as well as social heterogeneity are essential variables; but nevertheless, the social consequences are to him the essence of urbanism. The demographic variable is one of several. There is also a technological variable, inventions and discoveries which have transformed man's appreciation of resources and their exploitation. Above all, there is an organizational variable: societies have become specialized, differentiated, stratified, and this may have been a necessary condition for many technological changes. We look upon the city as a dependent variable, the outcome of processes in society itself. This is not to deny that the city can become the centre of initiation and change,[18] but merely to stress that it is no more than a focus for changes in society as a whole.

We are talking then about changes in society, particularly about changes in organization and in modes of production — which do not necessarily have to be identified entirely with the city as a built form.[19] The subsequent concentration of people is part of a 'way of life' composed of these variables. R. N. Morris has suggested a number of propositions arising from Wirth's ideas, of which these are the main ones:[20]

1. Growth and diversity are associated with relatively weak bonds among city dwellers, and consequently social control is formalized.
2. It is less likely that city dwellers will know one another personally, and contacts become impersonal, superficial, and transitory.
3. There is a highly developed division of labour: the large firm will displace the family business, and codes of etiquette are established for occupational groups.
4. The impossibility of assembling residents in one place leads to indirect communication.
5. Physical contacts are close, but social contacts superficial, so there

is an emphasis on visual symbols of control (e.g. traffic lights).

6. Land-use pattern is the result of competition for a scarce resource, leading to identification of uses — including grades of residential use — with specific parts of the city.
7. Competition and mutual exploitation replace co-operation.
8. A simple class structure is blurred because people fill a variety of roles.
9. Because he belongs to a variety of groups, the city dweller is likely to experience conflict, be less tied to a locality, i.e. more mobile.

In brief, secondary contacts replace primary, interest groups replace kinship, contract replaces obligation. The city's impersonality is stressed, as is the mobility and unattached nature of the people.

The number of times Wirth's essay has been analysed, criticized, or extended, shows it is still a valuable starting-point. But we should remember that if some of his concepts seem familiar and ring true, it is because he is describing the Western city. Indeed, we might go further and say that he is describing the American city which was produced by the social processes of the second half of the last century and the first few decades of this; and his ideas are firmly related to the Chicago school of sociologists who were strongly ecological. The model is fairly culture-specific. There is an assumption, too, that the city is an independent variable. Put in crude terms, a person moving into a city becomes like — or accepts — the models laid down by Wirth. It is also an ecological variable, for two of its basic criteria — size and density — are ecological, and the third — heterogeneity can be regarded as a consequence of these.[21]

THE RURAL–URBAN CONTINUUM

Wirth was highlighting a common, and repeated, assertion that life in the city can be contrasted strongly with life in the countryside. Many studies have collected evidence of this contrast, in economic terms — primary activities versus secondary, or food production versus industrialization, in demographic terms — differences in fertility, birth- and death-rates, and in social structure. When polarized, the distinction is a sharp one and it has been heightened by the habit of a succession of scholars, first of distinguishing these differences in terms of opposites and secondly of encapsulating many differences in one arresting concept. The German scholar Tönnies spoke of *Gemeinschaft* and *Gessellschaft*; the first word, translating as 'community', epitomized rural society, in sharp contrast to the second, meaning 'association', which characterized urban society. Here, as in other theories of contrast, it is suggested that one order has been destroyed and replaced by a radically different one. Many of the characteristics subsumed under these two words emerge in Weber, who emphasizes the 'rational' life of the city in contradistinction to the 'traditional' life of the country. Becker talked of the 'sacred' as opposed to the 'secular', and Maine of 'status' as opposed to 'contract' in the defining of relationships within the two spheres. Durkheim saw the 'mechanical' opposing the 'organic', arguing that the new interdependencies of city life gave rise to a more coherent social structure, a greater sense of community.[22] These phrases are no more than indicators of very complex differences and they do no more than signify that these scholars identified opposing forces fashioning society. Each word or phrase reveals aspects of either 'pole' which a person in Western society would recognize, e.g. the dominance of family relationship in rural communities and the dominance of associational links in the urban. But we should be very careful of the sweeping nature of some of these generalizations.

However, common to all these ideas is the concept of contrast, and of the change experienced when passing from one state to another – a change often implicitly for the worse, partly because of the nostalgic feeling urbanities have for a rural background which they suspect is the 'norm' from which urbanization is a departure. The implication is that we are dealing with a process, still going on in all parts of the world, but particularly in the developing world, by which 'ruralites' become 'urbanites'. While it should be made perfectly clear that very great changes are taking place, mainly by the economic transformation of simple societies, partly by the diffusion of technological advances, the evidence from the social and behavioural studies is that these changes do not produce the same effects, and they certainly do not enable us to identify a universal and fairly simple process.

Some scholars have tried to 'ease' the distinctions implied in the polar model by introducing the concept of a rural–urban continuum. Frankenburg has analysed a series of community studies in Britain, for example, and has arranged them along such a continuum, from the most rural to the most urban.[23] Pahl dismisses the idea for lack of empirical evidence, and doubts if the continuum has even a very useful classificatory purpose, at least in the form in which these 'ways of life' are identified with location in country or town. There is quite striking evidence, however, that in many towns people still behave rather as if they were living in village communities. Such 'urban villages' are common in most large metropolises. Abu-Lughod points to their function in Cairo as recreating, for the rural migrant, familiar conditions and thus easing his transition to the big city.[24] Many migrant groups in the United States cities have gone through stages of 'urban villages', which again acted as a 'cushion' to migrants in the radical environmental change they had made. Young and Wilmott found many attributes of 'community', of *Gemeinschaft* in life in the East End of London.[25] Correspondingly, there are villages which are ostensibly rural but which not only depend on cities but which exhibit many features of urban life. Pahl's own studies demonstrate strikingly that what he called 'metropolitan villages', were in effect fragments of urban life in the countryside.[26] The influence of city life, the advent of urbanism in the countryside, is enormous, measured by actual impact of town dwellers, for recreational use, or by the dispersion of goods, or, more particularly, by the spread of ideas by the media. This influence has blurred very effectively any compartmentalization that the two ways of life might have exhibited; but in addition the picture is made more complex, and more like a mosaic, by the territorial piecemeal pattern of one or the other. Pahl would prefer to see the idea of a rural–urban dichotomy abandoned, largely because it no longer corresponds to the physical distinction between town and countryside.[27] This distinction, more recently, and because of increasing communications, has become largely irrelevant, and Pahl suggests that a distinction between locally oriented and nationally oriented groups would be more useful.

This aspatial approach typifies interpretations of urbanism which emphasize (a) the interrelatedness of a city and its region, and (b) complete freedom of communication. The city has been increasingly loosening its bonds, and the old concept of containment – whether by wall or green belt, or even by citizenship – is becoming a thing of the past. For the last half century the Western city has witnessed an immense decanting of its population, leaving empty cores but adding to the periphery vast and loosely knit suburbs which are extending further and further from the centre (see Fig. 8.7). Suburbanization – in the West at least – can be seen as almost as significant a process as urbanization itself. But there is still a limit to this kind of extension. Much as they wish to escape it, people have been tied to the city, mainly by their jobs, partly by the desire to maintain service links – for we are tied to the city by drains, if nothing else. The suburb is still an extension of the city, certainly an escape from its worst industrial ills, certainly a more spacious, a greener, quieter appendage, but essentially a part of it. Only more recently have British new towns, beyond the green belt, given an impression of new urbanity, but they are physically akin to suburbia, and to some people have merely lengthened the extent of commuting. The spaciousness of suburbia, attenuation of the urban fabric though it is, is hardly more than a pointer towards

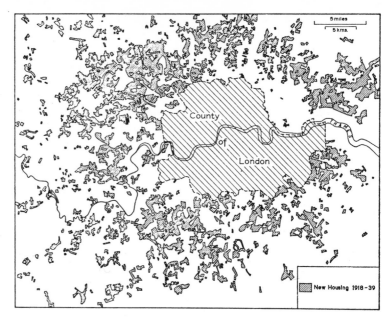

Fig. 8.7 Housing built between 1918 and 1939. Based on the Greater London Plan 1944. This was the peak period of suburbanization: the extent of expansion is the result of the comparative light density of residential building (Coppock and Prince (1963) *Greater London*, London, p. 146)

Webber's urban non-place realm.[28] It is a product of urban escapism within the industrial or post-industrial period.

Does this new suburban extension imply a different kind of urbanite? Much has been written on suburbia, suggesting a difference in quality of life which certainly distinguishes the suburbs from, say, the inner city. But this is hardly an attribute of the physical environment we call the suburb. Dobriner has been at pains to explode what he calls the myths of the American suburb, because they are based on our notion of middle-class suburbs and bear no relationship to the working-class suburb.[29] In other words, the social aspects of suburbia are the sum total of the attitudes and attributes of those who have decided to move to the suburb, and so they become a product of certain classes, age groups, occupations, etc., who share these attributes. People do not change because they move to the suburb: the suburb — largely because its housing stock attracts people of similar status — attracts like people. Gans's work points to similar conclusions.[30] Suburbanism is not a way of life as opposed to any other urban way of life. Concepts such as 'city' and 'suburb' allow us to distinguish settlement types from each other physically and demographically, but the ecological processes and conditions which they synthesize have no direct or invariate consequences for ways of life. No one has shown that the characteristics of a suburb are an ecological product of the environment — it is still a dependent or intervening variable.

Geographers need no reminding of the concept of the city region and the urban field of Dickinson and Smailes,[31] and Friedman and Miller's urban realms are reminiscent of both.[32] The idea underlying all is the interdependence of a centre and its field, demonstrable in many ways, e.g. the limits of distribution of services, the extent of common interests by local radio or newspaper, and increasingly by the area over which the central place attracts its working population, as Berry demonstrates in the United States.[33] (Fig. 8.1) The centripetal attraction of the centre and its relative accessibility results in a spiralling of rarer resources to that centre. Much of this is a function of accessibility expressed in means of communication. Webber replaces this model by one of dispersal to settlement and of resources and the virtual elimination of nodes.[34] This is dependent on two basic changes: (a) greater ease of movement, which means that all points in a given area become equally accessible, and (b) the fact that contemporary communication does not necessitate propinquity or movement, i.e. telecommunications have eliminated distance. The need for physical links is no longer paramount, and the accumulation of linkages between transactions — the very essence of the traditional city — is no longer essential. Community no longer presupposes propinquity.

The realization of this re-ordering of activities depends largely on universal access to the new means of communication; car, phone, television, etc. must be available to all. This is very far from being the case. Nor would this necessary condition inevitably become a sufficient one. In addition, changing the present stage of infrastructural technology would entail astronomical costs. However, there are pointers to this particular kind of future in the use of mobile homes and in increasingly sparse suburbanization in the United States where land shortage is not a constraint.

Webber's ideas reinforce the fact that urbanization as a social process is not necessarily tied to the city as an urban form. There are considerable constraints to a theoretically possible dispersal, not the least of which are the vast towns and cities which we have inherited, and which cannot conveniently be wiped off the face of the earth.

EFFECTS OF URBANIZATION IN THE NON–WESTERN CITY

The various arguments we have discussed, and indeed the very concept of the city, have concerned the West. To assume the processes are universal is to greatly over-simplify the real world. Urban scholars have been preoccupied with the European and American city, only rarely concerning themselves with alternatives to the Western model.[35] Yet the degree of urbanization in the developing world is unprecedented, and many students have assumed that the relatively simple evolutionary model of the West, its stages linked with industrialization and increasing social differentiation, will hold for all countries. But there are many reasons for arguing that a growing Third World metropolis need not duplicate the developmental stages of a Western city. The population explosion is far greater than that of the Western world in the nineteenth century, and in addition city populations themselves are undergoing natural increase. Development and change is often complicated by disorganization following decolonization. Economic growth can be controlled and planned in a way which was not envisaged in the West a century and a half ago. The technology of the West, whose growth was concomitant with city growth, is now available to everyone. Lastly, and probably most important of all, the value systems of the societies undergoing urbanization are different. Because the city is a dependent variable, we are interested in social change expressing itself in urbanization: the patterns of life and organization are bound to be very different.

The study of the pre-industrial city in its own right is a very large topic and here we will deal with one only of the outcomes of rapid urbanization — squatting — partly because it is so dominating an element in city form, and partly because it presents such a sharp contrast to the normal residential pattern of the Western city. We are so used to cities in which the richer suburbs are on the outskirts, that it is something of a shock to travel into a Latin American metropolis and seemingly traverse the 'slums' first before coming to the inner city.

We have already referred to the extent of urbanization in the developing countries and to the phenomenal growth of larger cities. There are, of course, slums in the conventional sense — and indeed in Calcutta, for example, overwhelming problems of street sleepers and homelessness of which we have little conception.[36] But the most obvious manifestation of urban growth is the shanty-town — the often spontaneous expression of lack of conventional urban housing.

Squatting is usually legally defined as building houses on land which is neither owned nor rented by the squatters. It is taking over by occupation: and it happens so quickly that legal action to prevent it is impossible. The comparatively recent phenomenon of squatting in Western cities, i.e. the taking over of unoccupied houses by groups of homeless,[37] although an important aspect of the ecology of small areas of the inner city, is insignificant compared with the phenomenon in the non-Western city, or even compared with the shanty-towns some European cities have now attracted. In Latin America, Asia, and Africa the movement involves millions, and the land occupied is almost invariably peripheral to the cities. In fact, much of the urban growth of inter-tropical cities is in the form of shanty towns. The rapidity of their appearance and phenomenal increase has led Dwyer to call them 'spontaneous' settlements.[38] The accompanying table gives some indication of the extent of squatting in selected 'developing' cities.[39]

Table 8.3. *Squatting in the Third World*

Country	City	City pop. 000s	Squatters 000s	% of city pop.	Year
Zambia	Lusaka	194	53	27	1967
India	Calcutta	6,700	2,220	33	1961
Indonesia	Djakarta	2,906	725	25	1961
Iraq	Baghdad	1,745	500	29	1965
Pakistan	Karachi	2,280	752	33	1964
Turkey	Ankara	1,250	750	60	1970
Latin	Brasilia	148	60	41	1962
America	Buenaventura	111	88	80	1964
	Mexico City	3,287	1,500	46	1966
	Lima	2,800	1,000	36	1969
	Caracas	1,590	556	35	1964
	Maracaibo	559	280	50	1966

(Berry, 1973, p. 84)

An example of squatting from Caracas[40] will give some idea of what the shanty-town implies, and much of the description will apply to the *favelas* of Rio de Janeiro, the *callampas* of Chile and the *villas de misera* of Argentina. In Venezuela the individual shanty is called a *rancho*, and a group of these forms a *barrio* (Fig. 8.8a). Although some *ranchos* are built near the centre — sometimes on very steep hillsides or in gullies — most are on the outskirts of the city (Fig. 8.8b and 8.9). Built of any kind of scrap, and lacking most amenities, *ranchos* appear overnight, often in very large groups. The very rapidity with which they are built defies official control. Organization comes from within, for often the movement to a new *barrio* is made by an entire community. Although most squatters will come directly from the countryside, many will arrive as the result of organized movements from the more conventional city centre slums, where they have already, to some extent, become

(a)

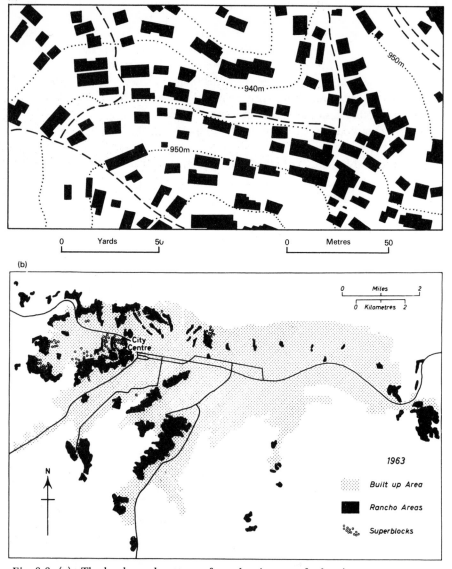

Fig. 8.8 (a)   The haphazard pattern of *ranchos* in part of a *barrio*
(b)   **Distribution of** *barrios* **in Caracas (1963) show a peripheral growth,**
together with the use of gullies along the northern length of the city (Jones, 1964)

accustomed to city life. The genesis of this underlines the contrast of the
barrio with the traditional slum. Not only is the location different, but
the shanty-town — however decrepit it looks — is *new*, not old: it

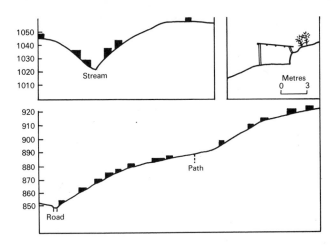

Fig. 8.9 Typical slopes on which *ranchos* are built (no vertical exaggeration). (Jones, 1964)

expresses a will to self-help, a positive desire to be near the opportunities a city offers — it is a 'slum' of hope, not of despair.[41] Very often the *rancho* owner will, in time, transform his wooden or zinc shack into an adobe brick house, and a *barrio* district might eventually become indistinguishable from another street. In other words, the shanty may be the city in the making. Although some have dismissed shanty dwellers as displaced persons — the surplus of an agricultural economy thrown on the mercy of an urban world — others have seen them as very positive elements, as people who are willing to organize themselves to build their own homes, and later to make themselves felt politically in obtaining services, schools, police, etc. Some would like to see the cities capitalize on this energy and self-help and go half-way to meet the needs of these people.[42] This could be done by preparing sites for squatters, by laying down the infrastructure, and perhaps even supplying the core — bathroom/kitchen — of future houses. In this way a shanty district would attain the status of a reasonably built environment much more quickly and in a more orderly way. To many squatters, their method of becoming city dwellers not only provides them with the shelter which municipalities cannot provide, but also meets the need for a sense of 'ownership' — at little or no cost — and that in itself confers a stabilizing element on an incipient urbanization.[43]

The social processes involved are as difficult to untangle as the physical forms of settlement which result. Demographically, we must refer back to the population explosion in the Third World, but this does not account for the displacement of people involved. Certainly there is some displacement from the rural economy which cannot carry the extra population, but in addition there is a tremendous pull element from the cities themselves. They do not necessarily provide work — perhaps they do no more than promise the *hope* for work and settlement; but to obtain even crumbs, one must be near the table. Cities like Caracas cannot absorb labour in the way that classic industrial cities could; they are already in a post-industrial stage, where tertiary activities predominate and quaternary activities are growing. Such activities cannot immediately absorb the labour. On the other hand, the city *does* have wealth, and this is the immediate attraction.

Squatting — a vast and visible consequence of urbanization — has been the subject of investigation in many parts of the developing world, and there is a considerable literature on the topic.[44] We might draw a very tentative parallel with squatting in some Western cities, insignificant though this may be in scale. One thing they have in common is that they are both illegal. But also common to all squatters is a deliberate budgetting of total resources and a reluctance — as well as an inability on behalf of most — to meet the cost of shelter passing through institutionalized channels.[45] Unlike Western examples, squatting elsewhere also reflects the projection of a peasant tradition in an urban setting.

Squatting in the Third World is only one consequence of urbanization, easier to deal with because it is tangible. There are many others. Some of these have been incorporated by McGee into his models of Asian cities.[46] Colonial cities still carry the marks of administration centres bearing little relation to the indigenous city — Delhi is an outstanding example. On the other hand, squalid slums indicate early stages of industrialization and the pressure of male migrants in many Indian cities. Socially the consequences of urbanization are no less dramatic: the ethnic mix of great entrepreneurial cities like Singapore; the multiplicity of 'urban villages' in Cairo; the clash of traditions and cultures in Latin America; the changes in family and group structure consequent on migration; the increase in stratification and the significance of new institutions like formalized education.

Much of the change implicit in the process of urbanization, therefore, is reflected in the social patterns of cities. Indeed, this is the basis of the process, and this is one theory that underlies a major approach at explaining those patterns, as we shall see in the next section.

INCREASING SOCIAL SCALE: ITS SPATIAL IMPLICATIONS

The growth and development of the city when it is viewed as a dependent variable is an excellent example of the impact of increasing social complexity on the environment. The achievement of a social surplus is a necessary condition for new forms of organization, as not everyone is now engaged in the struggle for physical survival; and consequently settlements grow in size and heterogeneity as more people are freed from food producing to fit new roles in the society. The very growth of settlements has wide implications for the way society and its use of space are organized. It may be that the non-agricultural element in the population will choose one particular settlement for their activities, and this will become the cultural centre of the people concerned. It is probable that the production, control, and distribution of food and other products will require an organization more elaborate than that of primary producers. Because of the relative slowness of transport, regional centres may be set up to carry out the tasks of control and distribution. What we are describing is the beginning of the development of a hierarchy of regional centres in a network of settlements. This is not the place to discuss the development of a system of cities,[47] merely to emphasize in a very oversimplified way that social change leads to spatial change. A modern example will clarify the point. The increasing real incomes of virtually all sections of the population in countries like Britain and the United States have had a great impact on patterns of residential development and movement. Increasing wealth leads to greater space consumption with more spacious suburbs, more roads, and more public facilities.

Spatial changes arise from social changes. The latter are often characterized as a dichotomy as society moves from one style to the other, and we have discussed some of these dichotomies (p. 202). We now want to look at one attempt to produce a theory of social change on the macro-scale which is, at the same time, coupled with a theory of residential differentiation at the micro-scale. Social area analysis is dealt with in this chapter because its proponents place great emphasis on the macro-processes that lead to change. The residential pattern — the social areas — are held to be simply the outcome on a micro-scale of macro-processes. Although social area analysts like Shevky and Bell developed the ideas of both the classical ecologists (p. 28) and of Louis Wirth (p. 200), they saw the city as a product of the 'complex whole of modern society: thus the social forms of urban life are to be understood within the context of the changing character of the larger containing society'.[48] Their way of understanding the city was through

Table 8.4 *Social Area Analysis*   *Steps in Construct Formation and Index Construction*

Postulates Concerning Industrial Society (Aspects of Increasing Scale) (1)	Statistics of Trends (2)	Changes in the Structure of a Given Social System (3)	Constructs (4)	Sample Statistics (Related to the Constructs) (5)	Derived Measures (From Col. 5) (6)	
Change in the range and intensity of relations / Differentiation of function / Complexity of organization	Changing distribution of skills: Lessening importance of manual productive operations — growing importance of clerical, supervisory, management operations	→ Changes in the arrangement of occupations based on function	→ Social Rank (economic status)	→ Years of schooling, Employment status, Class of worker, Major occupation group, Value of home, Rent by dwelling unit, Plumbing and repair, Persons per room, Heating and refrigeration	→ Occupation, Schooling, Rent	} Index I
	Changing structure of productive activity: Lessening importance of primary production — growing importance of relations centred in cities — lessening importance of the household as economic unit	→ Changes in the ways of living - movement of women into urban occupations — spread of alternative family patterns	→ Urbanization (family status)	→ Age and sex, Owner or tenant, House structure, Persons in household	→ Fertility, Women at work, Single-family dwelling units	} Index II
	Changing composition of population: Increasing movement — alterations in age and sex distribution — increasing diversity	→ Redistribution in space — changes in the proportion of supporting and dependent population — isolation and segregation of groups	→ Segregation (ethnic status)	→ Race and nativity, Country of Birth, Citizenship	→ Racial and national groups in relative isolation	} Index III

Source: Shevky and Bell (1955) p. 4.

the idea of 'societal scale', the scope of social interaction and dependency. They argued that increasing scale, from small to large, from primitive to urban-industrial, was accompanied by other changes, particularly in the range and intensity of relations, in functional differentiation, and in complexity of organization (Table 8.4, col. 1). Thus increasing scale, and the emergence of urban-industrial society, is primarily an outcome of changes in the economy, particularly technological innovations. As Column 2 in the table shows, increasing scale is reflected in three 'statistics' of trends: the changing distribution of skills, the changing structure of productive activity, and the changing composition of the population. While Column 3 shows how society may be affected by these trends, the rest of the table points to the constructs (Col. 4) and statistics (Cols. 5 and 6) used in measuring the increasing scale. Thus, changes in the distribution of skills is expressed by the construct *social rank* and measured by occupation, education, and rent; the changing structure of productive activity is expressed by *urbanization*, measured by fertility, proportion of women at work, and single family dwelling units; changing population composition is expressed by *segregation* and measured by the ratio of ethnic or racial groups.

The initial measurements were made in simple ratios which were then averaged to give a series describing the constructs. The latter were divided into four categories for social rank and urbanization on the basis of standardized score ranges. This gives a possible sixteen types of social area to which social segregation may be added as a characteristic when it is above the city average. Census tracts provided the areal bases for calculations, and where contiguous tracts exhibited similar construct scores, they identified larger areas of social homogeneity — social areas.

The example shown is that of Winnipeg.[49] The first diagram (Figure 8.10) shows how each census tract in the city scores along the two constructs 'social rank' and 'urbanization', and this places them within one of the sixteen boxes produced by the two constructs. Those tracts with high segregation can be easily distinguished from the others. The diagram is then translated into a map, each tract being shaded according to its position on the diagram (Fig. 8.11). The result shows that there is considerable bunching of tracts with similar characteristics, and this extended homogeneity gives us the social areas of the city.

Social area analysis has been criticized on several grounds. The three constructs are meant to be independent, but many studies have shown that there is a high correlation between variables in different constructs. In a study of Rome it was found that fertility was more highly correlated

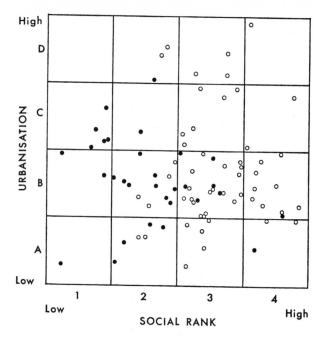

Fig. 8.10 Social space diagram for Winnipeg: Each circle shows the position of a census tracts in social space with shaded circles marking those tracts which are segregated (Herbert, 1972)

with social rank than with the other measure of urbanization.[50] Similar conclusions were drawn from a British study in which fertility and women at work were more highly correlated with social rank than with one another.[51] In Cairo, Abu-Lughod found that social rank and urbanization variables were combined in one factorial category,[52] reflecting, perhaps, a different cultural setting. As far as our own interest is concerned, a more important criticism is that there is no logical link between the theory of social change and the typology of city tracts. There is no linear relationship between increasing social scale and spatial pattern. In Western cities people themselves go through stages, e.g life-cycle stages, that are closely related to where they live (p. 153), but which are not necessarily linked with large-scale social changes. Some early critics, in more general vein, concluded that little attempt is made to tie in the notion of 'social area . . . with any of the underlying theory',[53] and 'it seems that social area analysis boasts no theory that cogently relates hypotheses about areal structure to propositions about social differentiation'.[54] Udry was more sympathetic

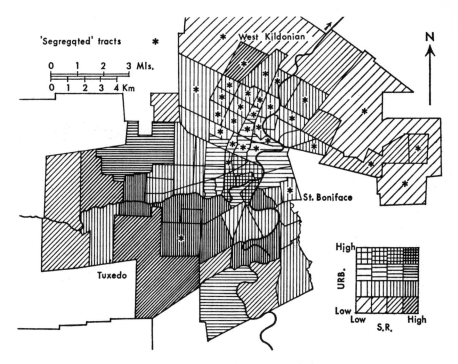

Fig. 8.11   Social areas in Winnipeg, 1961 (Herbert, 1972)

in suggesting that there are really two separate but co-ordinated theories involved, one of increasing scale, the other, using the same axes and variables but not deducible from the first, a theory of sub-area differentiation. The two theories are logically co-ordinated through the proposition that as a society increases in scale, its sub-areas are functionally differentiated.[55] Unfortunately, the significance of the three constructs to residential differentiation is left unexplained.

In his revision of Shevky and Bell's ideas, however, McElrath sees residential differentiation as a function of social differentiation. The macro-processes affecting society must be understood if we are to explain a particular residential pattern. McElrath sees two master trends in the changing structure of society — industrialization and urbanization;[56] and these have given rise to particular historical changes. Industrialization has led to changing distribution and rewards of skills and a change in productive activity. Urbanization has led to concentration of population and an increasing dispersal of resources (see Table 8.5). Each of these historical changes is measured by a construct, as the figure shows. Urbanisation and industrialization, then, yield four basic

Table 8.5. *Social Differentiation and Structural Change*

Master Trend	Distributive changes		Dimensions of social differentiation	
	Historical changes	Indicators of change	Constructs	Sub-area indicators
Industrialization	Changing distributions and reward of skills	Literacy Further education Commercial workers Non-manual workers	Social Rank	Occupation Education
	Changing structure of productive activity	Non-Agri-cultural workers Industrial Diversity Wage and Salaried workers	Family Status	Fertility Women in the work force
Urbanization	Aggregation of population	Urban con-centration Metropolitan concentration	Migrant status	Distance: birth-place Selection: age-sex structure
	Increasing dispersion of resources	External relations	Ethnic status Immigration rates	Culturally visible Minorities

Source: D.W.G. Timms, *The Urban Mosaic* (1971), p.132.

dimensions of social differentiation along which the rewards and resources of urban communities are distributed. In the city the range of opportunities available to an individual or family is subject to the multiple constraints of economic status (based on skills); family status (based on life-style option); migration status (based on migration experience); and ethnic status (based on social visibility).[57]

We have come back to one of our first ideas, i.e. opportunity space. In this instance we have examined, through the work of Shevky, Bell,

McElrath, and others, some of the macro-processes that determine its nature and extent. This is not to claim that the attempt to link macro and micro has been successful. Most analyses of the macro-processes tend to simplify the micro-outcome. Social change and increasing social complexity — whether it is called increasing societal scale, the emergence of urban-industrial society, or modernization — are vital considerations in social geography, as long as it is remembered that the type and effects of change will vary from society to society and from one kind of spatial structure to another.

NOTES AND REFERENCES

[1] A. Richmond (1969), 'Migration in Industrial Society', in J.A. Jackson (ed.), *Migration*, Cambridge.

[2] European movements are referred to in J.M. Houston (1953), *A Social Geography of Europe*, Oxford.

[3] Some African examples are dealt with in R.M. Prothero (1965), *Migrations and Malaria*, London.

[4] J.A. Patmore (1970), *Land and Leisure in England and Wales*, London.

[5] W. Petersen (1970), 'A General Typology of Migration', in C. Jansen (ed.), *Readings in the Sociology of Migration*, Oxford.

[6] G.K. Zipf (1946), 'The P_1P_2/D Hypothesis in the Intercity Movement of Persons', *Am. Soc. Rev.* 11.

[7] S. Stouffer (1940), 'Intervening Opportunities: a Theory Relating to Mobility and Distance', *Am. Soc. Rev.* 5.

[8] E.G. Ravenstein (1889), 'The Laws of Migration', *Journal Royal Stat. Soc.* 48, pp. 167–235.

[9] H.R. Jones (1965), 'A Study of Rural Migration in Upland Wales', *Trans. Inst. Brit. Geogs.* 37.

[10] K.R. Cox (1972), *Man, Location and Behaviour*, New York.

[11] F. Kant (1953), 'Inland Studies in Sector Analysis', *Lund Studies in Geog.*, Series B, 3, pp. 3–15.

[12] T. Hägerstrand (1957), 'Migration and Area', in D. Aannenberg (ed.), Migration in Sweden, *Lund Studies in Geog.*, Series B, 13.

[13] D.H. Pinkey (1955), 'Migration to Paris During the Second Empire', *Journal Mod. History*.

[14] B. Thomas (1955), 'The Economic Aspect', in *Positive Contribution by Immigrants*, UNESCO, New York, No. 77.

[15] K. Davies (ed.) (1973), 'Cities of the Developing World', *Sci. American* 213, p. 219.

[16] P.M. Hauser (1965), 'Urbanisation: an Overview', in P.M. Hauser & L.F. Schnore (eds.), *The Study of Urbanisation*, New York.

[17] L. Wirth (1938), 'Urbanism as a Way of Life', *Am. J. Soc.* 44.

[18] A thesis forcefully put forward by J. Jacobs (1969), *The Economy of Cities*, London.

[19] P. Wheatley (1968), 'Proleptic Observations on the Origin of Cities', in R.W. Steele (ed.) *Liverpool Essays in Geography*, Liverpool, pp. 315–345.

[20] R.N. Morris (1968), *Urban Sociology*, London.

[21] L. Reissman (1970), *The Urban Process*, New York, p. 114.

[22] P.H. Mann (1965), *An Approach to Urban Sociology*, London, Chapter 7. Reissman (1970), op. cit., Chapter 6.

[23] R. Frankenburg (1966), *Communities in Britain*, London.

[24] J. Abu-Lughod (1961), 'Migrant Adjustment to City Life: the Egyptian Case', *Am. J. Soc.* 67.

[25] M. Young and P. Willmott (1957), *Family and Kinship in East London*, London, pp. 198–212.

[26] R.E. Pahl (1965), *Urbs in Rure*, London.

[27] R.E. Pahl (1968), 'The Rural-Urban Continuum', in R.E. Pahl (ed.), *Readings in Urban Sociology*, London.

[28] M.M. Webber (1963), 'Order in Diversity: Community without Propinquity', in L. Wingo (ed.), *Cities and Space*, Baltimore. M.M. Webber (1964), 'The Non Place Urban Realm', in M.M. Webber *et al.*, *Explorations into Urban Space*, Philadelphia.

[29] M. Dobriner (1963), *Class in Suburbia*, Chapter 1, New Jersey.

[30] H.J. Gans (1968), 'Urbanism and Suburbanism as a Way of Life', in H.J. Gans, *People and Plans*, London.

[31] R.E. Dickinson (1967), *The City Region in Western Europe*, London, p. 161. A.E. Smailes (1947), 'Analysis and Delimitation of Urban Fields', *Geography* 32.

[32] J. Friedman and J. Miller (1972), 'The Urban Field', in E. Chinoy (ed.), *The Urban Future*, New York.

[33] B.J.L. Berry and F.E. Horton (1970), *Geographic Perspectives on Urban Systems*, Chicago, Fig. 2.18.

[34] M.M. Webber *et al.* (1964), *Explorations into Urban Space*, Philadelphia.

[35] G. Sjoberg (1960), *The Pre-Industrial City*, Glencoe; D.J. Dwyer (ed.), (1974), *The City in the Third World*, London; T.G. McGee (1967), *The South East Asian City*, London; T.G. McGee (1971), *The Urbanisation Process in the Third World*, London; G. Breese (1969), *The City in Newly Developing Countries*, Princeton; A.L. Mabogunje (1968), *Urbanisation in Nigeria*, London.

[36] C. Abrams (1968), *Man's Struggle for Shelter in an Urbanising World*, London.

[37] R. Bailey (1973), *The Squatters*, London.

[38] D.J. Dwyer (1975), *People and Housing in Third World Cities*, London.

[39] B.J.L. Berry (1973), *The Human Consequences of Urbanisation*, London, p. 84.

[40] E. Jones (1964), 'Aspects of Urbanisation in Venezuela', *Ekistics*, 18.

[41] C. Stokes (1962), 'A Theory of Slums', *Land Economics* 38, pp. 187–97.

[42] J.F.C. Turner (1972), 'Architecture that Works', in G. Bell & J. Tyrwhitt (eds.), *Human Identity in the Urban Environment*, London. J.F.C. Turner (1969), 'Uncontrolled Urban Settlements' in Breese (ed.), op. cit.

[43] L. Peattie (1969), 'Social Issues in Housing', in B.J. Fredin and W. Nash (eds.), *Shaping an Urban Future*, Cambridge, Mass.

[44] J.M. Mara (1961), 'Migration and Urbanisation, the Barriados of Lima', in P.M. Hauser (ed.), *Urbanisation in Latin America*. M. Mangin (1972), Latin American Squatter Settlements', *Lat. Am. Res. Rev.* 2, pp. 65–98. D.J. Dwyer (1964), 'The Problem of Migration and Squatter Settlements in Asian Cities', *Asian Studies* 2.

[45] Peattie (1969), op. cit.

[46] McGee (1971), op. cit.

[47] See, for example, D. Harvey (1973), *Social Justice and the City*, London, pp. 195–284.

[48] E. Shevky and W. Bell (1955), *Social Area Analysis*, Stanford. There is an excellent discussion of social area analysis and its critics in D.W.G. Timms (1971), *The Urban Mosaic*, Cambridge, pp. 123–210.

[49] D. Herbert (1972), *Urban Geography*, Newton Abbott, pp. 142–4.

[50] D.C. McElrath (1962), 'The Social Areas of Rome', *Am. Soc. Rev.* 27, pp. 376–91.

[51] D.T. Herbert (1967), 'Social Area Analysis: A British Study', *Urban Studies* 4, pp. 41–60.

[52] J. Abu-Lughod (1969), 'Testing the Theory of Social Area Analysis: The Ecology of Cairo, Egypt', *Am. Soc. Rev.* 34, pp. 189–212.

[53] A.H. Hawley and O.D. Duncan (1957), 'Social Area Analysis: A Critical Appraisal', *Land Economics* 33, pp. 337–45.

[54] O.D. Duncan (1955), 'Review of Social Area Analysis', *Am. J. Soc.* 61, pp. 84–5.

[55] J.R. Udry (1964), 'Increasing Scale and Spatial Differentiation: New Tests of Two Theories from Shevky and Bell', *Social Forces* 42, pp. 403–13.

[56] D.C. McElrath (1968), 'Societal Scale and Social Differentiation' in S. Greer (ed.), *The New Urbanisation*, pp. 33–52.

[57] D.C. McElrath (1965), 'Urban Differentiation', *Law and Contemporary Problems* 3, pp. 103–10.

IV · PLANNING

9 A fair society—concepts and measurement

SOCIAL JUSTICE AND A FAIR SOCIETY

In the main, the material we have already presented has aimed at explaining why particular spatial phenomena occur or why they are related in certain ways. We have been concerned, therefore, with scientific inquiry, with analysis and explanation. It is also true to say that some of the empirical work that we have set down has involved phenomena that are regarded as social problems or social *malaise*. We have seen that different groups and areas are differentially placed in the spatial system with respect to scarce and desirable resources, such as housing (see p. 148), public safety (see p. 98), and health and health care (see p. 90). To reiterate earlier mentioned themes, these social groups occupy particular opportunity spaces, to each of which accrues a greater or lesser degree of advantage and satisfaction. We want now to turn to a discussion of the position of those groups and areas that suffer the greatest disadvantage, i.e. to examine these social problems as problems.

The reason for doing this is the recent interest of social geographers in investigating such distributions in an effort to influence the directions taken by public and private policy. This particular view of social geography works from a specific value orientation. It is recognized, therefore, that the particular values that a researcher brings to a situation will influence both the problem he chooses to study and his approach to that problem. There are of course many different value positions that can be adopted. Even those who engage in pure research of an academic kind — to use the popular definition of the term — or who strive through their work for status recognition within their peer-group have made certain decisions about their aims. These decisions stem from their values. It is not an overstatement to say that no research is value-free.

We are more interested, however, in those who carry out applied research — work that may have an influence on policy. In this case; values are more explicit. The researcher on the bases of his studies and values advocates either that things stay as they are or that some change is necessary. Different types and methods of change can be advocated (see p. 262). Common to many is the desire to produce a better-ordered society where social ills based on inequality are eliminated. One aim, therefore, is to try and help produce a fairer, more just society, a society which allocates scarce resources on a more equitable basis.

This is, of course, not merely a recent goal. The structural shifts in the British economy, for example, produced in the 1920s and 1930s a noticeable imbalance of employment and prosperity between different regions. Action was taken in the mid-30s by the designation of special areas, although post-war government endeavour to redress this inequitable regional distribution of industry, jobs, and wealth was based on the minority recommendations of the Barlow Report. This report is central to British urban and regional planning. 'It united the national/ regional problem with another problem, the physical growth of the great conurbations, and presented them as two faces of the same problem.'[1] The Minority Report stressed that there should be controls on industrial location over the whole of the United Kingdom. In this example, a fairer society is defined as one in which jobs are directed to where people live, i.e. the aim is to reduce the regional differences in opportunities.

There is a more general difficulty with the terms 'fairer' and 'more just'. Nor must we assume that, in any objective sense, fairness can be equated with justice or justice with fairness. The definition again depends on one's value position. We do think that a more equitable distribution of resources is both fairer and more socially just. Although there is no generally accepted principle of social justice, attempts have been made to clarify the meanings of 'fair' and 'just'. Harvey has discussed the idea of social justice in relation to spatial systems. The first step in the process of clarification is to limit the scope of the term 'social justice'. Justice is limited to mean a principle for the resolution of competing demands. It is 'a particular application of just principles to conflicts which arise out of the necessity for social co-operation in seeking individual advancement.'[2] Individual advancement is thought of in terms of command over society's scarce resources, and it is this command that is to be distributed justly among different territories. This ignores an important scale problem, for a just distribution across a set of territories defined at one scale does not necessarily mean a just distribution achieved at another scale or among social groups. Thus providing a similar standard of health care in all British regions does not mean that all area health authorities, or districts, or social groups will enjoy a similar standard, i.e. localized spatial and social pockets of relative deprivation may continue to exist.

The idea of a just distribution is, however, embodied in three criteria: need, contribution to the common good, and merit. Need is a relative concept, but there are certain categories of activity which we need fairly constantly over time – food, housing, medical care, education, social and environmental services, consumer goods, recreational opportunities, neighbourhood amenities, and transport facilities. The problem is to attempt to define minimum standards for each category that could be equated with needs. Contribution to the common good is taken to mean 'a spatial organisation and pattern of territorial resource allocation which provides extra benefits in the form of need fulfilment (primarily) and aggregate output (secondarily) in other territories through spill-over effects, multiplier effects and the like'.[3] An area would contribute to the common good if its resource allocation – e.g. industrial investment – had the effect of stimulating necessary activity in another district – e.g. the manufacture of components or perhaps the provision of higher-order services. Merit is given a somewhat different meaning than would be expected. It does not involve an extra allocation of resources for being the 'best' territory, but such an allocation is used to compensate for a difficult social and/or natural environment. Thus extra resources will be allocated to areas with worn-out environments and infrastructures. In this way, merit is part of regional policy.

A just distribution is only part of the story. Socially just means must be devised to arrive at that distribution. This state of affairs occurs when the prospects of the least fortunate group or area are as great as they can be, within recognized constraints. There are then, limits set by national prosperity and methods of distribution that affect the chances of the worst-off region maximizing its prospects. The problem is to find the organizational structure which will help attain and maintain these prospects. Harvey argues that it is unlikely to be the market, as this structure usually leads to greater, not lesser, territorial inequalities as funds flow to the most profitable region. The need, therefore, is for a decentralized system of organization which replaces the market. Harvey's ideas can be summarized by saying that territorial social justice requires the following conditions:

the distribution of income should be such that (a) the needs of the population within each territory are met; (b) resources are so allocated to maximise inter-territorial multiplier effects; and (c) extra resources are allocated to help overcome special difficulties stemming from the physical and social environment; and the mechanisms (institutional, organizational, political and economic) should be such that the prospects of the least advantaged territory are as great as they possibly can be.[4]

Smith is also involved in the discussion of what constitutes a fair society,[5] i.e. the outcome of a just distribution justly achieved. His view is based on a broad American consensus of what should constitute a well society. We should add that there is less consensus on how to achieve it (see p. 260). In the well society, people have sufficient income for their basic needs of food, clothing, shelter, and a 'reasonable' standard of living. Poverty is, then, eradicated. People become socially and economically mobile and are respectful of the dignity of others. They will live in good quality housing in decent neighbourhoods, having access to good health and educational facilities, and to recreational amenities. Society will be socially stable with strong family structure, little social disorganization, little crime, and good public order. People will be able to participate fully in all aspects of social, economic, and political life.[6]

A pipe dream? Probably. But these ideas of social justice and a fair society demonstrate the concern of many to reduce the inequality in society. The general aim of such an approach is to redistribute command over the distribution of scarce and desirable resources (goods, services, facilities, wealth itself) in favour of the poorer sections of society. The existing inequitable distribution is easily demonstrated, although the desire for redistribution in favour of the poor depends on our own and society's values. First, we shall examine the aspatial situation.

Table 9.1. *Wealth of Individuals in Britain 1961 to 1973*

% of wealth owned by:	1961	1965	1966	1971	1972	1973
Most wealthy 1 per cent	28·4	24·4	23·6	20·4	22·1	21·8
Most wealthy 2 per cent	37·1	32·7	31·0	27·7	28·9	27·7
Most wealthy 5 per cent	50·6	46·4	43·7	40·1	41·8	38·8
Most wealthy 10 per cent	62·5	58·6	56·0	51·6	43·9	50·9
Most wealthy 25 per cent	79·2	77·7	75·1	72·1	73·9	72·6
Most wealthy 50 per cent	92·5	92·5	90·9	90·2	91·0	91·4
Bottom 50 per cent	7·5	7·5	9·1	9·8	9·0	8·6
Total Wealth (£ billion)	54·5	74·3	76·8	112·7	138·4	163·9

Sources: Social Trends, 1974, p.144; Social Trends, 1975, p.106.

Table 9.1 shows the distribution of wealth in Britain. The trend towards redistribution in favour of the poorer half was in fact reversed in 1972 and 1973, and over the whole time-span there has been little wealth filtering down to the bottom of the social hierarchy. The position is similar in the United States. In the 1960s the top 5 per cent owned 53 per cent of the wealth and the top 20 per cent owned 77 per cent.[7] Not only is wealth unequally distributed, but Table 9.2 shows that in 1974 in Britain 25 per cent of all households had a weekly income of under £30, the bulk of which came from social security

Table 9.2. *Household income: average weekly income by source, 1974*

United Kingdom

	Average total weekly income (= 100%)	Percentages of total weekly income						Percentage of all households
		Wages and salaries	Self-employ-ment	Invest-ments	Annuities and pensions	Social security benefits	Other sources	
	£							
All households:	58·33	72·4	7·5	3·4	2·5	9·4	4·8	100·0
Weekly income range:								
Under £12	10·15	1·7	0·9	3·2	1·7	86·3	6·2	4·1
£12 but under £20	15·75	5·0	1·0	3·7	5·9	75·7	8·7	11·1
£20 but under £30	24·68	23·7	3·7	5·3	7·7	51·1	8·5	9·8
£30 but under £40	35·20	58·4	8·7	3·6	5·6	17·6	6·1	10·3
£40 but under £60	50·02	77·2	6·9	2·2	2·4	6·9	4·4	23·5
£60 but under £80	69·43	81·7	5·8	2·1	1·7	4·0	4·7	19·1
£80 but under £100	88·89	84·3	4·6	2·3	1·6	3·0	4·2	11·0
£100 or more	138·24	73·8	12·6	5·8	1·7	1·7	4·4	11·1

Source: Social Trends, 1975, p.108.

benefits. And in fact, an increasing proportion of those people in
receipt of national insurance benefits also received supplementary
benefits.

Inequalities in income form the basis of most other inequalities.
The quality of housing obtained is dependent, to a large extent, on size
and security of income (see p. 149). Cullingworth has shown how the
possession of certain housing amenities varies according to social group
membership (see Table 9.3).[8] In fact, in 1971 9·1 per cent (or about

Table 9.3. *Housing Conditions and Social Group*

% households having exclusive use of	Profess-ional	Small Employers	Clerical	Foreman & Skilled Manual	Other Manual	Retired & Un-occupied	All House-holds
Fixed Bath	92	90	77	72	62	62	71
Flush Toilet	96	94	90	91	83	85	89
Hot Water from Tap	96	94	84	80	68	67	77
Garden	83	80	70	68	63	67	69
Garage	47	47	24	14	7	13	19

Source: Cullingworth (1965).

1·6m.) of households lacked exclusive use of a fixed bath. This compares
with 15·4 per cent (about 2·6m.) in 1966. In 1971 14·6 per cent (about
2·9m.) of households were without the exclusive use of an inside toilet.
This compares with a 1966 figure of 22·7 per cent (3·8m.). The 1967
Housing Condition Survey of England and Wales showed that a total of
1·8m. dwellings (12 per cent) were statutorily unfit for human habi-
tation. To this must be added 151,000 dwellings (9 per cent) in
Scotland.[9]

As well as having a group dimension, these inequalities are varied
spatially. Coates and Rawstron have demonstrated the regional
variations in income distribution, with incomes tailing off in general
towards the north and west from the financial core of the south-east
(see Figs. 9.1a–9.1e)[10] The same authors also point out the regional distribution of poverty, using as one of their measures the distribution of
free school meals. Again, a similar pattern emerges with the percentage
of children obtaining such meals being highest in the industrial counties
of South Wales and the north, inner London and isolated rural areas.
The county borough picture is more complicated, although there is, on
the whole, an increase in the provision of free school meals from south
to north (see Fig. 9.2). If further evidence is required concerning the
regional imbalance of the distribution of goods and services, reference

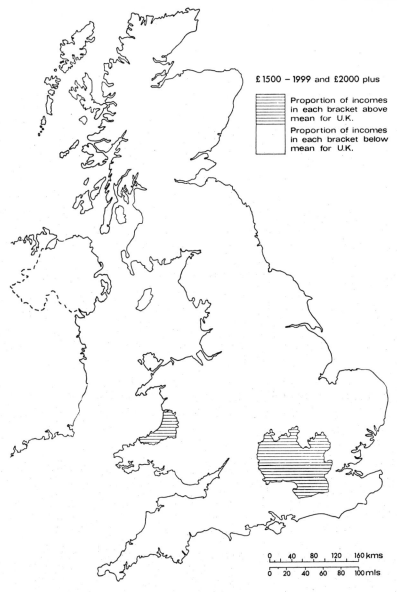

£1500 – 1999 and £2000 plus

Proportion of incomes in each bracket above mean for U.K.

Proportion of incomes in each bracket below mean for U.K.

0   40   80   120   160 kms

0   20   40   60   80   100 mls

Fig. 9.1(a)   Regional Distribution of Income in the U.K. £1500—1999 and £2000 plus, 1964—5 (Coates & Rawstron, 1971)

£1000 – 1499 and £1500 – 1999

Proportion of incomes
in each bracket above
mean for U.K.

Proportion of incomes
in each bracket below
mean for U.K.

Fig. 9.1(b)   Regional Distribution of Income in the U.K. £1000–1499 and £1500–
1999, 1964–5 (Coates & Rawstron, 1971)

Fig. 9.1(c)   Regional Distribution of Income in the U.K. £700–999 and £1000–1499, 1964–5 (Coates & Rawstron, 1971)

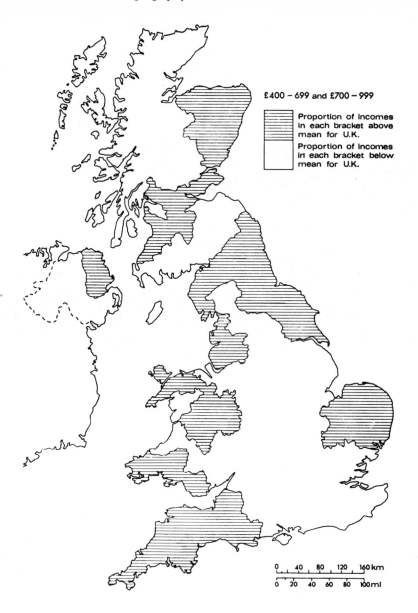

£400 – 699 and £700 – 999

Proportion of incomes
in each bracket above
mean for U.K.

Proportion of incomes
in each bracket below
mean for U.K.

| 0 | 40 | 80 | 120 | 160 km |
| 0 | 20 | 40 | 60 | 80 | 100 ml |

Fig. 9.1(d) Regional Distribution of Income in the U.K. £400–699 and £700–999,
1964–5 (Coates & Rawstron, 1971)

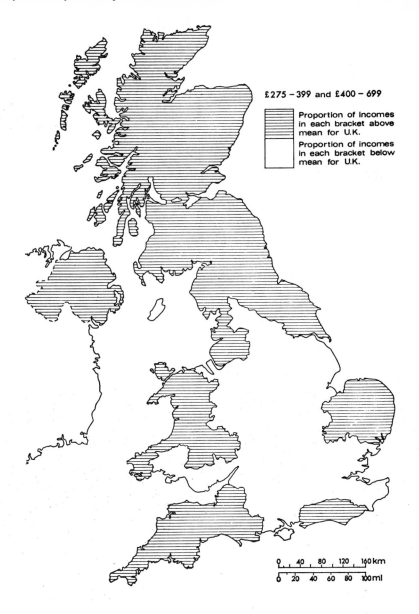

£275 – 399 and £400 – 699

Proportion of incomes
in each bracket above
mean for U.K.

Proportion of incomes
in each bracket below
mean for U.K.

0   40   80   120   160 km

0   20   40   60   80   100 ml

Fig. 9.1(d) Regional Distribution of Income in the U.K. £275–399 and £400–699,
1964–5 (Coates & Rawstron, 1971)

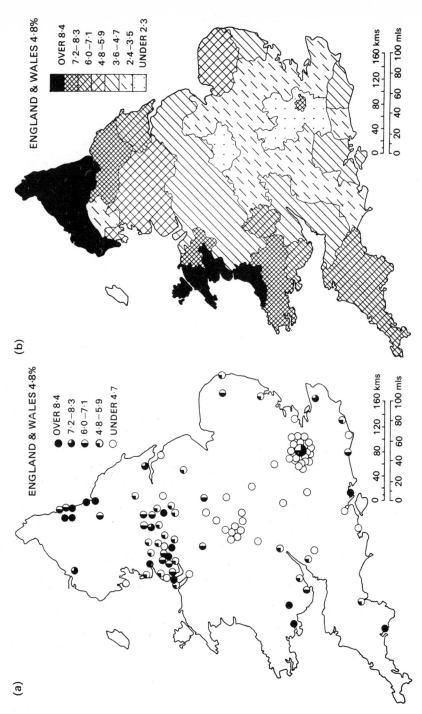

Fig. 9.2 The Distribution of Free School Meals in England and Wales in 1966 (a) Percentage of children present: county boroughs only (b) Percentage of children present: counties include county boroughs (Coates & Rawstron, 1971)

(b)

ENGLAND & WALES 4·8%

■	OVER 8·4
▨	7·2–8·3
▨	6·0–7·1
▨	4·8–5·9
▨	3·6–4·7
▨	2·4–3·5
☐	UNDER 2·3

0 40 80 120 160 kms
0 20 40 60 80 100 mls

(a)

ENGLAND & WALES 4·8%

●	OVER 8·4
◗	7·2–8·3
◑	6·0–7·1
◔	4·8–5·9
○	UNDER 4·7

0 40 80 120 160 kms
0 20 40 60 80 100 mls

can be made to the statistics of Gross Domestic Product per head per region in current prices at factor cost, with the United Kingdom as a whole measuring 100.[11] In 1972, and in descending order, the standard regions were placed as follows: South-East 116·2, West Midlands 102·5, East Midlands 95·8, South-West 95·3, East Anglia 95·0, North-West 93·5, Yorkshire and Humberside 93·3, Scotland 90·6, Wales 87·3, North 85·3, and Northern Ireland 71·5. Just considering the highest and lowest regions, this represents a 36·1 per cent share of total United Kingdom GDP for the South-East, and a mere 2·0 per cent share for Northern Ireland.

We have simply been trying to show the economic basis of the inequitable nature of modern British society with certain groups and territories having a less than adequate share of total U.K. resources. It is precisely this poverty and inequality that has led to the increasing concern with the notions of social justice and a fair society: for as Harrington has said, in the context of the United States, 'poverty should be defined absolutely, in terms of what man and society could be. As long as America is less than its potential, the nation as a whole is impoverished by that fact. As long as there is the other America, we are, all of us, poorer because of it.'[12]

MEASUREMENT AND SOCIAL MONITORING

We must now briefly turn to the problem of discovering whether or not the society in question is progressing to a just distribution justly arrived at. Here we encounter again two previously mentioned aspects of social geographical study. The first is the time element — we have to decide on the time-span over which we are going to monitor any changes in the organizational or distributional structure of society. A one-year time-span is obviously too short a period to detect significant trends, and it may be that the period between decennial censuses is too long. Intuitive judgements will have to be made on the right time-span in different situations. An attempt to monitor change over time, albeit only one year, is provided by Smith. It is a study of the quality of life in eighteen metropolitan areas.[13] Smith summed the ranks of each area to try and develop a general indicator of metropolitan change. The smaller the sum of ranks, the better the city performed (see Table 9.4). The most improved cities turn out to be Chicago, Minneapolis, and Boston, while the least improved ones are San Francisco, Buffalo, and Cleveland. This analysis is merely indicative of what might be achieved given better time-series data.

The second aspect was implicit in the discussion of the time element:

Table 9.4. *Rankings on change for eighteen metropolitan areas, on ten 'Quality of Life' indicators*

City or Metropolitan Area	Adjusted per capita Income 1966-67	Unemployment Rate 1967-68	Low Income Households 1967-68	Housing Costs 1967-68	Service Mental Test Rejections 1967-68	Infant Mortality 1966-67	Suicide Rate 1966-67	Robbery Rate 1967-68	Traffic Deaths 1966-67	Voting in Presidential Election 1964-68	Sum of Ranks	Final Ranking
New York	5·5	2	5	5	6	11	3·5	17	11	17	83	4
Los Angeles	10·5	3	15·5	11	8	7	11·5	6	7	16	95·5	12
Chicago	10·5	8	4	1	10	4·5	5	2	5·5	12	62·5	1
Philadelphia	10·5	5	7·5	8·5	16	17·5	9	13	18	9·5	114·5	15
Detroit	18	4	7·5	12	18	12·5	11·5	4	3	7	91·5	8
Boston	2	6	2	8·5	7	9	11·5	15	4	7	72·5	3
San Francisco	14	7	15·5	18	14·5	7	8	18	13	12	127	18
Washington, D.C.	16·5	18	7·5	10	11	1	2	14	15	3	98	13
Pittsburgh	5·5	10	12	6	17	14·5	11·5	16	14	4·5	111	14
St. Louis	14	1	12	4	4·5	12·5	14	12	8·5	12	94·5	10
Cleveland	16·5	12	12	15	12	14·5	7	1	12	14·5	116·5	16
Baltimore	10·5	10	18	2	9	7	1	11	17	9·5	95	11
Houston	5·5	15	7·5	14	14·5	2	17	7	10	1	93·5	9
Mineapolis	1	17	12	3	2	16	3·5	9	2	4·5	69	2
Dallas	5·5	10	2	13	13	10	18	3	8·5	2	85	5·5
Cincinnati	5·5	16	17	7	4·5	3	16	8	1	7	85	5·5
Milwaukee	5·5	14	2	16·5	1	4·5	6	5	16	18	88	7
Buffalo	14	13	12	16·5	3	17·5	15	10	5·5	14·5	121	17

Source: Smith (1973b), p.107.

it is the problem of measurement. There is wide recognition of the inadequacy of information that can be used to monitor the social performance of a territory, a group, and so on. In recent years, this problem of monitoring and, therefore, measuring social change has received much attention, mainly in 'the social indicators approach'. A social indicator may be defined as

a statistic of direct normative interest which facilitates concise, comprehensive and balanced judgment about the condition of major aspects of a society. It is in all cases a direct measure of welfare and is subject to the interpretation that, if it changes in the 'right' direction, while other things remain equal, things have got better, or people are 'better off'.[14]

In other words, in a geographical context a social indicator is a method of comparing the performance or quality of territories on the basis of certain criteria. It is in essence a measure of areal differentiation, dividing good from bad, improving from static or declining.

The axiom of the social indicators approach, then, is that man can improve the performance of the social system with respect to the achievement of stated goals. In summary, such indicators

should ideally (1) measure the state of and change over time in (2) major aspects or dimensions of (3) social conditions that can be judged normatively, as (4) part of a comprehensive and inter-related set of such measures embedded in a social model, and (5) their compilation and use should be related to public policy goals.[15]

Of course, the idea of improvement implies a value judgement — there may well be disagreement about the direction in which society should change. It is even more likely though that there will be disagreement over how to achieve desired states. Such difficulties may be alleviated by the use of different types of social indicators.

Carlisle identifies four types of social indicator:[16]

(a) Informative Indicators — descriptions of social conditions at a particular time and place.

(b) Predictive Indicators — informative indicators linked to a model of social change.

(c) Problem-oriented Indicators — quantitative measures of particular problems, designed to provide the basis of policy decisions.

(d) Programme-evaluation Indicators — monitoring devices to test the progress and effectiveness of particular policies.

These are not mutually exclusive, and to date most effort has been concentrated on (a) and (c). Knox exemplifies both of these approaches. A study of the prosperity of the South-West region of Britain is one of the informative indicator type. The conditions in this region could be represented by five factors — money, property, growth, opportunity, and employment structure. Interestingly, it was noted that there was little correspondence between the real pattern of prosperity and the pattern used as a basis for giving government assistance to particular districts. Assisted areas were defined principally on the grounds of unemployment. In a way we can suggest that there may be a programme-evaluation dimension (d) in this work. The educational priority programme exemplifies the uses of problem-oriented indicators (see pp. 247—9).[17]

Knox's over-all aim is similar to that of Smith. It is to produce a set of social indicators that can measure territorial well-being, or levels of living. The similarities are also apparent in their definitions and measures.

Knox has said that

> The level of living of persons resident within a geographical area is constituted by
> the overall composition of housing, health, education, social status, employment,
> affluence, leisure, social security and social stability, aggregately exhibited in that
> area, together with those aspects of the demographic structure, general physical
> environment and democratic participation which may determine the extent to
> which the needs and desires relating to the foregoing constituents of level of living
> can be, or are, met.[18]

Smith has proposed measuring territorial well-being by seven major
criteria — income, wealth and employment; the living environment;
health; education; social order (or disorganization); social belonging
(alienation and participation); and recreation and leisure.

Conceptually, these are both grand schemes of the informative
indicator type. Problems arise when the mechanics of measurement are
considered. For the most part, social indicator studies along with those
of social geography in general have tended to rely on published data
sources. Such data, though, are not always in a form suitable to be
employed as the input of multivariate analyses (see pp. 112—20). These
data sometimes fail to provide us with the measures we require for our
studies. In many cases, that which is available is still used. The variable
from the published source — for example the census — becomes a surro-
gate measure. Such measures can be ambiguous or even downright poor.
For example, can social disintegration be adequately measured by
known narcotic addicts per 10,000 population or community concern
by the contributions per head to charity appeals?[19] In his inter-state
study, Smith used the following surrogates to measure health: malnu-
trition, infant mortality, deaths from tuberculosis, expenditure per
patient in hospital, availability of hospital beds, number of doctors,
number of dentists, and insurance coverage. There are other measures
for mental health. While such surrogates could be used in the field of
health, recreation had to be discarded completely. Data so compiled
'can hardly be described as an *integrated* system of indicators that
identify *major dimensions* of social well-being'.[20] Still, such surrogates
produce some interesting spatial patterns. Such patterns may also be
useful as a starting-point for discussing policy needs, as long as their
limitations are realized.

Figure 9.3 shows the patterns produced by Smith's six criteria. The
southern states perform poorly on all criteria except social disorganization. Figure 9.4 shows us some of the results from a principal
components analysis. On component one, general socio-economic
well-being, the south performed poorly, whereas for component two,
social pathology, those states with major cities containing deprived

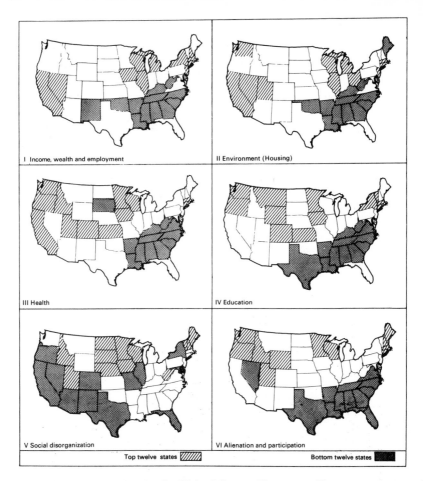

Fig. 9.3 Social Well-Being in the United States. The top and bottom states, on six social indicators. (Smith, 1973)

minority populations performed worst of all.

The influence of the quality and quantity of data on the results produced can be seen from a study of Tampa, Florida. In this case, less census data were used than is normal in a conventional city-based analysis. More material on social problems was available than for the usual factorial ecology. A very different picture of city structure was, therefore, produced (see Fig. 9.5). It is interesting to note how information input determines the nature of the study and of the results. In the study of Tampa, it had been hoped to incorporate attitudinal surveys on people's perceptions of their neighbourhoods and the city.

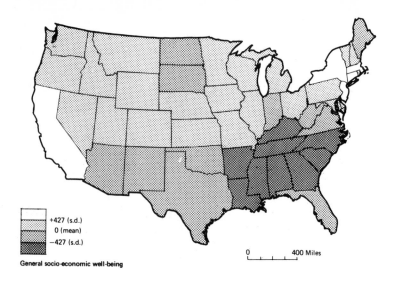

General socio-economic well-being

+427 (s.d.)
0 (mean)
−427 (s.d.)

0   400 Miles

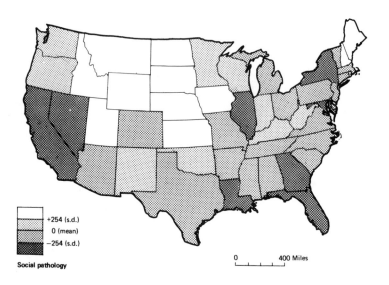

Social pathology

+254 (s.d.)
0 (mean)
−254 (s.d.)

0   400 Miles

Fig. 9.4 United States: state performance on two leading components of social well-being, based on factor scores standardized so that mean=0 and standard deviation (s.d.) = square root of eigenvalue. (Smith, 1973)

This proved to be impossible. It is true to say, though, that until attitudes, aspirations, and preferences are included, we shall not obtain

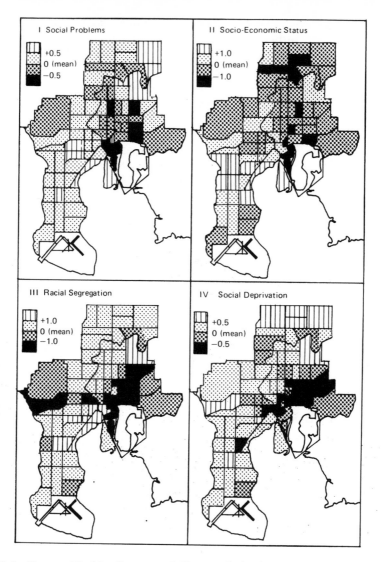

Fig. 9.5   Tampa, Florida: Scores on indicators derived from four leading factors of social well-being (Smith, 1973)

a complete picture of social well-being, despite the great importance of objective measures. A study of the Deeplish district of Rochdale in fact points to the importance of taking attitudes into consideration when assessing environmental conditions. Objectively, Deeplish is run down with old housing with less than the national average of standard amenities. Despite such a physical environment, only 12 per cent were 'rather dissatisfied' with their housing, and 10 per cent with their neighbourhood.[21] It would have been impossible to discover this by using only published data sources. Thus an important part of work on social indicators must be the measurement and monitoring of attitude change over time. A start is being made. There have been attempts by the Institute of Social Research, University of Michigan, to measure the effective evaluations of the life-concerns — society, home, self, family — of Americans.[22] Abrams has described similar British studies that have examined people's satisfactions with life-domains — health, housing, standard of living. It was found that the domains of greatest importance were marriage, family life, and work. Those domains in which there had been steady advances in recent years in objective terms — leisure, housing, standard of living, education — were placed bottom.[23] Finally, Allardt has examined the subjective welfare values of having, loving, and being, in the context of Scandinavia. He found that Finland was lower in value realization on almost all variables related to welfare values than Denmark, Norway, and Sweden. The welfare values of having, loving, and being proved to be largely independent of each other.[24] These studies are simply examples of an important addition to the social indicators approach. Perhaps they demonstrate how to tackle the problem of surrogates. The main problem then becomes one of efficient and effective sampling.

NOTES AND REFERENCES

[1] P. Hall (1974), *Urban and Regional Planning*, Harmondsworth, p. 93.

[2] D. Harvey (1973), *Social Justice and the City*, London, p. 97. In this work, Harvey relies heavily on Rawls for ideas concerning distributive justice and Runciman for the criteria of a just distribution. See J. Rawls (1971), *A Theory of Justice*, Cambridge, Mass., and W.G. Runciman (1966), *Relative Deprivation and Social Justice*, London.

[3] Harvey, op. cit., pp. 107–8.

[4] Ibid. pp. 116–17.

[5] D.M. Smith (1973a), An Introduction to Welfare Geography, *Department of Geography and Environmental Studies, University of Witwatersrand, Occasional Paper* 11.

[6] D.M. Smith (1973b), *The Geography of Social Well-Being in the United States*, New York.

[7] These figures are taken from C.H. Anderson (1974), *The Political Economy of Social Class*, Englewood Cliffs, p. 112.

[8] J.B. Cullingworth (1965), *English Housing Trends*, London.

[9] These housing condition figures are reported by J.B. Cullingworth (1973), *Problems of an Urban Society*, London, ii. 69.

[10] B.E. Coates and E.M. Rawstron (1971), *Regional Variations in Britain*, London. Reference must be made to the excellent geographical study of poverty in the U.S. by R.L. Morrill and E.H. Wohlenberg (1971), *The Geography of Poverty in the United States*, New York.

[11] These data have been obtained from *Social Trends* 6, 1975, p. 103.

[12] M. Harrington (1963), *The Other America*, New York.

[13] Smith (1973b), op. cit., pp. 104–8. The study was in fact carried out by M.V. Jones and M.J. Flax (1970), *The Quality of Life in Metropolitan Washington, D.C.*, The Urban Institute, Washington, D.C.

[14] U.S. Department of Health, Education and Welfare, quoted in Smith (1973b), p. 54.

[15] Smith (1973b), p. 54.

[16] E. Carlisle (1972), 'The Conceptual Structure of Social Indicators' in A. Shonfield and S. Shaw (eds.), *Social Indicators and Social Policy*, London, pp. 23–32.

[17] P.L. Knox (1975), *Social Well-Being: A Spatial Perspective*, Oxford. The informative indicator is illustrated by the study of I.R. Gordon and R.M. Whittaker (1972), 'Indicators of Local Prosperity in the South-West Region', *Regional Studies* 6, pp. 299–313.

[18] Knox, op. cit., p. 31.

[19] The use of these surrogates is discussed briefly by M. Abrams (1973), 'Subjective Social Indicators', *Social Trends* 4, pp. 35–50.

[20] Smith (1973b), op. cit., pp. 84–5.

[21] Ministry of Housing and Local Government (1966) *The Deeplish Study: Improvement and Possibilities in a District of Rochdale*, London.

[22] F.M. Andrews and S.B. Witney (1974), 'Assessing the Quality of Life as People Experience it', paper presented to the Conference of the American Sociological Association, Montreal.

[23] Abrams, op. cit.

[24] E.A. Allardt (1973), About Dimensions of Welfare, *Research Group for Comparative Sociology, University of Helsinki, Report* 1.

10 Public policy and social planning

SOCIAL PLANNING AS SOCIAL ENGINEERING

As well as developing important diagnostic tools to measure inequalities, the social indicators approach has as a major aim an attempt to influence public policy decisions. We shall concentrate on discussing the social planning part of public policy as this seems to relate more closely to events in social geography than do economic or manpower planning. Social planning is the 'real world' counterpart of our concern for social justice and a fair society. Social planning is planning for people in space, rather than for space with people in it. Planning is a necessary activity because it is unlikely in a complex, capitalist society that the maximization of the collective welfare of the community will come about from individual decisions. Even during the middle and late nineteenth century, confronted by overcrowded, insanitary conditions and unsafe buildings, it was realized that only a collective response could ameliorate these conditions. In a way, then, planning has always been social. It was a response to the social as well as physical problems of the cities of the day. But in the main, physical solutions were thought to solve these problems. Then, as perhaps now, it was easier to plan towns than people; for example, compare the success of the sanitary reformers such as Chadwick in improving public health facilities in British towns with the eventual failure of social and moral experiments such as that of Owen at New Lanark, Scotland in creating a happy industrial community.[1] There is widespread agreement on the need for and methods of providing health care, but much disagreement on how to achieve happiness. So for the most part the early public health and housing improvement legislation was aimed at the physical conditions of overcrowding and sanitation.

A second aim has, however, received wider recognition — that the social and moral lives of the people be improved by these schemes. The debate on the Housing, Town Planning, etc. Act of 1909, contained the following statement: 'The object of the Bill is to provide a domestic condition for the people in which their physical health, their morals, their character and their whole social condition can be improved by what we hope to secure in this Bill. The Bill aims in broad outline at, and hopes to secure, the home healthy, the house beautiful, the town pleasant, the city dignified and the suburb salubrious.'[2] Physical planning was thus seen as being able to determine social conditions. It is an extreme view of planning as social engineering. This view that good sanitation produces good behaviour had, and may still have, other proponents. For example, the social philosophy of planning has accepted the importance of community and so planners have actively promoted the furtherance of group relationships. It is thought that a particular small-scale arrangement of dwellings can engender a spirit of neighbourliness through spontaneous co-operation. This is, of course, neighbourhood planning — a means of stimulating direct primary associations between people and so permanently enriching community life (see pp. 120—2). In many neighbourhoods, however, a sense of neighbourliness has not been awakened. In fact, the main reason for social ties developing in such districts seems to be the need to deal with common problems and frustrations. Tenants' and residents' associations often develop so as to present a united front to the landlord or any other perceived threat. Once the problem has been solved though, the association is more than likely to be disbanded.[3] The idea that social cohesion can result from physical planning is, of course, an example of environmental determinism. The influence of environment and architecture on social life cannot be completely dismissed. Newman has found that individual regard for communal property (open spaces, stairways, etc.) is increased where such property is small-scale and observable. For the sake of social order, therefore, a small stairway serving four to six apartments, is preferred to a high rise complex with all its unattended public spaces.[4] But the nature of social activity depends not only on the simple determination of social life by the physical environment, but also on the residents' themselves, and it is true to say that all physical planning has social implications. The control of land uses through zoning, for example, often has the effect of keeping unwanted social groups out of certain suburban areas (see pp. 167—8).

Many of these social implications may be undesirable. In fact, the role of physical planning in relation to social goals and issues has been extensively criticized. Simmie, for example, has said that creating equal life chances, combating poverty, providing adequate housing, and preventing unemployment are central to the *raison d'etre* of physical planning. Its attempts to carry out these tasks, however, have been inadequate, due to its narrow outlook, lack of competence, and predominantly paternalistic ideology.[5] Until recently, the mass of planners have been trained in 'non-social' disciplines, with strong architectural, surveying, and land-use biases and into a profession that saw its role as providing the local authority (not the public) with the 'best' scheme as seen by the profession irrespective of public demands (see pp; 250–7, and 259–261). There is however, a growing realization by planners that social issues require more explicit attention and social solutions.

SOCIAL REMEDIAL PLANNING

'Town planning, *together with other instruments of social policy*, plays a crucial role in a mixed economy in redistributing spatial resources.'[6] In recent years, many local authorites as well as academic researchers, have tried to lay the basis for such redistribution by instigating studies to identify areas of social problems or *malaise*. In doing this, they are taking up one of the key issues in planning in Victorian times. Liverpool, for example, has carried out a very detailed social *malaise* study, while Nottinghamshire has produced a county deprived area study.[7] In the latter case, deprivation was measured by published statistics on income, employment, education, housing, population, and crime. Figure 10.1 shows the distribution of deprivation in the county. The highest levels of deprivation are found mainly in urban and industrial districts as, for example, in Nottingham (NO on the map), Mansfield (MA), Newark (NC), Worksop (BA) and Ollerton and Boughton (NE). Many planning departments have now produced such studies, which tend to be mainly descriptive, although they can lead to proposals for the establishment of priority areas, such proposals being reinforced on occasion by public policy.

General Improvement Areas and Housing Action Areas. Priorities in improvement policy has changed over the years. At first, emphasis was placed on the improvement of individual houses, then on areas of houses, and finally on general environmental improvement. This led, under the auspices of the 1969 Housing Act, to the setting-up of general improvement areas (GIAs). Within these areas, the local authorities have power to spend up to £200 per house on improvements such as landscaping and pedestrianization. In a study of GIA designation in Huddersfield, Duncan found that the areas chosen were not those of the greatest deprivation in terms of lack of facilities and overcrowding, but were in the lower middle and middle range of property values in peripheral areas of nineteenth-century housing. GIAs, therefore, are not designated necessarily to alleviate conditions in areas of housing stress, but in those that would seem likely to benefit from improvement.[8]

A further example of priority areas dealing particularly with housing are the areas of housing stress. Several authorities have located their stress areas, although they have few legislative powers to deal with the

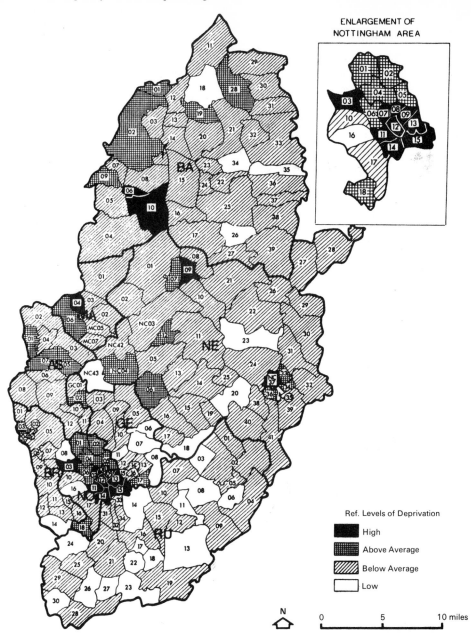

Fig. 10.1 Nottinghamshire: distribution of deprivation (Notts Co. Council (1975), *County Deprived Area Study.*

problems in such districts. The Greater London Council used seven
census-derived variables to designate its areas of housing stress. These
were percentage of households living at a density of more than 1·5
persons per room; percentage of households with more than 3 people
living at a density of more than 1·5 persons per room; percentage of
households without access to a fixed bath; percentage of households
in multiple occupation; percentage of households without access to
hot and cold water supplies; percentage of households in multi-
occupation having no access to their own stove or sink; and percentage
of households of 3 or more persons in multi-occupation. Figure 10.2
shows that these areas are concentrated in inner London. In such areas

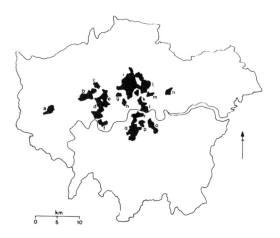

Fig. 10.2 Areas of Housing Stress in Greater London, 1966. Shaded areas indicate
the 10 per cent of wards with the highest stress index. An indication of their
location is given by the letters: (a) Southall; (b) Harlesden/Willesden; (c) Dollis
Hill; (d) Shepherd's Bush/Notting Hill; (e) Kilburn; (f) Fulham; (g) Kentish Town;
(h) Somers Town; (i) Finsbury/Highbury/Holloway/South Hornsey/South Totten-
ham; (j) Stoke Newington; (k) Shoreditch; (l) Wapping; (m) South Hackney;
(n) West Ham; (o) Deptford; (p) Camberwell; (q) Brixton/Clapham/Tulse Hill;
(r) Newington.(P.L. Knox 1975, p.17)

of multi-occupation and overcrowding, increased powers have been
granted to control abuses. Further powers were granted by the Housing
Act of 1974. This allowed for the identification and establishment of
housing action areas (HAAs). Local authorities were to select groups of
around 300 to 400 houses and complete their upgrading in five or at
most, seven years. In 1974 about 3·5 per cent (600,000) of all dwellings

qualified for HAA treatment. Half the expenditure for general environmental improvements comes from central government, as does 75 per cent of a maximum of £3,200 for the upgrading of dwelling units. Several planning authorities have already begun to initiate HAA programmes. The London Borough of Islington, for example, has identified ten potential HAAs, on the basis of present dwelling conditions and household conditions and composition. The four areas with the worst deprivation — Offord Road area, Beresford Road area, Arthur Road area, Tabley Road area — were then compared using data on health complaints, evictions, harassment, applications for conversion (as a measure of willingness to improve one's property), and so on. Offord Road is a district where much private improvement is already occurring, so it was decided that Beresford Road would be the first HAA.[9]

Educational Priority Areas. The Plowden Committee was set up in the 1960s to investigate all aspects of primary education. An examination of the social conditions in different areas, using measures such as socioeconomic status of parents, the lack of home amenities, the proportion of children with language difficulties, the proportion of families receiving welfare subsidies, found that there was a co-existence of deprivations (slum housing, widespread poverty, unskilled employment) in certain districts. The Report, therefore, recommended a national policy of 'positive discrimination' to make schools in the most deprived areas as good as the best in the country.[19] Thus education was seen as one of the keys to the alleviation of deprivation. So particular areas and schools were selected as for example in Liverpool and Inner London. The ILEA produced an index for designating educational priority areas (EPA) schools and Table 10.1 shows some of the differences in disadvantage.[11]

It is perhaps unfortunate that the concept of EPA has become somewhat diluted, being replaced by the educational priority school, i.e. resources are given to schools not areas. Of course, education itself will do little to solve the problem of poverty. The £16m. announced in 1967, which is being shared among 150 schools in fifty-one local education authorities, will improve parts of the school system and may help the school become an integral part of its community, but it is hardly likely to alter greatly the pattern of deprivation in these areas. It is even doubtful whether all these resources are being concentrated on the right schools and children. Resources going to EPA schools in Inner London, for example, reach 13·6 per cent of *all* children, but only 20·2 per cent of the most disadvantaged children in the ILEA area. It has also been found that for every immigrant child in an EPA school

Table 10.1 *The Inner London Educational Authority (ILEA) Index of Educational Priority Designation*

					Criteria					
School in order of degree of disadvantage	Social class	Family size	Over-crowding	Housing stress	Cash supplements	Absenteeism	Immigrants	Retarded & Handicapped children	Teacher turnover	Pupil turnover
1st	47·8	43·4	15·9	35·6	29·5	14·7	68·1	75·0	83·3	55·5
50th	42·1	39·1	10·7	30·4	34·3	12·3	53·0	65·0	71·4	39·1
100th	39·3	36·6	9·1	26·2	13·5	10·8	35·0	49·4	66·7	28·5
150th	32·7	33·2	5·4	22·2	11·4	9·5	21·8	38·9	57·1	23·5
England & Wales Average	31·9[1]	26·7[1]	1·2	19·8	5·1	n.a.	2·5	25·0	35·6[2]	9·5[1]
	%	%	%	%	%	%	%	%	%	%
Variables:	semi-skilled & unskilled	Children in families of 6 +	Households at densities $> 1\frac{1}{2}$	Households without inside W.C.	Children receiving free school meals	Absent in sample work week May '67	Immigrant children Jan '67	Children of low ability at 11+ stage	Teachers in school July '67 there for $<$ 3 yrs	Pupils with incomplete yr.1966-7

[1] 1961 figs. not 1966 census material from 1966 sample.
[2] From Plowden, not strictly comparable.

Source: After Halsey (1972).

there are three that are not.

There are 5 times as many children at risk because they come from large families outside EPA schools than there are inside them. There are 5 times as many un-skilled workers' children, 3 and a half times as many children receiving free school meals and four and a half times as many children with low verbal reasoning outside EPA schools than there are in them.[12]

These facts present a serious challenge to an area-based policy in the field of education (see p. 250).

The Urban Aid Programme. A similar basis — the identification of areas of multiple deprivation — underlies a more comprehensive approach to delapidated parts of cities. This is the Urban Aid Programme, examples of which are the twelve community development projects (CDPs) set up between 1969 and 1972. The CDPs are located at Hillfields, Coventry; Vauxhall, Liverpool; Newington, Southwark; Glyncorrwg, Glamorgan; Canning Town, Newham; Batley, West Yorkshire; Benwell, Newcastle; Cleaton Moor, Cumberland; Saltley, Birmingham; Ferguslie Park, Paisley; Percy and Trinity, Newcastle; and Clarksfield, Oldham. As the Inter-Project Report stated,

The experiment was originally conceived and planned on a number of basic assump-tions. It was assumed that the problems of urban deprivation had their origins in the characteristics of local populations — in individual pathologies — and these could best be resolved by better field co-ordination of the personal social services, combined with the modernisation of self-help and mutual aid in the community.[13]

As the projects got under way, their emphases changed. They discovered several key issues in all the areas — employment, housing, and social income and resources (i.e. grants and welfare rights). Their general perspective also changed; they rejected the idea of individual pathologies and, as their Forward Plan has said, 'Poverty is seen to be a consequence of fundamental inequalities in our present political and economic system. . . The projects' experience has led them largely to discount the value of attempting to influence policy and promote technical strategies for change in isolation from working class action.'[14] They see CDPs as being simply political education programmes for local populations and the first final report to be published — Coventry — is written with these perspectives in mind.

Whether or not it has been caused by this changed perspective, the Home Office appears to be running down the projects and seems to intend to replace them with Comprehensive Community Programmes (CCPs). There is little detail available on CCPs at the time of writing, except that they will identify and analyse the whole range of economic, social, and physical or environmental problems of areas and contain proposals for action to deal with these problems within a five-year time scale.

The views expressed in the CDP reports and the findings of the latest EPA analysis, however, must lead us to question the utility of area-based approaches to social problems. These approaches have been introduced for the best of motives. It has been considered that if extra resources are concentrated in the most deprived localities then the eradication of these ills will be achieved in the shortest possible time. There are, however, two related difficulties. First, it is assumed that these deprivations are localized. Indeed they do appear to be concentrated in particular districts, but it all depends again on the scale of analysis. It may be that the census units used to date allow us to fall yet again into the ecological trap of assuming that the majority if not all individuals in a sub-area conform to the pattern of characteristics derived from aggregate data — an error illustrated by the EPA material. Second, it appears to be true that the inner city as a whole is more deprived than other urban and rural areas, but this concentration has led to policies that treat the inner city as a place apart, a place of isolated causes and effects, where forces deriving from the rest of the spatial system are irrelevant. As the CDP perspective indicates, this may not be the case. The inner city is, therefore, an integral part of society, albeit one in which poverty and deprivation are most easily seen. Thus the concentration of the poor in, the poor housing and environmental conditions of, and the disappearance of economic activity and productive investment from, this area can only be understood with reference to what is going on elsewhere in society.

PARTICIPATION AND PRESSURE GROUPS

The official position on CDPs and CCPs seems to be that they are examples of an effort to involve local populations in what is happening in their areas. They can be seen as attempts to provide some substance to the rather bland recommendations of the Skeffington Report on participation. This report concluded, for example, that people should be kept informed throughout the preparation of plans for their area; that plans should be published for the benefit of the affected people; and that people should be encouraged to participate in the preparation of plans.[15] Participation often takes the form of a series of public meetings to discuss a series of alternative proposals put forward by the planning department. The A1–M1 link in Northamptonshire is a case in point. Figure 10.3 presents the material given to interested members of the public. Alternative routes with their advantages and

The Problem...

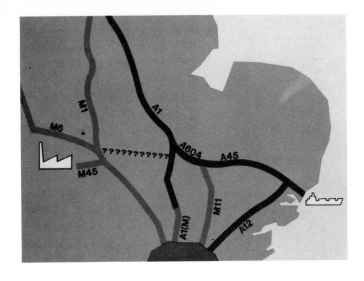

In recent years there has been considerable growth of commercial traffic using the East Anglian ports and this trend is likely to continue. There is no convenient rail link to carry this traffic and good road communications are therefore important.

The A45/A604 is being improved westward to the A1; as part of this programme a by-pass of Bury St Edmunds and an improved approach to Felixstowe Docks have already been provided whilst by-passes for Huntingdon, Godmanchester, Newmarket and Stowmarket are now under construction. Other improvements, including a northern by-pass of Cambridge are planned.

To the west of the M1, the M6 and M45 give access to the industrial Midlands. Between the M1 and the A1, however, there is no adequate direct route.

In consequence traffic uses several unsuitable roads to cross this area. Since much of the traffic consists of heavy lorries, environmental damage is inflicted on towns and villages en route and difficulties are caused for local life. Kimbolton, shown on the front cover, is typical of this problem.

We are now asking for your views on the possible routes for a high quality east-west link in this area which would improve the situation. Such a link was shown diagrammatically in the recent proposals for a national network of lorry routes though it would in fact cater for through traffic generally.

The Link Road

At the request of the Department of the Environment, Freeman Fox and Associates, the Transportation and Planning consultants, have investigated the suitability of a large number of alternative corridors for an M1-A1 link road in the general area between Leicester and Bedford.

It became apparent that the most feasible routes started near Catthorpe at the M6/M1 junction, then passed Kettering to finish near Huntingdon. In their recent report the Consultants have presented four possible corridors for consideration. These are described overleaf.

It should be emphasized that the lines shown represent broad corridors within which the chosen route would lie. They do not therefore represent detailed alignments and it is not possible at this stage to identify their effect on individual properties. The detailed route alignment within the chosen corridor will be the subject of further study.

The predicted traffic levels do not warrant the construction of a dual carriageway motorway. It is likely that the link would be a high class single carriageway road for most of its length.

What The Link Would Achieve

The link would effectively close the gap in the national road network as shown on the map above. By providing a direct and suitable route for lorries it would relieve many towns and villages from noise and pollution; otherwise they would eventually suffer from more than one lorry passing every minute.

There are a number of developing towns in the area that would benefit from improved east-west communications. It is expected that a new link road would reduce the cost of transport between the Midlands and the East Coast, whilst local traffic would also gain from the reduction in congestion due to the removal of through traffic from existing roads.

Public transport would benefit from the improved traffic conditions on local roads and would, in addition, be able to use the link for longer journeys.

How You Can Help

We would like you to take part in the early planning of this new link road which could become an important feature of your area in the future. You can do this by visiting one of the exhibitions where more information will be on display and where staff will be available to discuss and answer any questions you may have.

The main exhibitions will be held in Kettering, Wellingborough, Rushden, Huntingdon and St Neots, whilst an exhibition caravan will visit smaller towns and villages in the area. Full details are given on the enclosed leaflet.

Whether or not you are able to visit an exhibition we would be grateful if, when you have decided which choice would be best for the area, you would complete and return the enclosed pre-paid questionnaire. We are also consulting the local authorities and other interested parties.

What Happens Next?

The completed questionnaires and any other comments received will be examined and the Secretary of State will take your views into account before he decides where the new link should run. His decision will be made public.

After the decision is taken there will be further studies to select a detailed route within the preferred corridor. Following this a specific proposal will be worked up in still greater detail and formally published. This could lead to a public inquiry. Inevitably these procedures will take a number of years to complete.

The arrangements for compensation for those affected by road proposals have recently been improved by the Land Compensation Act 1973. Explanatory leaflets will be available at the exhibitions or can be obtained by writing to the address shown on the front cover.

Fig. 10.3   Participation in Planning: A1—M1 Link

The 4 Possible Choices...

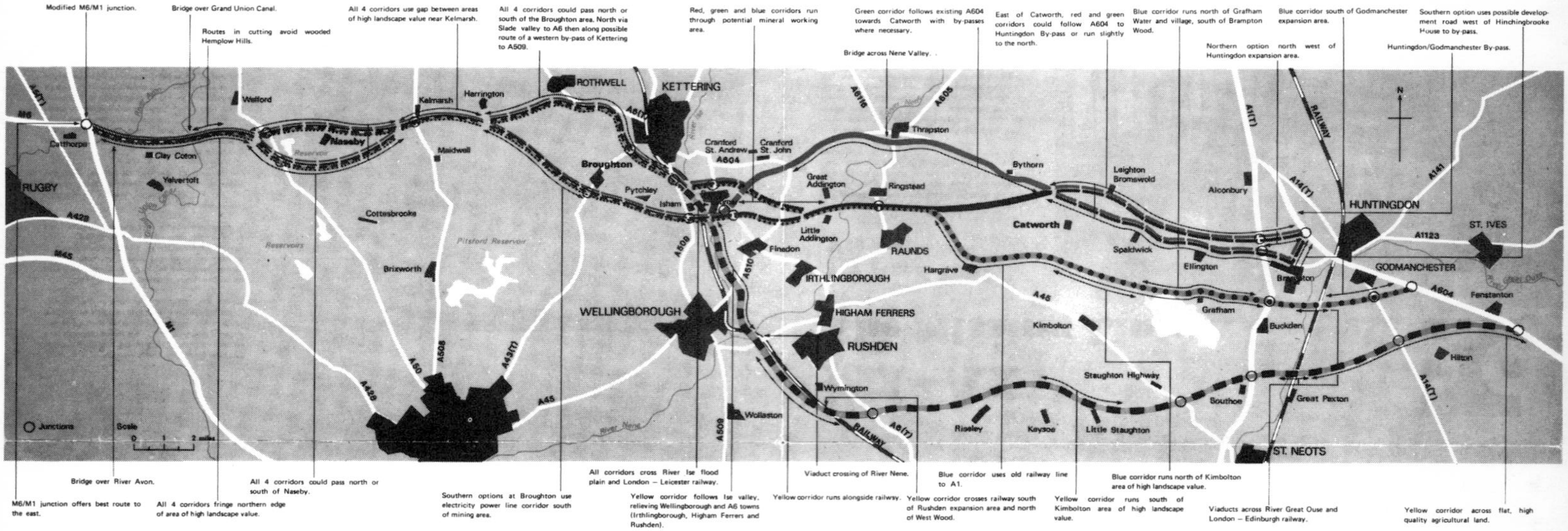

Fig. 10.3 (contd.)

Which Do You Prefer..?

The 4 Choices

From the M6/M1 junction the green corridor would cross the Avon Valley and rise to the Hemplow Hills. Then, passing either north or south of Naseby and fringing an area recognised by the County Council as being of high landscape value, it would continue east to Harrington. From there it could run either north or south of Broughton. Crossing the River Ise near Burton Latimer it would swing north east to join the A604 east of Cranford St John. From here it would follow the general line of the A604 with village by-passes where necessary. From the junction of the B660 near Catworth it could either continue to run along the A604 or lie slightly to the north. Both these alternatives would meet the Huntingdon-Godmanchester By-pass north of Huntingdon.

This choice would follow the same corridor as the green alternative as far as Burton Latimer. It would then pass between the Addingtons and across the Nene Valley before continuing eastward to the A604 near Catworth. From here to Huntingdon the same alternatives apply as for the green choice.

●●●● The blue corridor would be identical to the green choice as far as Burton Latimer. It would then, like the red corridor, pass between the Addingtons and across the Nene Valley and run eastward to Raunds. Here, however, it would swing south east to run along a disused railway line to Hargrave then eastward towards Grafham. At Grafham it would swing north for a short distance to avoid the village and reservoir. East of the A1 it would leave the line of the old railway to cross the Great Ouse Valley and pass south of Godmanchester before joining the A604.

Following the same corridor as the green alternative to the River Ise it would then turn south along the valley between Wellingborough and Rushden to cross the Nene Valley and run alongside the railway line to Wymington. From here it would swing eastwards to run in open country north of Riseley, Little Staughton and Southoe to the A1. Crossing the Great Ouse Valley and the railway north of Great Paxton it would continue eastward passing north of Hilton to join the A604 east of Fenstanton.

Important Points to Consider
Before Filling in Your Questionnaire

			●●●●	▬ ▬ ▬
Length (miles)	47	43	47	53
Estimated construction costs (1974 prices)	£9M	£13M	£14M	£15M
Houses taken	Probably not more than 15.	Probably not more than 15	Probably not more than 15.	Probably not more than 15
Houses affected by noise	Probably not more than 35	Probably not more than 25	Probably not more than 40.	Probably not more than 45
Length through Grades I and II Agricultural land (miles)	3	2	14 (includes 9 miles along disused railway line)	20
Advantages	Reduces visual, agricultural and urban severance to a minimum by following A604. Relieves A45 Takes little good quality agricultural land. Provides some relief to St. Neots.	Improves traffic conditions on A45, A604. Takes little good quality agricultural land. Provides some relief to St. Neots.	Reduces agricultural severance to a minimum by following railway corridor. Relieves A45, A604. Provides some relief to St. Neots.	Provides a by-pass for the A6 towns and relieves A45. Makes savings on road proposals in the Wellingborough area. Provides most relief to St. Neots.
Disadvantages	Increased traffic would affect existing houses on A604. Increases traffic on Huntingdon/Godmanchester By-pass through built-up area. Conspicuous crossing of River Nene at Thrapston.	Increases traffic along scenic Nene Valley on A605 and on Huntingdon/Godmanchester By-pass through built-up area.	Introduces new major road near Grafham Water and village. Engineering and environmental problems with crossing of River Great Ouse and main railway near Brampton. Increases traffic along attractive Nene Valley on A605.	Engineering and environmental difficulties with crossings of River Nene at Wellingborough and of A1, River Great Ouse and main railway north of St. Neots. Intrudes on the existing village/agricultural pattern in north Bedfordshire. Less traffic relief to A604. Longest route taking most good quality agricultural land.

Detailed Points

ADVANTAGES OF ALTERNATIVES IN THE FOLLOWING PLACES:—

	NORTH	SOUTH
NASEBY (All Choices)	Shorter length. Less conspicuous. Avoids areas of high landscape value.	Avoids severance of Naseby Field from village. Could use reclaimed mineral working land near Naseby reservoir.
BROUGHTON (All Choices)	Reduces agricultural severance. Cheaper to build. Less conspicuous. Makes use of possible line of a future western by-pass of Kettering providing A6 by-pass for town.	Affects fewer existing properties. Reduces traffic pressure on A6. Less construction period nuisance.
EAST OF CATWORTH (Red and Green Choices only)	Avoids existing villages and houses on A604 and improves local traffic conditions. Less construction period nuisance. Avoids need to upgrade possible local development road at Huntingdon.	Less conspicuous. Cheaper to build. Avoids breaking up the existing attractive village and agricultural field pattern.

The lines shown are diagrammatic. At this stage route corridors only have been studied and therefore the possible effects on individual properties cannot yet be forecast.

This figure has been reproduced from a multi-coloured original. Although modified, some detail has been lost. We think the figure is still useful in that it provides an example of the choices presented to the public in participation exercises.

Fig. 10.3 (contd.)

QUESTIONNAIRE

A LINK ROAD BETWEEN THE M1 AND A1

Please answer the questions below by ticking the appropriate boxes.

1   Bearing in mind the needs of the locality as a whole, which THREE of the following factors do you consider most important in choosing a route corridor?

Tick THREE boxes only please.

a. Avoiding noise and pollution. ☐

b. Avoiding adverse effect on agriculture. ☐

c. Avoiding adverse effect on attractive countryside and recreational areas. ☐

d. Keeping costs to a minimum. ☐

e. Effect on shopping, schooling etc. due to removal of through traffic. ☐

f. Improvement in safety. ☐

g. Effect on traffic:- reduction of congestion, delays etc. ☐

h. Any other factor.(please write below) ☐

....

....

		GREEN	RED	BLUE	YELLOW
2	Which would be your first choice?	☐	☐	☐	☐
3	Which would be your second choice?	☐	☐	☐	☐
4	Which would you consider the worst choice?	☐	☐	☐	☐

5 Please show whether you prefer the north or south choice at the following places.

	NORTH	SOUTH	NO PREFERENCE
NASEBY	☐	☐	☐
BROUGHTON ~~BOUGHTON~~	☐	☐	☐
EAST OF CATWORTH (Red and green choice only)	☐	☐	☐

6 Any other comments:- ....

....

....

....

....

....

....

....

7 Please write your name and address.......................................

....

When you have completed this form please post it to reach us by
13th, December ▓▓▓▓▓▓▓▓1974.   THANK YOU.

Fig. 10.3 (contd.)

disadvantages were laid down. The views of the public were canvassed by a questionnaire and meetings were held for them to air these views. But in this, as in many cases, the limits of the debate have been set by the planners — no scheme outside the list of alternatives is usually considered. Participation may, therefore, simply be a way of educating the public into the planners' ways of thinking and not vice versa.

Participation can occur over a variety of planning issues. In the case of the Rhondda a report, in which the cases for the continuation of Rhondda as a major urban settlement, a new road system, new industrial sites, and the improvement of existing housing and environmental conditions were put forward, was the basis for public participation. Participation took the following forms — film shows, exhibitions, and public meetings, the latter being attended by about 7,000 people. At these meetings discussion often ranged far beyond the report and in fact it was thought that publicity for them was inadequate. Involvement in the discussion was often dominated by action groups and the views of the 'silent majority' were seldom canvassed.[16]

It has been generally noticed that many people will organize themselves into action or pressure groups to fight for or (usually) against a particular plan or proposal. Pressure groups are, however, not limited to planning issues and public inquiries. They play an important role in the democratization of decision-making, at least at the local level. Thus, for example, tenants' or residents' associations have been set up to fight for particular amenities or against certain problems on housing estates. Amenity groups can become permanent sources of pressure if the object of their attention is continually threatened or troublesome as, for example, the Council for the Preservation of Rural England and Friends of the Earth. We should not forget that trade unions — those important national pressure groups — can have an environmental impact either implicitly as in the case of trade union involvement in the Dockland Joint Committee on the future of London's riverside, or explicitly as in the case of the construction unions in Sydney with their 'green bans' on property development that would be detrimental to agricultural or recreational land. Such interests are tangential to the main concern of trade unions. In any event, most environmental pressure groups are localized and small-scale, although they can grow to become of national significance. One example is the siting of London's Third Airport. This issue produced many such groups, some against the airport, as at Cublington, Foulness, and Wing, some in favour as at Wing (for work). Pressure groups are, of course, not always successful, as the unsuccessful demands for the re-siting of the new runway at Edinburgh airport demonstrates. It can be said, though, that pressure groups add bite to public inquiry and participation procedures. This is at present necessary with there being little need for planners to consult the public before alternative schemes are worked out. Indeed, as Skeffington remarked: 'Public participation would be little more than an artificial abstraction if it became identified solely with planning procedures rather than with the broadest interests of the people.'

But who are the people? Is participation in planning an exercise with which few people are concerned? A National Opinion Poll Survey, which interviewed 1,676 adults in 100 U.K. parliamentary constituencies in November 1974, found that 70 per cent of those interviewed had heard nothing at all connected with public participation in planning. Only 7 per cent of respondents and their families said that they had been to public meetings, 9 per cent to exhibitions, 3 per cent had completed planning questionnaires, and only 1 per cent had been interviewed by planning officials. Only 12 per cent of the sample could in fact be classified as being active participants. They were, on the whole, more middle-class, more middle-aged, better educated, more politically active and more often members of interest (action) groups than the rest of the sample.[17] That such characteristics are typical is borne out by many studies, and considering one particular area — Cheshire — we find that involvement was heavily concentrated in existing voluntary groups. Only 5 per cent of those attending public meetings had no affiliations with existing groups. Professionals, managers, owner-occupiers, and the university-educated were again over-represented in those involved.[18]

The fault of low public involvement may well lie with the planning authority, although it is difficult to generate interest from mass apathy. (NOP) Survey found that only 13 per cent of their sample were 'very interested' in local affairs. Even so, different approaches to participation have been tried by different authorities, ranging from Humberside's invitation to the public to fill in an almost blank map of the county with anything important they think has been left out, Lincolnshire's attempts to involve an uninterested public with comic strips, newspapers and some door-to-door interviewing, to South Yorkshire's more sophisticated efforts. South Yorkshire divided its population into three groups — the great majority who were neither interested in the structure plan nor willing to get involved (their views on the quality of their lives were obtained by sample survey); those interested but not wanting to become involved (they were provided with information by the mass communications system); and those both interested and prepared to be involved in formulating the plan (a wide range of interest groups and voluntary bodies were approached and provided with information on the structure plan).[19]

It is doubtful that many authorities go as far as South Yorkshire. It does appear, however, that much could be done to improve adherence even to the letter of Skeffington's ideas which, under the 1968 Town and Country Planning Act, are now a statutory responsibility. Public meetings are often inadequately advertised at very short notice. The 'silent majority' is seldom tapped as it should be, even if their involvement is likely to be minimal. Above all, the attitudes of officials to participation is not, in some instances, very promising. A letter from the Department of the Environment states that 'Our experience has shown that public meetings are not a good way of getting information across to the public as the floor tends to be dominated by protest groups on these occasions and our officials are then put in the invidious position of being convenient Aunt Sallys for abuse.'[20] It appears that paternalism still exists and participation is (still) often thought of as a way of educating the public into the planners' perspective.

SOCIAL DEVELOPMENT PLANNING

The introduction of participation in planning has helped to widen our discussion of social planning. Important though the remedial side of social planning is, we must remember that those living in deprived areas form only a small proportion of the population. We should not see social planning as solely concerned with this type of problem. It has a more creative function as well. This is best seen in relation to redevelopment schemes and new and expanded towns, i.e. 'new' communities. The difficulties faced by any such community will depend to a large extent on the type of family that has been selected to go there. Careful monitoring of social, demographical, and occupational characteristics of the incoming populations are, therefore, required. Again, solutions that suggest a linear relationship between social type and physical factors have been seen not to work. For example, the idea that the tolerance of social differences and the provision of a wider range of facilities could be met by 'social mix' has been proved unsupportable. Studies in both the United States and Britain have shown that people prefer neighbours to be like themselves (see p. 152).

But more often than not the need is for the provision of certain social facilities — a meeting hall, a church, or pub, and so on. A study carried out in the Isle of Dogs showed that most of the perceived needs of the residents could have been met by the provision of a multi-purpose community centre. The inadequate provision of these facilities has also been documented by The Needs of New Communities Report.[21] The Report suggested that each community should have a social development plan. Social development was defined as policies and programmes directed towards meeting social needs. Such a plan would promote the provision of social facilities and of welfare, advice, and information services, and would consider their management, staffing, and implementation. The social planner, therefore, acts as a 'stimulator' of other departments, who have the statutory responsibility for providing the needed facilities. Most new and expanded town development corporations have set up social development departments (e.g. Milton Keynes, Peterborough) or arrivals offices (e.g. Northampton). To be more specific, in the case of Greater Peterborough, social development officers are expected to contribute to the formulation and implementation of policies. They conduct research into the settling in of families, the provision of meeting places, recreation facilities for the young and elderly, and for the arts. As an integrative function, social development provides the institutions through which people can exercise choice in what they do.

In fact, it may be that social development planning is the harbinger of a more comprehensive social planning, one which sees the social system as being a dynamic entity and which gives greater emphasis to the consideration of social processes. Cherry sees planning as needing not to determine the future pattern of land-use and activity, but to provide a framework which gives people the widest opportunities and which removes the constraints that limit people's enjoyment of the benefits of social change.[22] So we can say that social planning must encourage and facilitate the expression and fulfilment of the needs and aspirations of citizens. Policy, of course, provides a vital and realistic part of this. It must be carefully worked out and co-ordinated. This is, to use Gans's term, societal planning — the evaluation of social goals and the development in broad outline of the kinds of programme required to achieve the chosen goals.[23] But it is the precise means of achieving broadly agreed goals, and the utility of planning itself in this context, that are the subject of much debate.

THE EFFICACY OF SOCIAL PLANNING

It may be worthwhile briefly summarizing the discussion so far on social planning. There are three aspects to social planning:

(a)   the monitoring of the social implications of physical planning, or social engineering;

(b)   the identification of areas of social malaise and the attempt to ameliorate such conditions, or remedial planning, or social problems perspective;

(c)   the promotion of social and welfare facilities to meet defined
        social needs, or social development planning.

In all this, the planner is concerned with the spatial distribution of
scarce resources. In this distribution, some groups gain and others lose.
It is because the same groups lose nearly every time that the social
problem perspective has come to dominate social planning. Because
there is no concensus in British society on how wealth is distributed,
i.e. there is an unprincipled scramble for money, goods, and services,
social planning is beginning to attempt to differentiate between different
sections of society, to discriminate in favour of those in most need.
Whether it can be successful in this in a capitalist society must now be
discussed.

The willingness and ability of planners to so discriminate depends
partly on their position in society and partly on the nature of society in
which they operate. We have already examined the nature of our
society (see p. 224). The position of planners in society is important
because it affects the way they see the world, i.e. it affects their
ideology. There has been some confusion of the meaning of the term
'ideology'. In some cases, the term 'work orientation' may be more
apposite. For example, Foley describes the three main ideologies (work
orientations) in British planning.[24] Firstly, planners see themselves
as umpires, reconciling competing claims for scarce land. Secondly,
some see themselves as promoters of a better way of life by improving
the quality of the physical environment. Thirdly, some see their role
as providing a better physical design for a better community life. The
emphasis is thus on the planners' view of their own roles (work orientation) rather than on how they see social life (ideology). Of course,
there is a two-way relationship, but we would argue that ideology
is the prime determinant. Another scheme of work orientations is
provided by Boskoff.[25] Planners may have:

(a)   corrective physical orientation, e.g. downtown redevelopment
        schemes — attempting to 'correct' part of the spatial structure;
(b)   creative physical orientation, e.g. green belts — attempting to
        create a new spatial pattern by control;
(c)   corrective social orientation, e.g. casework programmes — this
        sees the social worker as planner attempting to correct 'wrong'
        aspects of people's characters;
(d)   creative social orientation, e.g. well-designed new communities —
        attempting to create new styles and ways of living.

All these different work orientations are, to a large extent, dependent
on the ideology of the planner, i.e. his model of how society operates
and changes.

The CDP Inter-Project Report considered that there were three possible ideologies or models of social change. These are:

(a) Consensus models 'based on the assumption that social problems are "malfunctions" which can be cured by adjustments and re-arrangements within the existing operating systems'. Thus areas of deprivation are seen as inefficiencies in the market mechanism, that can be cured by a concentration of funds in these areas. Problems are seen then mainly as failures of co-ordination and communication and the focus of change is thus on management and administration.

(b) Pluralist models 'based on the assumption that social problems arise from "imbalances" in the democratic and bureaucratic systems'. Problems are seen as failures of participation and of representation of certain interests in the political process. The focus of change is thus on politicians, policy-makers, and the disenfranchised.

(c) Structural conflict models 'based on the assumption that social problems arise from a fundamental conflict of interests between groups and classes in society'. Problems are seen as inequalities in the distribution of power. The focus of change is on the centres of organised power.[26]

These models and a consideration of different levels of activity produced nine possible related and overlapping strategies for the planner, policy-maker, and public (see Table 10.2). Of these strategies,

Table 10.2. *Models of Social Change and Possible Strategies on Three Levels of Operation*

Basic Assumptions / Level	Consensus	Pluralism	Structural Conflict
National	1. Social planning	4. National Lobby	7. National Pressure
Local	2. Organizational & Service Development	5. Local Lobby	8. Local Pressure
Grass-Roots	3. 'Traditional' Community Development	6. Community Organization	9. Community Action

Source: National Community Development Project (1974), p.24.

we can see that 1, 2, and 3 dominate the thinking and action of the planner. He has basically a consensual model of society. Interests are

seen as reconcilable and problems as technical. By planning compre-
hensively (1), better communications and co-ordination (2), and
community integration into the wider society (3), the planner and
social worker seek solutions to the problems of areal and group
deprivation. The ideas of lobbying (4 and 5) are perhaps best exemplified by pressure groups and interest groups bargaining for their own
vested positions (see p. 255). When groups or areas appear to be
powerless to organize their own pressure, help can be provided by
community organization (6). They can be provided with information
or with access to relevant experts or, especially in the United States,
to advocates. Advocacy planning, the employment of experts to present
and fight for the case of particular groups and territories, is quite widespread in the United States. The problem is that such advocacy tends
to be limited to immediate and pressing issues — the fight against a
motorway or office development — and the energy, like that of the
tenants' association of old, tends to vanish when the issue disappears.
Advocacy may not, therefore, be the answer for long-term improvement
and change. If such bargaining as posited by strategies 4, 5, and 6 does
not work, then the answer may be national and local pressure (7 and 8)
and community action (9). 'These assume a longer term historical
analysis, and aim to relate selectively to the local community, forging
links between its more active members and groups, and organised
sections of the working class. The intention is to sharpen local consciousness of the underlying problems, and relate action and pressure
to the activities of the wider labour movement.'[27] The CDPs appear to
have adopted these strategies, although at the local and grass-roots
levels there are problems such as the parochialism of many such groups.
Community groups are bound together by issues rather than ideals or
ideology. Their support is also narrowly based by definition, and their
main value lies in their bringing issues to the attention of the rest of
the community and the local political system. At the national level,
it is likely that non-environmental problems will predominate — wages,
inflation, unemployment, investment, and so on.

Of course, the strategies employed will depend on the model of
society or ideology possessed. We have argued that planners have
mainly favoured a consensual model. This creates particular problems
in dealing with deprivation which is seen as a localized phenomenon,
requiring simply the injection of funds or new strategies such as housing
action areas and comprehensive community projects for them to
disappear. They have not disappeared yet, despite all the localized
efforts. This could mean that yet more similar strategies are required
or that the model of society is incorrect. The latter may well be the

case, for in a fundamentally inegalitarian society it would appear that there are, in the very least, different interest groups who do not always see eye to eye. It may be necessary to spend more time and resources employing strategies 4 to 9 and it should be said that the distinction between lobbying and pressure is perhaps more apparent than real.

SOCIAL GEOGRAPHY AND PUBLIC POLICY

It is legitimate to ask where social geography stands in this discussion on social planning. We have thought it necessary to discuss the policy field as this is the area that social geographers must influence if they want their discipline to be truly problem-oriented. The examination of some of the tools of the policy-makers, together with the efficacy of such tools, has enabled us to clarify the idea of change. Earlier we said that there was more than one way of achieving desired transformations in society. In essence, there appear to be two. First, change can occur within the framework of existing institutions, although the change itself may modify these. Whether we have a consensual or pluralist view of society, the approach is evolutionary and gradual. Second, change can be of such a magnitude that it overthrows existing institutions and erects radically different ones in their place. If we have a structural conflict view of society, the approach is revolutionary.

By and large, geography — it is difficult to give separate treatment to a fairly new, small specialism in this matter — has adopted an evolutionary approach. It would be difficult for it to do otherwise. Geography exists within the institutional structure of our society — among the professions, universities and colleges, experts, and so on — and works within that structure, i.e. it works within it because it is part of it. Geography has not, however, had a very significant part to play in influencing and formulating policy. As a subject, its impact has been particularly small, although a major reason for this may well be external to geography in the lack of spatial awareness of British civil servants and politicians. Geographers as individuals have played a greater part. House has documented some of these achievements, which occur mainly in advisory committees, local government consultancy, and so on, i.e. in a formal, defined setting.[28] There are, however, limitations to the impact of any individual. Many well-argued, colleague-supported research papers and policy recommendations have been rejected or substantially modified because of 'political necessity'.

Morrill has put forward some ideas that may help increase this geographical contribution.[29] He starts from the position that geographical expertise will be important at the level of policy implementation.

Basic causes of disadvantage are economic, social, and political, and spatial rearrangements will have little affect on these. They will, however, assist in the implementation of any change. This change will not come about simply because we choose to study 'relevant' problems. There is a need to organize, to communicate findings, to form interest committees, to lobby. The geographer is seen as a specialist who must use his particular skills for the transformation of society. As specialists in the environment and location we could become the custodians of the landscape. Morrill attempts to provide an action programme for the profession as a whole and for its individual members. This means not only involvement with each other, but also with government and the disadvantaged. To date, we can conclude that the impressions geography and geographers have made on public policy have been small.

Against this small success we must introduce a different line of thought, i.e. the structural conflict conception of society. In this view, the geographer must 'reject co-optation into the corporate state'.[30] Geographers must work with and for disadvantaged groups, supplying them with information so that they can better understand the nature and causes of their deprivation and so that their level of political consciousness can be heightened to the point at which they demand radical change. In this way, these groups will be in a strong objective and subjective position to challenge the existing order. This approach appears as yet to be strong on hypothesis but weak on action. In the final analysis, we must return to one of the opening points of Chapter 9 — whether an individual geographer will aim either to influence policy through direct links with government or advocacy or to heighten the political consciousness of the disadvantaged depends on his own value position. In any event, it is likely that many social geographers will pursue their traditional academic concerns which form the bulk of this book, i.e. the examination of socio-spatial phenomena in a non-policy context in order to identify patterns as a first stage of attempting to explain such occurrences in terms of the significant process operating, and eventually by the practical application of theory.

NOTES AND REFERENCES

[1] Detailed discussion of the work of the sanitary reformers can be found in W. Ashworth (1954), *The Genesis of Modern British Town Planning*, London. The work of Owen is described by C. Bell & R. Bell (1969), *City Fathers*, London (Penguin, 1972).

[2] Quoted by J.B. Cullingworth (1973), *Problems of an Urban Society*, London, ii. 123.

[3] See for example, R. Durant (1968), 'Community and Association in a London Housing Estate' in R.E. Pahl (ed.), *Readings in Urban Sociology*, Oxford, pp. 159–85.

[4] O. Newman (1972), *Defensible Space*, London.

[5] J.M. Simmie (1971), Physical Planning and Social Policy, *Journal of the Town Planning Institute* 57, pp. 450–3.

[6] R.E. Pahl (1970), 'Spatial Structure and Social Structure', reprinted in R.E. Pahl *Whose City?*, Longman, p. 188.

[7] See D. Cullingford, P. Glynn, & R. Webber (1975), Liverpool Social Area Analysis (Interim Report), *Planning Research Applications Group, Technical Paper* 9; Nottingham County Council (1975), *The County Deprived Area Study.*

[8] S.S. Duncan (1974), 'Cosmetic Planning and Social Engineering? Improvement Grants and Improvement Areas in Huddersfield', *Area* 6, pp. 259–71.

[9] The Islington programme as documented in the London Borough of Islington, Housing Committee Reports, 14 Jan. and 15 May 1975.

[10] Central Advisory Council for Education (1967), *Children and their Primary Schools* (Plowden Report), London.

[11] A. Little and C. Mabey (1972), 'An Index for Designation of Education Priority Areas' in A. Shonfield and S. Shaw (eds.), *Social Indications and Social Policy*, London, pp. 67–93. These findings are also reported in A.H. Halsey (1972), *Educational Priority: EPA Problems and Policies*, vol. 1, London.

[12] J.A. Barnes (1975), *Educational Priority: Curriculum Innovation in London's EPAs*, vol. 3, London.

[13] National Community Development Project (1974), *Inter-Project Report*, p. 1.

[14] National Community Development Project (1975), *Forward Plan 1975–6*, p. 1.

[15] Report of the Committee on Public Participation in Planning (1969), *People and Planning* (Skeffington Report), London.

[16] See G. Walker and A.G. Rigby (1971), 'Public Participation in the Rhondda Valleys', *Journal of the Town Planning Institute* 57, pp. 157–60. This issue of the *JTPI* and vol. 59 (1973) of the same Journal demonstrate the range of participation exercises.

[17] See Report Section, *New Society*, 11 Sept. 1975.

[18] See Report Section, *New Society*, 9 Oct. 1975.

[19] See, G. Weightman (1975), 'Your Country Needs You', *New Society*, 4 Sept.

[20] This letter concerns the Brighton Station development proposals and is quoted in P. Ambrose and R. Colenutt (1975), *The Property Machine*, Harmondsworth, pp. 153–4.

[21] See J. Eyles (1976), Environmental Satisfaction and London's Dockland: Problems and Policies in the Isle of Dogs, *Queen Mary College, Department of Geography, Occasional Paper* 5; and Ministry of Housing and Local Government (1967), *The Needs of New Communities*, London.

[22] G. Cherry (1968), *Town Planning in its Social Context*, London.

[23] H.J. Gans (1968), *People and Plans*, New York, p. 85.

[24] D.L. Foley (1960), 'British Town Planning: One Ideology or Three?' *Brit. J. Soc.* 11, pp. 211–31.

[25] A. Boskoff (1970), *The Sociology of Urban Regions*, New York.

[26] National Community Development Project (1974), op. cit., p. 23.

[27] Ibid., p. 26.

[28] J. House (1973), 'Geographers, Decision Takers and Policy Makers' in M. Chisholm and B. Rodgers (eds.), *Studies in Human Geography*, London, pp. 272–305.

[29] R.L. Morrill (1973), 'Geography and the Transformation of Society' in M. Albaum (ed.), *Geography and Contemporary Issues*, New York, pp. 1–8.

[30] D. Harvey (1974), 'What Kind of Geography for What Kind of Public Policy?', *Trans. Inst. Brit. Geogs.* 63, pp. 18–24.

Selected Bibliography

We have tried to select works that will complement our own text. We have placed emphasis on books rather than articles — there are 16 books and 2 long articles listed below — because we see this bibliography as the core of a social geography library. Originally we inteded to provide a selected bibliography for each chapter, but on further reflection thought that such lists would be too long, too subjective, and perhaps a little daunting. We have, therefore, simply provided a few follow-up sources in 'Notes and References'. We are sure that there will even be some disagreement with this list. Our main concerns have been to keep the bibliography as short as possible and to ensure as much complementarity as possible with our text. We are, however, certain that such selections will have to be modified as social geography grows and develops.

B.E. Coates & E.M. Rawstron (1971), *Regional Variations in Britain.* London.

J.B. Cullingworth (1973), *Problems of an Urban Society, Vol. 2*, London.

J. Eyles (1974), 'Social Theory and Social Geography', *Progress in Geography*, vol. 6., London.

R. Frankenberg (1966), *Communities in Britain*, Harmondsworth.

H.J. Gans (1968), *People and Plans*, New York.

P. Gould & R. White (1974), *Mental Maps*, Harmondsworth.

D. Harvey (1973), *Social Justice and the City*, London.

R.J. Johnston (1971), *Urban Residential Patterns*, London.

E. Jones (ed.) (1975) *Readings in Social Geography*, Oxford.

R.E. Pahl (ed.) (1968) *Readings in Urban Sociology*, London.

C. Peach (ed.) (1975), *Urban Social Segregation*, London.

P.H. Rees (1970), 'Concepts of Social Space' in B.J.L. Berry & G. Horton (eds.) *Geographic Perspectives on Urban Systems*, Englewood Cliffs, N.J.

L. Reissman (1964), *The Urban Process*, New York.

B.T. Robson (1975), *Urban Social Areas*, Oxford.

J. Shepherd *et al.* (1974), *Social Atlas of London*, Oxford.

D.M. Smith (1973), *Geography of Social Well-Being in the U.S.*, New York.

G. Theordorson (ed.) (1961), *Studies in Human Ecology*, New York.

D.W.G. Timms (1971), *The Urban Mosaic*, Cambridge.

Author Index

Wirth, L., 182, 200, 201, 211, 217
Wohlenburg, E.H. 240
Wolpert, J., 51, 64, 164
Wood, P.A., 86

Young, M., 24, 128, 163, 218

Zorbaugh, H., 29, 30, 63
Zelinski, W., 85, 87
Zipf, G.K., 217
Zweig, S., 143, 163

Subject Index

Accommodation 166
Action space 159
Activity space 62
Adventitious population 124
Advocacy 261
Africans 110
Age-structure 154, 155
Aggregate 132, 133, 194, 250
Amenity group 255
Applied research 221
Ascribed membership 15, 16
Asians 110
Assimilation 165, 177, 196
—models 178, 180ff
Atlas of Mortality 90
Attitudes 237ff
—Deeplish 239
—life concerns 240

Barlow Report 222
Behaviour and behavioural approach 11, 13, 14, 17, 40, 67, 77, 120, 131ff.
Belfast 40ff, 71ff, 73, 74, 82, 84, 89, 154, 174ff.
Bethnal Green 127
Biotic Community 28-9
Black belt 170ff
Borough 6, 77
Boston 32, 33, 47ff, 157
Bureaucratization 22, 23

Cairo 19
Calcutta 119
Caracas 143, 207ff, 210
Caste society 141

Census data 78ff, 131, 236, 240, 244, 246
—units 75, 77, 173, 175, 213
Ch'ang-an 37
Chicago 8, 22, 29, 30, 43, 44, 98, 99, 105, 112ff, 157, 170, 179
China 36, 37, 67, 141ff
Christians 104
Cholera 88
City 97ff
—as dependent variable 200, 205, 206, 211
—region 203, 205
Civil lines 108
Class 20, 23, 86, 141, 144, 145ff, 156, 166ff, 201, 249
—consciousness 145, 261, 263
Communication 201, 203, 205
Community 13ff, 22, 31, 120, 122, 123, 124, 125, 203, 205, 243, 261
—area 75
Community Development Project 249, 250
Competition 29, 201, 222
Comprehensive Development Project 249
Concentric zones 118
Concommitance 88
Conflict 18, 19, 20, 21, 23, 201, 222
Consensus 18, 20, 189, 190, 259
Constraints 62, 138, 147, 148, 152, 156, 158, 160, 190, 288
Core-periphery 92, 143
Crime 77, 78
Cultural change 24
—geography 8, 9
—landscape 34, 85
—patterns 85ff
Culture 7